Jonathan Harbour

Sams **Teach Yourself**

Android
Game Programming

in **24**
Hours

SAMS   800 East 96th Street, Indianapolis, Indiana, 46240 USA

Sams Teach Yourself Android Game Programming in 24 Hours

ISBN-13: 978-0-672-33604-1
ISBN-10: 0-672-33604-9

Library of Congress Cataloging-in-Publication Data is on file.

Printed in the United States of America

First Printing November 2012

Trademarks

Warning and Disclaimer

Bulk Sales

Sams Publishing offers excellent discounts on this book when ordered in quantity for bulk purchases or special sales. For more information, please contact

U.S. Corporate and Government Sales
1-800-382-3419
corpsales@pearsontechgroup.com

For sales outside of the U.S., please contact

International Sales
international@pearsoned.com

Editor-in-Chief
Greg Wiegand

Acquisitions Editor
Neil Rowe

Development Editor
Mark Renfrow

Managing Editor
Kristy Hart

Project Editor
Elaine Wiley

Copy Editor
Barbara Hacha

Indexer
Joy Lee

Proofreader
Chrissy White,
Language Logistics

Technical Editor
Chris Bossardet

Editorial Assistant
Cindy Teeters

Cover Designer
Mark Shirar

Compositor
Nonie Ratcliff

Contents at a Glance

Table of Contents

Foreword

When Jonathan Harbour asked me to write the foreword to this book, I was quite honored. I first met Jon when I started teaching game design at the University of Advancing Technology in Tempe, Arizona. As a novice teacher, I was very grateful to Jon for offering his advice and assistance. Because he taught game programming and I taught game design, it was natural that we would work together.

We also hit it off simply as gamers. We both love strategy games, and we found that we are both huge board wargame fans. We especially enjoyed a WWII battle game called Memoir '44, but our most intense confrontations were in Twilight Struggle, a game covering the entire Cold War period in an innovative card-driven format.

We soon discovered that we also shared similar philosophies about teaching and game development—that game development is hard work, and to prepare our students for careers in the game industry requires that we challenge them and hold them to the highest standards. So when Jon asked me to work with him and a team of students on a small XNA game project, I jumped at the opportunity! We assembled a strong team and spent some time getting to know each other in order to understand our collective skills and strengths.

After a period of brainstorming, research, and concept development we chose to do a 2D side-scrolling platformer, but not just another run-of-the-mill platformer! We really wanted to have some fun, but we also wanted to see if we could find a way to innovate a little. The game we ended up making was Aquaphobia: Mutant Brain Sponge Madness. As the game developed, we found that we were attracting a lot of attention at the school. People were charmed by the main character, the setting, and the overall art style—and the basic gameplay was undeniably fun! UAT honored us with a sponsorship to the Game Developer's Conference (GDC) Austin that summer.

Our follow-up was a more ambitious project. We proposed and received approval to merge Jon's mobile game programming course with my handheld game design course and to have all of the students in both classes work together on a single project. We would make a game for the Nintendo DS, and the concept we pitched was a straightforward translation of the popular board game Memoir '44. The project didn't pan out for a variety of reasons, but as any teacher will assure you, you learn more from your mistakes than you do from your successes! I think our students learned a LOT from that experience, and I know that Jon and I both did!

The bottom line is this: Jonathan Harbour is deeply passionate about making games. He also loves teaching. The book you hold will help you learn to make games, too. Enjoy!

David Wessman
Game Designer

About the Author

Jonathan Harbour is a writer and instructor whose love for computers and video games dates back to the Commodore PET and Atari 2600 era. He has a Master's in Information Systems Management. His portfolio site at www.jharbour.com includes a discussion forum. He also authored *Sams Teach Yourself Windows Phone 7 Game Programming in 24 Hours*. His love of science fiction led to the remake of a beloved classic video game with some friends, resulting in Starflight—The Lost Colony (www.starflightgame.com).

Dedication

This book is dedicated to my friend and colleague, David Wessman. I enjoyed working with David as a fellow instructor at UAT during 2009-2010. Among his many game credits is TIE Fighter (LucasArts).

Acknowledgments

This book was a challenging project because of the quickly evolving Android platform. I am thankful to the production team at Pearson for their patience during the long writing process (including missed deadlines) and hard work to get it into print. Neil Rowe; Mark Renfrow; Barbara Hacha; Elaine Wiley; and technical reviewer, Chris Bossardet.

We Want to Hear from You!

As the reader of this book, you are our most important critic and commentator. We value your opinion and want to know what we're doing right, what we could do better, what areas you'd like to see us publish in, and any other words of wisdom you're willing to pass our way.

We welcome your comments. You can email or write to let us know what you did or didn't like about this book—as well as what we can do to make our books better.

Please note that we cannot help you with technical problems related to the topic of this book.

When you write, please be sure to include this book's title and author as well as your name and email address. We will carefully review your comments and share them with the author and editors who worked on the book.

Email: consumer@samspublishing.com

Mail: Sams Publishing
           ATTN: Reader Feedback
           800 East 96th Street
           Indianapolis, IN 46240 USA

Reader Services

Visit our website and register this book at informit.com/register for convenient access to any updates, downloads, or errata that might be available for this book.

QR Barcodes

You may use these quick reference barcodes with your smartphone scanner to receive links to information about the book!

Publisher's Book Detail Link

Author's Website Link

Introduction

Since Google acquired Android, Inc., to compete with Apple and Microsoft in the smartphone and tablet markets, competition has heated up in this lucrative market. These are two tough competitors, but Android quickly gained a strong market share in a short time, with Google celebrating its 500 millionth Android OS sale. (Although Android is a license-free OS, devices are still registered with Google—at no cost). Both Apple and Microsoft have invested *billions* to develop and market their proprietary platforms, whereas Google has taken the open standards approach of releasing the source code to Android (which is based on the Linux core). This has allowed smartphone and tablet manufacturers to customize the OS for their devices while maintaining "app" compatibility across the line. Android literally is comparable to Apple's iOS devices in quality and performance, with an equally impressive online shop for purchasing music, books, movies, and apps: Google Play.

Android 4 was an especially important update to the OS, which seems to have been such a big hit that hardware manufacturers are largely leaving it alone—the stock OS—rather than customizing it for their devices. In the past, companies like Toshiba and Samsung have released custom versions that gave their devices a unique look and feel. But that practice is in decline as the OS gained notoriety and branding. An exclusion today is Amazon's Kindle Fire HD, which runs the Android 4 OS with many custom Amazon apps to give the dwevice a uniqueness that leverages the equally impressive Kindle Fire brand.

This book is about writing games for the Android 4 mobile operating system used in smartphones and tablets. The ideal reader for this book is a programmer who knows Java and has already dabbled in game programming before, and who needs a primer for the Android platform. This book is not extremely advanced; the reader level is beginning to intermediate, with absolutely no 3D covered (via OpenGL ES 2.0). An entire book is needed to cover OpenGL ES properly, and our goal with this book is to introduce the most important concepts in developing games for Android 4, not to address high-performance rendering. However, this book *will* take you right up to the point where you will be able to look into OpenGL ES. You will gain a solid understanding of the Android hardware, including the display system, audio system, sensors, and touch screen. A sample game engine is demonstrated in the final hours.

The Android SDK is based on the Java language, so this book's code revolves around Java. The SDK and development tools are free to download and install, and this book explains step by step how to do so, making it suitable for a beginner. The approach taken is that the reader is a knowledgeable person, with some experience at programming already, and is looking for a quick head-start to developing games on the Android platform. The book moves along at a leisurely pace, not getting too technical right away, simply showing the reader how everything works in a step-by-step fashion—in other words, how to get an Android game up and running fairly quickly. The Android SDK is a challenge to set up and use for a complete novice, so we cover every detail on getting started with the tools. Although a reader will greatly benefit from having at least some experience with the Java language, we do not make the assumption and will explain the code for each example. Then, after the basic hurdles are overcome, the latter half of the book delves into some serious gameplay code at a higher level.

In Part I, covering Hours 1–4, you learn how to install and configure the development tools and the Android SDK.

In Part II, covering Hours 5–14, you learn all about the Android OS and how to use the Android devices supported by the SDK, such as the graphics system, touch screen, audio system, and sensors (such as the accelerometer).

In Part III, covering Hours 15–24, you learn how to create a basic game engine for the Android platform with helper classes covering the common gameplay features needed to program most video games, such as sprites and a customizable animation system. The last two hours present game examples to demonstrate the concepts.

To download the source code for this book (as an Eclipse workspace), see the author's website at http://jharbour.com or the publisher's website at http://www.informit.com/store/product. aspx?isbn=0672336049.

PART I

Introduction

HOUR 1
Introducing Android 4

What You'll Learn in This Hour:

- ▶ New features in Android 4
- ▶ History of the platform
- ▶ Android hardware specifications
- ▶ Dev system requirements

The first four hours are very hands-on with step-by-step tutorials on setting up the Android SDK using two development environments: NetBeans and Eclipse. We will go over the steps to configure either Eclipse or NetBeans (your choice) for Android development.

This hour begins our exploration of game programming on Google's new smartphone platform, Android 4. There are two versions currently in circulation at the time of this writing: 4.0 (Ice Cream Sandwich) and 4.1 (Jelly Bean) with additional sub-versions expected in the coming year. Android 4 feels like a whole new platform, not just an upgrade of 3.2. One exciting thing about making games for Android is the excellent software development kit and development tools. We'll discuss the devices, feature set, and specifications in this hour, and we'll dig into the development tools right away. I assume you already know how to use your Android phone and want to get started writing code as soon as possible. You'll be up and running with Android code in no time! This hour is intended to help you choose an appropriate target for your game because there are so many Android devices. We'll look at the most common phones and tablets and compare their hardware specifications to see what types of games most devices will run.

Hello, Android 4

The most surprising thing about Android is that it has fully matured as a competitor in the smartphone market in *only three years*! From concept to the present version in three years is a remarkable feat. But there's a reason: Android is based on Linux core 3.0. Yes, it is essentially a derivative of the Linux operating system.

That Android competes successfully with Apple's powerhouse iPhone is significant given that Android was late entering the market, after Apple had a two-year head start. Microsoft continues to take market share away from both Google and Apple with its Windows Phone platform, which has seen similar fast-track improvements in the past year. As a result of the pacing, Google's Android SDK and OS developers tend to rely on creativity to get through challenges that normally require more time (see Figure 1.1).

FIGURE 1.1
Android 4.0, Ice Cream Sandwich. Image courtesy of Google.

Figure 1.2 shows the home screen for an Android 4 smartphone in portrait orientation. Note the simple layout of the interface. At the bottom are three *soft buttons*: Return, Home, and Tasks. The Return button is a generic Back button. The Home button returns to this screen.

The Tasks button brings up the screen shown in Figure 1.3, which shows running apps (including games) for quick task switching (also called Recent Apps). At the top is the Google search field with voice recognition.

Before learning all about Java SE 7, source code projects, compiler configurations, Android Market, and other great things that will interest a game developer, we need to first understand this new platform. Android is an operating system for smartphone devices. Android is also *non proprietary*, meaning that licensing the OS from Google is free. The source code for Android is *open source*. In contrast, Microsoft and Apple have a tight grip on the source code for their operating systems: Windows Mobile and iOS, respectively. These companies strictly regulate the release of their OS.

Microsoft licenses the Windows Mobile OS, aka "Windows Phone," to manufacturers, who then use the OS on their devices. This is a middle position on licensing: not as wide open as Google, not as restrictive as Apple.

FIGURE 1.2
The Android 4 home screen. Image courtesy of Google.

FIGURE 1.3
Browsing the running apps using the Tasks (Recent Apps) button.
Image courtesy of Google.

Apple maintains its proprietary control over both the OS and hardware, fine-tuning both exceptionally well. Although Apple iOS devices do not enjoy the broad offerings and versatility of Android, they do offer a more refined and consistent experience because one company designs both the hardware and software to work together.

Figure 1.4 shows the Apps installed on an Android 4 smartphone.

FIGURE 1.4
The Android 4 Apps screen. Image courtesy of Google.

There is a price to pay for open source, though. Releasing the source code for the OS does not automatically mean Android will dominate the market. On the contrary, one challenge for Android game developers is the large number of nonlicensed hardware manufacturers building Android phones and tablets without "permission" from Google. These manufacturers follow a guideline or "hardware API" for their devices to ensure broad compatibility among devices, but there are exceptions. Some Android phones and tablets use a different CPU, so they will not run some apps and games!

DID YOU KNOW

If you're planning to port your smartphone games to other platforms, see my other recent book from Sams, titled *Teach Yourself Windows Phone 7 Game Programming in 24 Hours*.

There was a time not too many years ago when just having a PC was enough to do your work: programming, software engineering, computer-aided design (CAD), word processing, accounting. Even in the 1980s it was rare for every employee to have a PC at his or her desk, and even more rare for families to have a PC in their homes. A lot of kids might have had a Nintendo Entertainment System (NES), a Sega Master System (SMS), or the older Atari 2600, all of which used cartridge-based games. A step up from these video game systems were the true PCs of the time, such as the Apple II, Commodore 64, Amiga, Atari 400/800, Atari ST.

No computer enthusiasts at the time used an IBM PC at home! MS-DOS was a *terrible* operating system compared to the other, more user-friendly ones. If you wanted to do programming, you would naturally gravitate to the consumer PCs, not the business-oriented IBM PCs. At the time, the Apple Macintosh was pretty expensive, and the ordinary kid would prefer an Apple II, but that was the start of the Mac back in the 1980s (although it has been completely redesigned several times before reaching the modern OS X).

Today the world is a different place. Even if we ignore how powerful computers are today, just look at all the handheld systems. The Nintendo DS family and the Sony PSP family are the two leading competitors of handheld video game systems, and they can do almost anything that their big brothers (Nintendo Wii and Sony PS3) can do, including online play. These things are everywhere! You can't walk through a store or a mall without seeing kids carrying some sort of mobile video game system with them, not to mention smartphones. And it's not just kids, but adults have their toys, too, like iPhone, iPad, Windows Phone, and Android devices.

One of my favorites is Plants vs. Zombies by PopCap Games. This game has been ported to most systems, including Xbox 360, Mac OS X, Windows, Nintendo DSi, iPhone, Android, and dozens of other systems. And you know what? Some of the higher-profile games are starting to come out for Android 4 already, ported from other systems like Windows, Xbox 360, and iPhone.

So what is Android 4 all about? Obviously, because you're reading this book, you are interested in programming games for the device. But what is development for this platform really like? What's it all about? We have to ask ourselves these questions because developing a game that you want to be taken seriously requires a pretty big investment of time, if not money. Most likely, anyone looking at Android 4 for game development is already experienced with Java SE 7. If you have never used this development tool, the next two hours will be really important because we'll be creating projects and working with both NetBeans and Eclipse quite a bit. I'll assume that you might not have any experience with the development tools.

About the Android SDK

The Android SDK is based on the Java language. Java programs are compiled with the Java Development Kit (JDK). All apps and games are written in Java and run on Android devices using the Java Runtime Environment (JRE). A Java program has an extension of .class, and the source code file has an extension of .java. Programs built with the Android SDK are compiled into a package that can run on the Android platform. There are two primary development environments for Java: Eclipse and NetBeans. Both have strong points and weak points, and neither is really superior to the other—it's more a matter of preference. Instructions on installing and configuring the Android SDK are coming in the next two hours.

If you are a beginner to both Java and the Android SDK, you should still be able to follow the instructions and get started writing Android code. But, if you have never programmed in a language like Java before (such as C#, C++, or Lua), you may find the code difficult to understand. A programming novice may want to read a primer on basic Java programming before continuing on with the Android SDK. Because many concepts are shared among all programming languages, it is helpful to know at least one of these languages. Some programming experience is really important to feel confident with the code in this book because we don't go over basic programming concepts—there's just too much to cover!

If you are already an experienced Java developer, you will still want to peruse the information over the next two hours to get a handle on the installation and structure of the Android SDK and development tools.

About the Android NDK

The Android *NDK* (which differs from the SDK) lets you write components of an app or game in native C++ code instead of Java. The NDK is a separate tool installed after the Android SDK is already installed. The NDK does not allow you to write an entire app or game in C++. Rather, it is used to supplement the SDK with support for C++ code and libraries and is meant to operate as a bridge to many hardware devices for which no Java library is available. We can use the NDK to optimize our game code. In addition to many C++ libraries, the NDK also supports OpenGL ES 2.0 for 3D rendering, OpenSL ES for audio, and pixel buffer access. The Android developers do not recommend using the NDK for most apps and games, but a game developer always looks for every edge!

Android Dev System Requirements

The Android SDK supports these operating systems:

- ▶ Windows XP, Vista, 7 (32- or 64-bit);
- ▶ Mac OS X 10.4.8 or later (x86 only)
- ▶ Linux (32- or 64-bit); any dist with GLibc 2.7 or later

We will be using the Windows version of NetBeans and Eclipse, giving you the choice of which IDE to use. The installation and configuration of both IDEs and the Android SDK is covered in the next two hours.

History of the Platform

Android 4 follows a very short history, dating to the first Android SDK in 2008. Android competes directly with Apple's iOS, which includes iPhone, iPod, and iPad devices. Although Microsoft's Windows Phone 7 follows in market share, it is also a worthy competitor.

Interestingly enough, I would not consider Apple's iPhone an evolutionary leap beyond Palm Pilot (the first "PDA"). The iPhone does not follow in the lineage of "mobile computer" dating back to the Palm Pilot and Pocket PC; instead, iPhone (that is, iOS) was derived from Apple's iPod. The iPod might have been invented by Sony, the company responsible for the Walkman generation of portable music players. Everyone in the 1980s or 1990s had at least heard of a Walkman at one time or another.

You have surely heard the term *podcast*. The term is rather generalized today to mean digital audio streamed for playback on the Web or on a portable player. The concept was invented by Apple for the iPod and iTunes, which now support video as well. While many of us were caught up in the Napster lawsuits over music sharing, Apple was busy developing iTunes and began selling music in a revolutionary new way: per track instead of per album.

Have you ever heard a catchy new song on the radio and wanted to buy it for your iPod, Android music player, or similar media device? In the past decade, you would buy the whole CD and then rip the tracks into MP3 with software such as Windows Media Player or Winamp. This point is debatable, but I would argue that Apple iTunes proved that digital music sales can be a commercial success, highly profitable both for the recording artists and for the service provider. Amazon has also shown that digital media is a successful industry.

iPod was so successful that it evolved into the iPhone and iPad, and competing companies have been trying to keep up with Apple in both of these markets now for several years. The iOS operating system works great. It does what users want, rather than what software engineers *think* users want—that's a key difference. Although Android is derivative of iOS, it offers its own innovations, such as being based on a grounded, established core in Linux.

What did customers want? Not a do-everything poorly device, but a do-the-most-useful-thing great device. In contrast, many companies hire "experts" to conduct consumer studies and then spend millions trying to convince customers that they really want and need that product. This might be one good way to break into a relatively unknown market or to adjust the feature set of a product according to consumer interest. The situation Apple found itself in back in 2007 with the release of iPhone was enviable, and with that came emulation.

Where Google has placed its mark is in licensing to attract hardware manufacturers. Most of Google's awesome web services—Earth, Maps, Picasa, and Documents (known as Google Drive for Android users)—are available for Android as free apps. The free licensing is compelling to device manufacturers, which has allowed Android to claim over a third of the market share in the smartphone and tablet markets.

BY THE WAY

Android OS 1.0 was released in September of 2008. That is a very quick-to-market time considering the maturity and stability of the OS in its current form.

Table 1.1 charts the very brief history of this awesome OS.

TABLE 1.1 **History of Android OS**

Date	Version	Code Name	Linux Kernel
Nov 2007	1.0 Beta		2.6
Sep 2008	1.0		
Feb 2009	1.1		
Apr 2009	1.5	Cupcake	2.6.27
Sep 2009	1.6	Donut	2.6.29
Oct 2009	2.0	Eclair	
Jan 2010	2.1		
May 2010	2.2	Froyo	2.6.32
Dec 2010	2.3	Gingerbread	2.6.35
Feb 2011	3.0	Honeycomb	2.6.36
May 2011	3.1		
Jul 2011	3.2		
Oct 2011	4.0	Ice Cream Sandwich	3.0.1
Aug 2012	4.1	Jelly Bean	

Android Hardware Specifications

Android OS is used on many types of devices, not just smartphones, although that is the largest market by far. Figure 1.5 shows a Samsung Galaxy Nexus smartphone. As you can see in Figure 1.6, the design of the tablet is very similar in the Samsung Galaxy Tab. This is by no means an endorsement of any one brand; it is simply meant to show a comparison between a smartphone and tablet from the same manufacturer.

FIGURE 1.5
The Samsung Galaxy Nexus (Android phone). Image courtesy of Samsung.

FIGURE 1.6
The Samsung Galaxy Tab (Android tablet). Image courtesy of Samsung.

Table 1.2 shows the common hardware specifications among the most popular Android models available at the time of this writing. The most notable thing about the specifications is that they now follow a basic standard across all manufacturers. Apple has demonstrated that too much openness and flexibility are not always desirable traits in mobile hardware. One of the difficulties facing Android developers today is the need to support many different hardware devices in a single code base. We will address this problem when covering the Android display system.

TABLE 1.2   Android 4 Hardware Comparison

Component	Nexus	Tab
CPU	1.2GHz Cortex-A9	1GHz nVidia Tegra 2
Cores	2 (dual)	2 (dual)
GPU	PowerVR SGX540	
Screen Size	4.65" HD	10.1" HD
Resolution	1280×720	1280×800 WXGA
Video Output		1080p (via HDMI)
Memory	1GB	1GB
Storate	16GB	16GB
Wi-Fi		802.11n
Gyroscope	Yes	Yes
Accelerometer	Yes	Yes
Proximity	Yes	No
Barometer	Yes	No
Compass	Yes	Yes
GPS	Yes	Yes
Camera	F:1.3MP, R:5.0MP	F:2MP, R:3MP
Video	720p	720p
Bluetooth	Yes	Yes

The Android OS has rapidly become a leading contender to Apple iOS with nearly 40% market share. We'll be seeing a lot more of the friendly Android logo (Figure 1.7) in the years to come. This is definitely a strong platform, a worthy investment of your time.

FIGURE 1.7
The Android OS logo. Image courtesy of Google.

Summary

The Android operating system has matured very quickly in only three years. The latest version, Android 4, is fully capable of competing with iPhone and Windows Phone. You will be using the Java language and the Android SDK to program games on this platform.

Q&A

Q. Android OS was developed and released rapidly in a very short time and quickly gobbled up market share from Apple's iOS. What possible ramifications will there be long term because of this rapid development?

A. Answers will vary.

Q. Because the Android OS is open source software, the source code for the OS is freely available. Is this a strength or a weakness? Explain your reasons.

A. Answers will vary.

Workshop

Quiz

1. What language do you use to program with the Android SDK?

2. What is the nickname of Android OS 3.0?

3. Which version of the Android OS has the nickname of Ice Cream Sandwich?

Answers

1. Java

2. Honeycomb

3. 4.0

Activities

Go online to Google and search for the Android SDK. Look up version 4.0 or 4.1 and note the URL to the documentation page. Bookmark this page for future reference—you'll need it!

HOUR 2
Installing the Development Tools

What You'll Learn in This Hour:

▶ Installing the Java Development Kit
▶ Installing the Development Environment
▶ Installing the Android SDK
▶ Using the Android SDK Manager

If you are an experienced developer, you may want to skip this hour because it is designed to assist a beginner with the development tools. This hour explains what is needed for Android development using either Eclipse or NetBeans (though we focus more on Eclipse in this book).

The Android SDK can be challenging to set up for someone who is not familiar with these development tools. We go over the steps in this hour to get your development environment installed configured for the Android SDK. This might seem like a no-brainer task, but the Android SDK is famously difficult to set up for the first time! We're going to take it one step at a time, with plenty of figures to show each step, so that over the next two short hours you will be up and running with a working Android project. From there, we will dig into game programming on this great platform!

This hour will show you how to install the Java Development Kit (JDK) and the Android Software Development Kit (SDK). Experienced developers tend to dislike tutorials like this. But I think the JDK was designed with ease of use in mind, and even a complete beginner should be able to follow the directions in this hour to get the development tools installed. Although this might be very easy to an experienced developer, we are going to cover each step in these first few hours. If you have already installed the software, you may skip to the next hour. We take it extremely slow at first but then ramp up very quickly to subjects like 3D rendering with OpenGL ES 2.0 in no time!

Please understand that "complete beginner" here is used to refer to Java development and does not at all imply that one is not skilled with other tools and languages! Even a highly experienced programmer may find the install and configuration of the Android tools problematic.

Installing the JDK

The quickest way to get set up if you have never before installed the Java Development Kit (JDK) on your PC is to download the prepackaged combination of Java with NetBeans. The version we're using in this book is Java SE 7, short for Java Standard Edition 7 (there is also an Enterprise Edition for developing server applications). If you prefer Eclipse, just get the JDK alone. I recommend Eclipse for Android development, mainly because this is the environment recommended by Google and used by the Android team.

There is a Java Development Kit (JDK) and a Java Runtime Environment (JRE). It is possible to install just the JRE for running Java applications and web-based applets on an end-user PC. But installing the JDK automatically includes the JRE, so if you have the JDK, you do not need to also install the JRE.

If you are using Java SE 6 or earlier, I recommend updating to Java SE 7 before doing any Android development. It will still work with SE 6, so if you're committed to that version, that's fine. I just find it helpful to use the latest version of software when it comes to development (including game programming).

You can install the JDK separately if you prefer. Perhaps you are an experienced programmer who has already installed the JDK? If that is the case, the steps will be slightly different, but the Android tools and settings should be similar in either IDE. If you are using NetBeans, be sure to also download the JDK plug-in for NetBeans. Again, Eclipse is the preferred IDE for Android development, officially supported by Google and the Android team. But, if you are a NetBeans user, you can use NetBeans with the Android SDK.

There are so many acronyms to remember! An integrated development environment, or IDE, is productivity software used to manage software projects, edit source code files, and build, debug, and run programs. An IDE is an all-in-one solution for software development.

The latest version of NetBeans at the time of this writing is 7.1. Eclipse is also free, and the latest version at the time of this writing is Helios Service Release 1. In either case, I recommend updating to the latest version of the IDE for best results.

Downloading the NetBeans Package

The download package is currently called Java SE 7 with NetBeans 7.1. A list of JDK versions is found at http://www.oracle.com/technetwork/java/javase. If you want to skip directly to the download page, it is located here: http://www.oracle.com/technetwork/java/javase/downloads.

On the download page, you should see the tab called Downloads shown in Figure 2.1. Click the NetBeans image to download the JDK with NetBeans. That's perfect—exactly what you need!

FIGURE 2.1
Locating the NetBeans download link.

WATCH OUT

Websites are constantly in a state of change! If you are reading this long after the book's publishing date, odds are the page will look quite different or may no longer even be online at the same location. Google is usually helpful at finding the "jdk with netbeans download" page for you.

Installing the Package

The installer begins with Figure 2.2. The versions (especially the update number) will likely have changed by the time you read this.

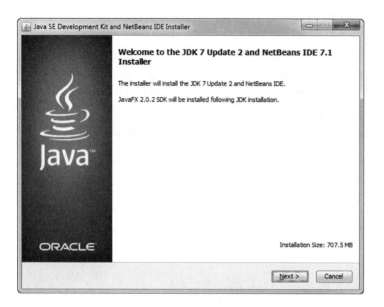

FIGURE 2.2
Preparing to install the JDK 7 Update 2 and NetBeans IDE 7.1.

The next dialog screen that comes up shows the license agreement, shown in Figure 2.3. If you accept the license agreement, highlight that option and proceed to the next step.

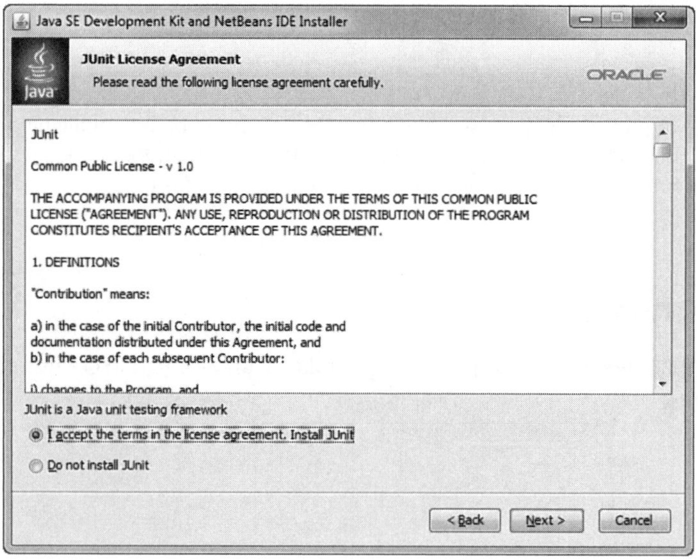

FIGURE 2.3
Accepting the license agreement.

The next dialog screen, shown in Figure 2.4, allows you to change the default install location for the JDK on the hard drive. I recommend leaving it at the default.

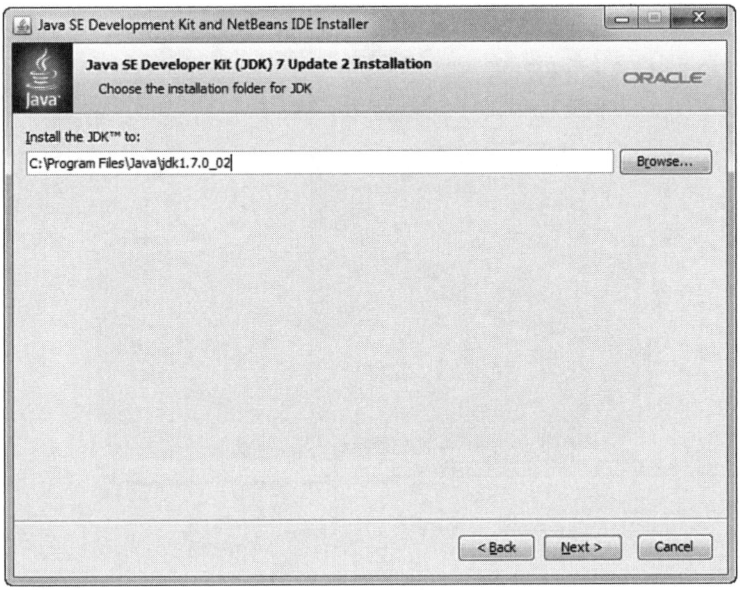

FIGURE 2.4
Choosing the install location for the JDK.

The next dialog screen, shown in Figure 2.5, enables you to change the default install location for NetBeans, including the JDK plug-in. Again, I recommend leaving these at their default values.

Installing the Android SDK

Now that the JDK has been installed, you will be able to install the Android SDK. In actual practice, these do not need to be installed in this order. You could install the Android SDK first without incident. We have to manually configure NetBeans to use the Android SDK anyway, so the install order is not important. We also cover the brief install process for Eclipse later in this hour.

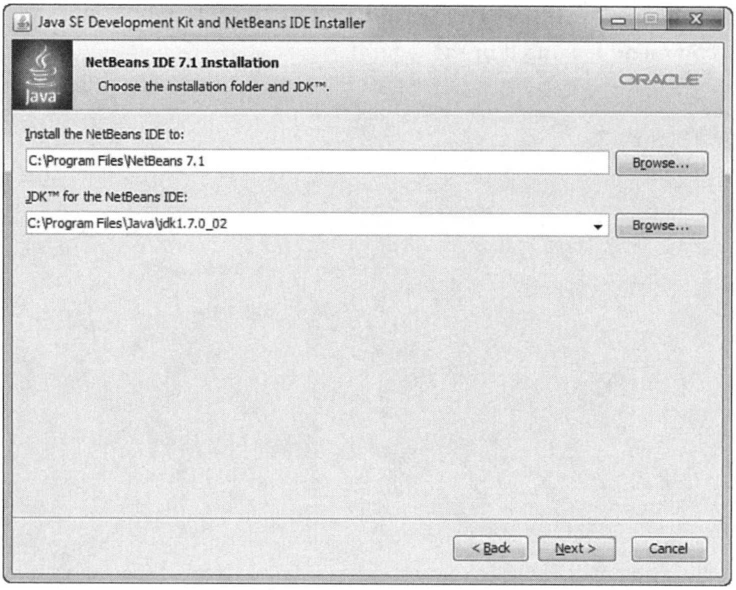

FIGURE 2.5
Choosing the install location for NetBeans.

Downloading the SDK

First, if you haven't already, you need to download the Android SDK. Browse to this URL to find the developer tools: http://developer.android.com. On this page are resources for Android developers. If you choose the SDK tab at the top, it will take you to the Android SDK download page located here: http://developer.android.com/sdk.

You might have noticed that Android SDK is not packaged for a specific OS version, such as 4.0 (Ice Cream Sandwich) or 4.1 (Jelly Bean). The Android SDK includes targets for all the versions of the Android OS. At the time of this writing, the latest SDK is version 1.6, and the Windows version is about 30MB. Not too bad for an SDK—they do tend to get pretty big. The DirectX SDK, for instance, weighs in at over 500MB, although a lot of that size is due to the examples. If you are using Mac OS X or Linux, versions of the SDK are also available for those platforms.

After downloading the Android SDK, we can begin going over the installer, starting with Figure 2.6.

Installing the SDK

The next dialog screen, shown in Figure 2.7, verifies the version of the JDK detected by the Android SDK installer. If you do not have the JDK installed, the Android SDK won't be able to add itself to the classpath (the list of folders where Java libraries are found), among other things. So, it's important to do this in the right order. If the JDK was not found, I recommend aborting this install and installing the JDK first.

FIGURE 2.6
Preparing to install the Android SDK.

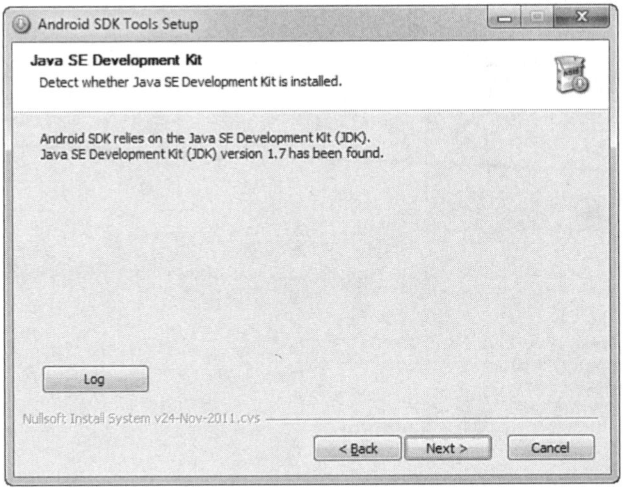

FIGURE 2.7
Identifying the JDK before proceeding with the install.

The next dialog screen, shown in Figure 2.8, shows the default install folder for the Android SDK. You may change the folder if you like, but I recommend leaving it at the default.

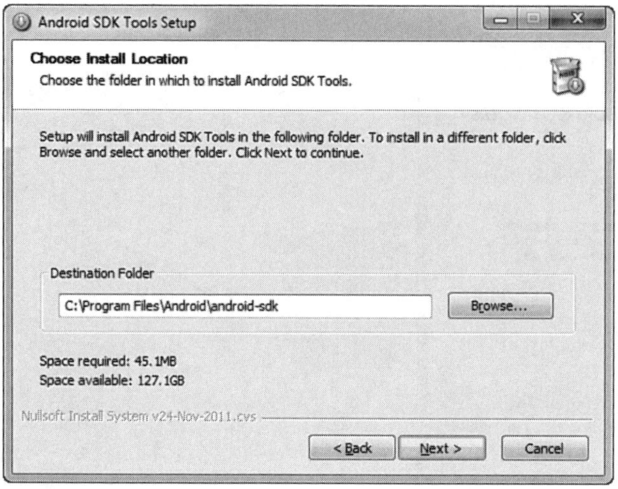

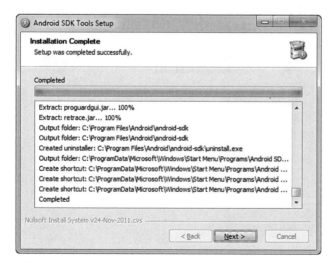

FIGURE 2.8
Choosing the install location.

Next, the install of the Android SDK begins. After a few minutes, if the install completed successfully, the dialog shown in Figure 2.9 comes up.

FIGURE 2.9
The Android SDK installation has completed.

Before closing, we want to recognize an option on the final dialog screen (see Figure 2.10). You *do* want to start the SDK Manager after the install finishes, so keep this option checked. This is an essential step—the Android SDK is not actually installed yet! All we have installed so far is the SDK Manager. If you miss this step, that's okay--the *SDK Manager* can be found in the Start menu under Program Files (or All Programs if using a newer version of Windows).

FIGURE 2.10
Completing the install—starting the SDK Manager.

Running the Android SDK Manager

The Android SDK is a rather small install package because it just installs core files and the SDK Manager, which we will be using next to download and install specific SDK packages. Figure 2.11 shows the Android SDK Manager. Near the bottom of the dialog are two check boxes labeled Updates/New and Installed; they should both be checked.

Some of the choices shown checked in this screen are optional, but it doesn't hurt to include such options. At minimum, select Android 4.0.3 (API15). If you have installed a newer version (which is very possible), it may be a higher API number. Just focus on Android 4.0.x and check all items under it.

If you choose Android 4.1 (API 16), it's possible you *might not* be able to run that code on a 4.0 device (unless it has the 4.1 update applied). Just something to keep in mind if you plan to test your code on a device using a USB connection—which is *highly* recommended for seeing actual performance of your game. The emulator can run 4.1 fine, but it should really only be used to verify that code runs on different devices; it is not a good choice for testing high-performance code.

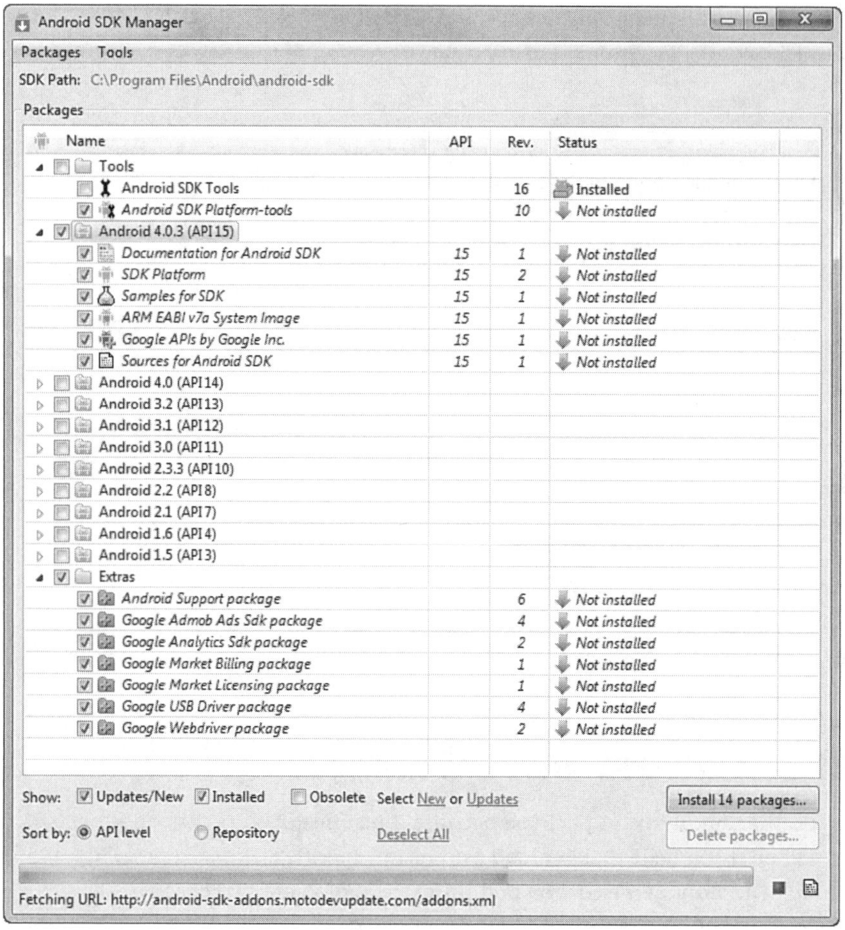

FIGURE 2.11
Installing the Android SDK using the Android SDK Manager.

Next, you might want to select all the Extras, which include Android Support package and others. Though not strictly required, some extra packages may be needed to deploy your game to the Android Market.

You do *not* need any earlier version of Android unless you plan to support older models. It's *very* possible that you will need to do just that. If that is the case, you can always run the Android SDK Manager again to install additional SDKs.

Down at the lower right of the Android SDK Manager dialog is a button that should say something like Install 14 packages.... Click this button to continue. This will bring up the verification dialog shown in Figure 2.12: Choose Packages to Install.

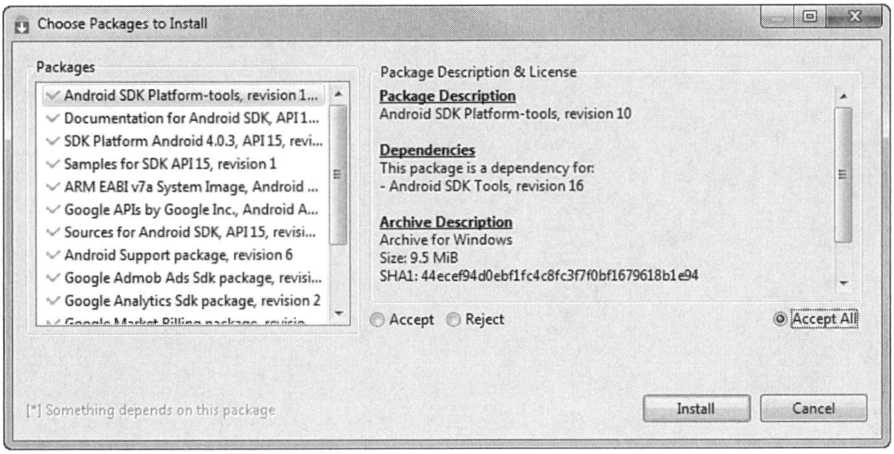

FIGURE 2.12
Verifying the chosen packages to be installed.

The list shows all the packages to be installed. Check the Accept All option if it isn't already checked, and then click the Install button to proceed. The Android SDK Manager screen will come up again and begin downloading and installing the chosen packages. If you opt to install 4.1 (SDK 16), then the list will appear as shown in Figure 2.13.

Installing the ADT Plug-in for Eclipse

Eclipse is the official IDE for Android development, supported by the Android development team. Although NetBeans is also supported via a third-party plug-in, it will not be as up to date as Eclipse because this is the tool of choice for the developers.

Let's go over the steps to install the Eclipse plug-in for Android development, although it's likely an experienced developer may have already done so. This is a lot easier to set up than NetBeans.

If you haven't already downloaded and installed Eclipse, the web location for downloading the Eclipse IDE is here: http://www.eclipse.org/downloads.

Among the many versions of Eclipse listed, you will most likely want to download and install the one titled Eclipse IDE for Java Developers. The Eclipse Classic version also works but will need additional updates after installing. Be sure to get the Eclipse Helios release (version 3.6.2 or later).

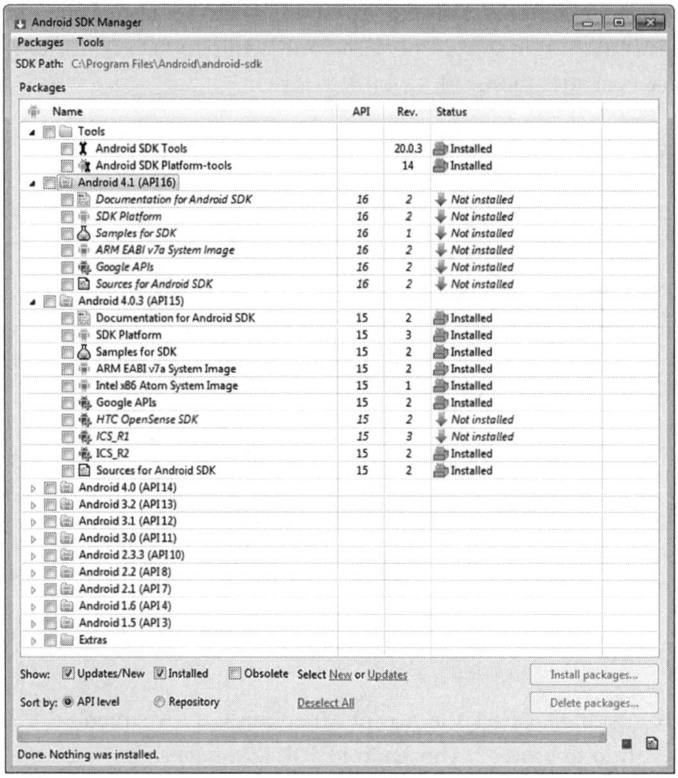

FIGURE 2.13
Perusing the list of SDKs including 4.1 Jelly Bean.

ADT is short for Android Development Tools. This is the package you want to add Android support to Eclipse (in addition to the Android SDK). This is equivalent to NBAndroid for NetBeans.

Next, you need the ADT Plug-in for Eclipse. Open the Help menu and choose Install New Software.

A dialog for adding new updates and add-ons to Eclipse appears, as shown in Figure 2.14. Click the Add button at the upper right.

A mini dialog with two text fields will come up, titled Add Repository. In the Name field, enter this: **ADT Plugin**. In the Location field, enter this: **https://dl-ssl.google.com/android/eclipse/**. The Add Repository dialog is shown in Figure 2.15.

Eclipse uses the URL entered into the Add Repository dialog to search for any packages. The Install New Software dialog will now show the Developer Tools for Android, as shown in Figure 2.16.

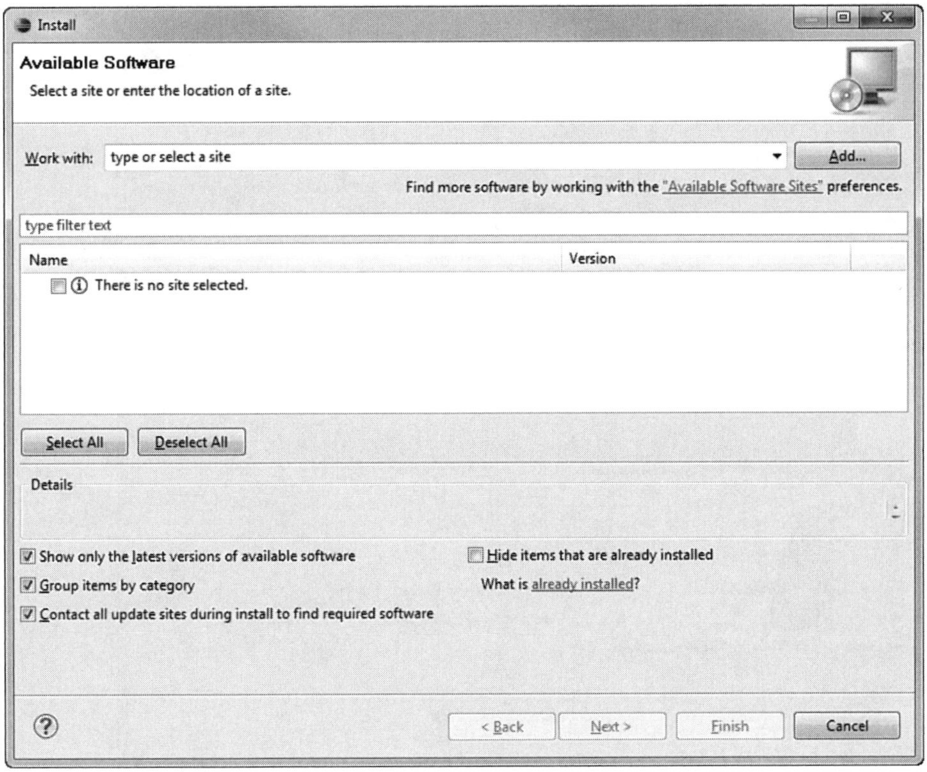

FIGURE 2.14
The Eclipse Software Install dialog.

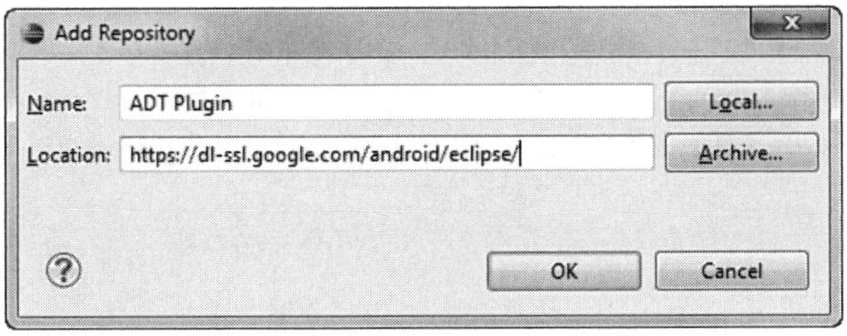

FIGURE 2.15
The Add Repository dialog.

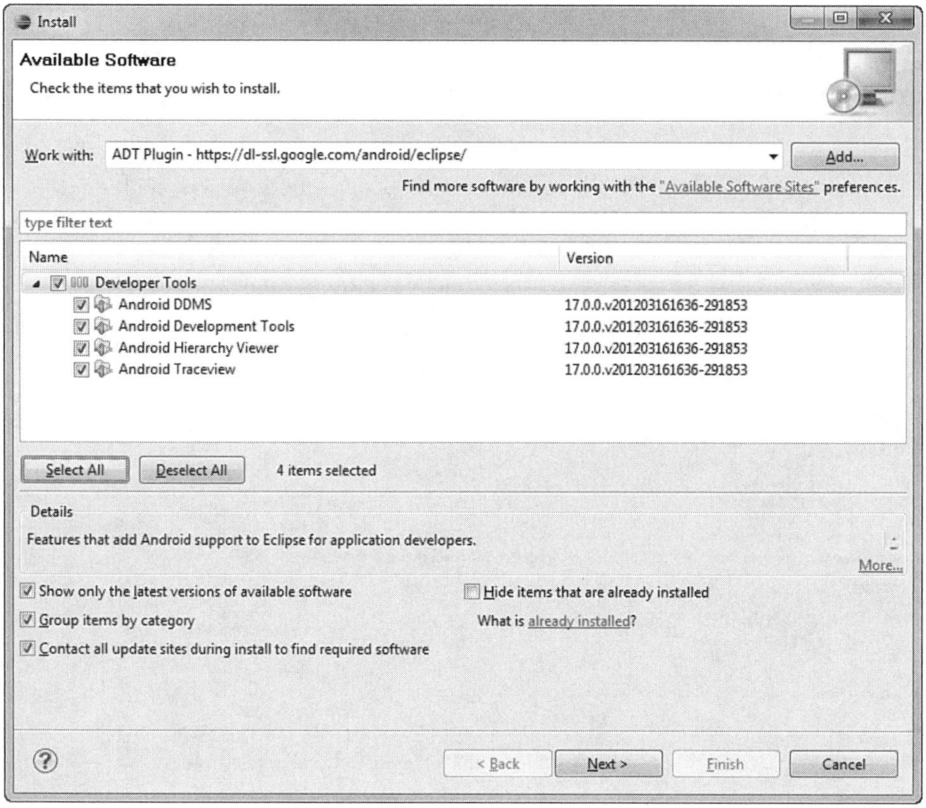

FIGURE 2.16
Installing the Developer Tools for Android in Eclipse.

After these steps, the Android plug-in will be installed, along with any additional packages needed by Eclipse. Some of these packages might look familiar if you also installed NetBeans, but the packages are also needed separately by Eclipse because it has a different configuration from NetBeans.

Summary

I recommend you try both NetBeans and Eclipse with the full Android SDK working in both IDEs before ultimately deciding which one to use. Each has strengths and weaknesses, and it's likely one or the other will appeal to you. It's helpful to make this determination early on so you will be more productive as you delve into the inner workings of the Android's game and graphics libraries! NetBeans is easier to use, in my opinion, but Eclipse has better features and official support from the Android development team. For a beginner, NetBeans is a better choice because it's easier to use. NetBeans can open a folder as a project, whereas Eclipse has to import a workspace and tends to write workspace settings files without confirmation (leading to confusion for a beginner).

Q&A

Q. Eclipse and NetBeans have a comparable toolset for Java development. If you have spent any time with either IDE, what are your impressions? If you are new to both, what are your *first impressions* after using either IDE for the first time?

A. Answers will vary.

Q. There are a lot of steps required to get started doing Android development for the first time. But someone who is already programming in Java using either NetBeans or Eclipse might see the Android tools as a mere add-on. How do these open-source tools compare to comparable commercial software such as Visual Studio?

A. Answer will vary.

Workshop

Quiz

1. What is the name of the software that enables you to compile Java programs?

2. What is the name of the Android development library?

3. What is the official IDE for Android development?

Answers

1. Java Development Kit (JDK)

2. Android SDK

3. Eclipse

Activities

▶ After installing your preferred IDE, go through the steps to update the software to the latest versions (either Eclipse or NetBeans, as the case may be). This will prepare you for the serious development work coming up in future hours.

Configuring NetBeans and Eclipse with the Android SDK

What You'll Learn in This Hour:

▶ Creating an Android emulator device

▶ Running the emulator

▶ Adding the Android plug-in to NetBeans

▶ Adding the Android plug-in to Eclipse

This hour covers additional prerequisites needed to use the Android SDK with an IDE. We're taking this in small steps now with plenty of figure examples to act as a quick reference for your Android programming projects to come. In this hour, you learn how to use the Android Virtual Device Manager to set up the emulator to run your Android programs. Then you learn how to add the Android SDK to NetBeans and Eclipse. The SDK was already installed in Hour 2, "Installing the Development Tools," so if you skipped that step, you will need to go back and install it.

Creating an Android Emulator Device

If you think that there are a lot of steps required just to get up and running with Android, you would be right! But we're on the right track and almost done with all of the prerequisites. Soon we will be writing game code. First, what you need to do is configure an Android emulator. An emulator is called Android Virtual Device, or AVD. You must use the Android Virtual Device Manager, shown in Figure 3.1, to create an emulator device.

The reason for needing an emulation *manager* is because of all the Android OS versions that have come out so quickly, in just the past three years. Also, developers might need to test their programs on more than one version of the Android OS to ensure that they work correctly.

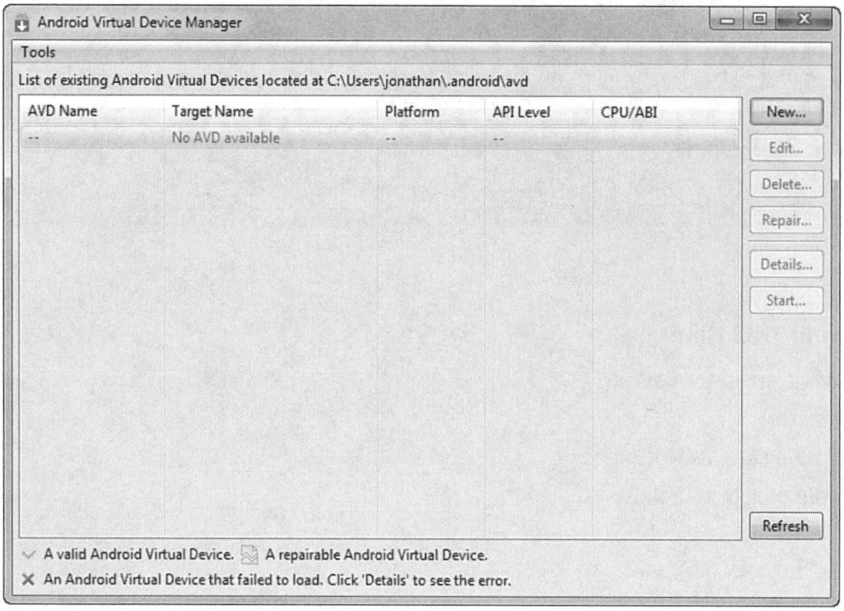

FIGURE 3.1
The Android Virtual Device Manager is used to set up the Android emulator.

Creating a New Emulator Device

First, we'll create an emulator device. Click the New button on the right side of the AVD Manager. This brings up the dialog shown in Figure 3.2, Create New Android Virtual Device (AVD). If AVD Manager is not running, you can find it in Program Files under Android SDK Tools.

As you can see, a lot of options exist for the emulator! First, we'll focus on the Target field, which has a drop-down list of Android OS targets. This list will be quite small if you installed only 4.0 or 4.1 (using the Android SDK Manager in the previous hour). If multiple SDKs are installed, you will be able to choose the version you want to emulate.

Give your new emulator device a name, such as MyAndroid (or a descriptive name related to the settings chosen).

Choose the target for Android 4. It might say 4.0.3 or 4.1 or some other revision, depending on the specific version you installed on your dev PC.

The CPU/ABI field should be grayed out for Android 4 because devices use a standard CPU. If, for any reason, this field is not grayed out (for instance, if you are targeting API 14 or earlier), be sure to set it to ARM. Again, this shouldn't be necessary if you're using the latest version of the API.

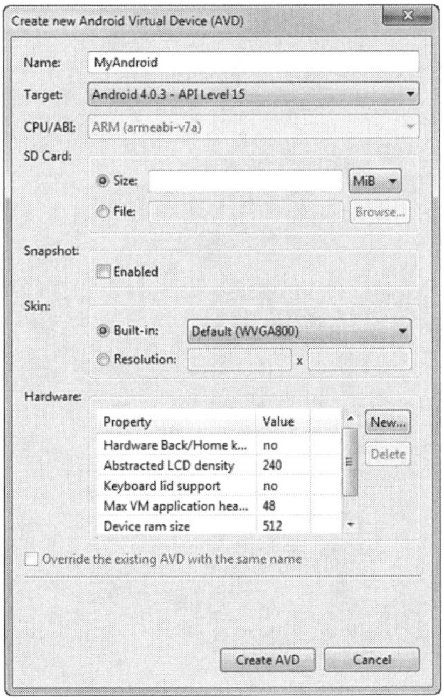

FIGURE 3.2
Creating a new emulator—Android Virtual Device.

If you want to simulate an SD Card in the emulator, you can specify the size of the SD Card.

The display setting is a challenge because there are so many options. It's probably safe to go with WVGA800, although there are others. This will differ quite significantly depending on the hardware you want to emulate. For instance, if you want to emulate a specific smartphone model, you would look up the screen resolution for that phone. But if you want to emulate a tablet, it will likely have a different screen. This allows you to create more than one emulator device for these various possibilities in the hardware.

Figure 3.3 shows the AVD Manager with the new device added to the list. An emulator device called MyAndroid has been added. If you want to quickly peruse the settings for any device, double-click the device in the list to bring up a mini detail dialog.

Running the Emulator

Choose your emulator device in the list and click the Start button on the right. This brings up the mini launch dialog shown in Figure 3.4. You can tweak a few options if desired and then click the Launch button.

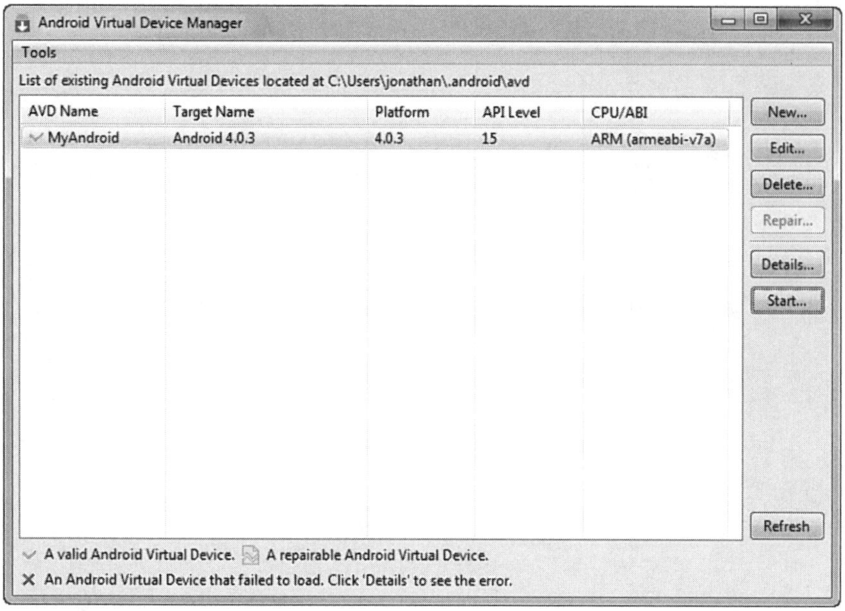

FIGURE 3.3
A new Android Virtual Device has been added.

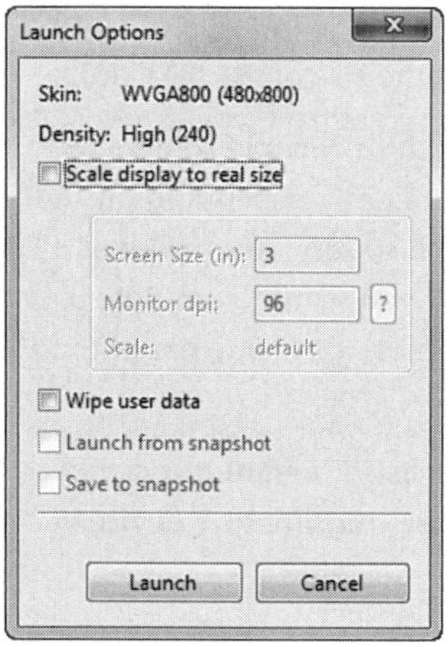

FIGURE 3.4
Preparing to launch the emulator.

The emulator device is shown in Figure 3.5, running Android OS 4.0. It may take a few minutes for the emulator to bring up the home screen shown here. The emulator must install the OS and then run it. Because this is rather time consuming, you will want to keep the emulator open while writing Android code so it's available anytime you build and run your code.

FIGURE 3.5
The Android OS 4.0 emulator is running.

Plugging Android SDK into NetBeans

Although the Android SDK has been installed, NetBeans doesn't automatically know about it, so we have to configure NetBeans to recognize Android projects. This is done with a special plug-in. We'll go over the configuration step by step with plenty of screenshots so you can refer to this hour if needed.

The plug-in has to be downloaded from within NetBeans and is available from a file repository at kenai.com. The plug-in is called NBAndroid, which is short for "NetBeans Android."

First, open the Tools menu in NetBeans, as shown in Figure 3.6, and choose the Plug-ins menu option.

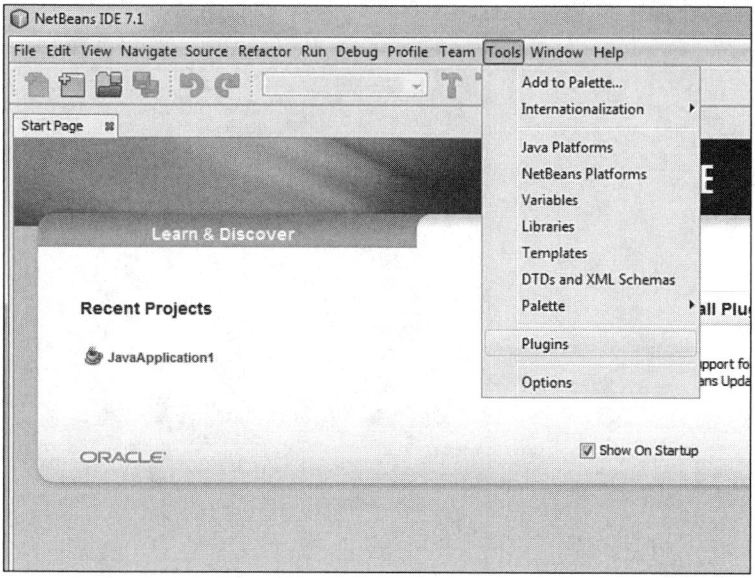

FIGURE 3.6
Invoking the Plug-ins dialog using the Tools menu.

If this is a new install of NetBeans, you likely will not have any additional plug-ins installed yet (as expected). The Plug-ins dialog is shown in Figure 3.7. This first tab shows only updates and is normally empty.

Open the Settings tab, shown in Figure 3.8. Three update centers will be listed (or more, if you are using a more recent version than NetBeans 7.1). The options are not important, but just for reference: Certified Plug-ins, NetBeans Distribution, and Plug-in Portal. We will be adding our own new plug-in source.

On the right side is a button labeled Add. Use this button to bring up the Update Center Customizer dialog (see Figure 3.9). This dialog has two fields where you can specify a new source for plug-ins.

In the Name field, enter **kenai.com**. In the URL field, enter this URL: **http://kenai.com/down-loads/nbandroid/updatecenter/updates.xml**.

Click the OK button to proceed.

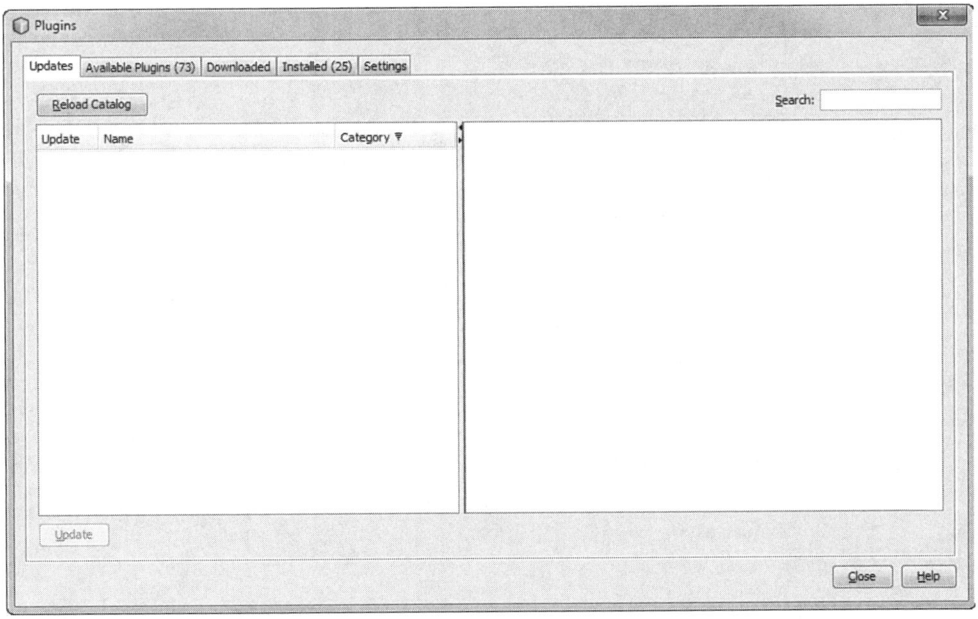

FIGURE 3.7
The Plug-ins dialog has several tabs.

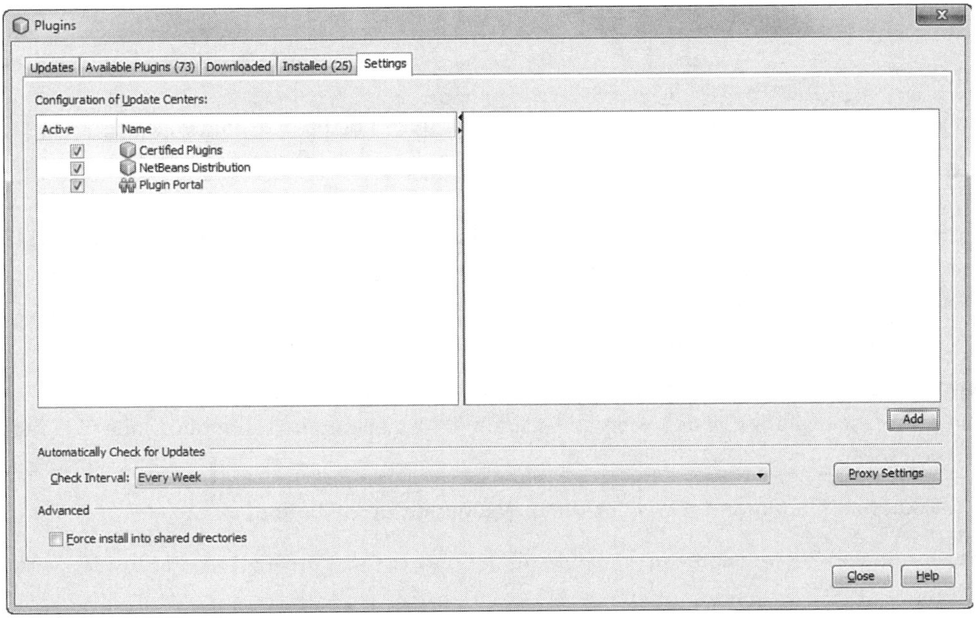

FIGURE 3.8
Viewing the list of plug-in sources.

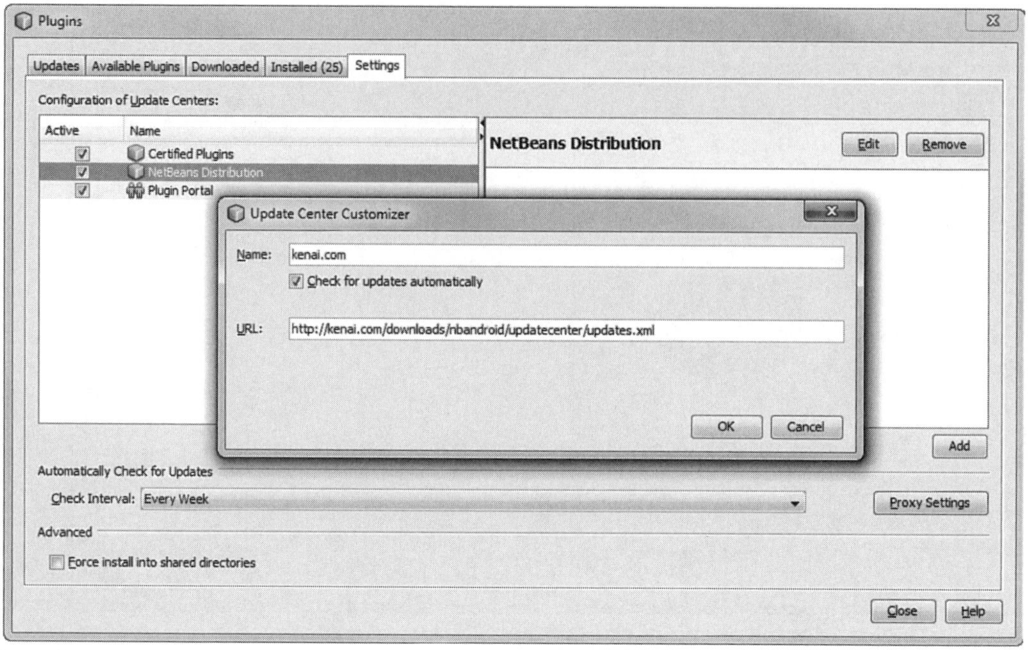

FIGURE 3.9
Adding a new plug-in source (kenai.com).

BY THE WAY

Remember that URLs tend to change without notice! Your best friend is a search engine: Try searching Google for "netbeans android sdk" and you should find the latest tools and plug-ins.

NetBeans then parses the URL specified for any available NetBeans plug-ins. Nothing more will come up—just switch over to the Available Plug-ins tab. The Android plug-ins appear at the top of the list (see Figure 3.10). If the list is not sorted alphabetically, click the Name field heading to sort by Name.

The only plug-in really needed is Android. Two have been selected in Figure 3.11, but the Android Test Runner plug-in is not essential—usually it's for testing larger applications. You may skip it if you like.

Check the Android plug-in and then click the Install button at the bottom left.

A confirmation window will come up showing all the plug-ins you have selected to install. Click Next.

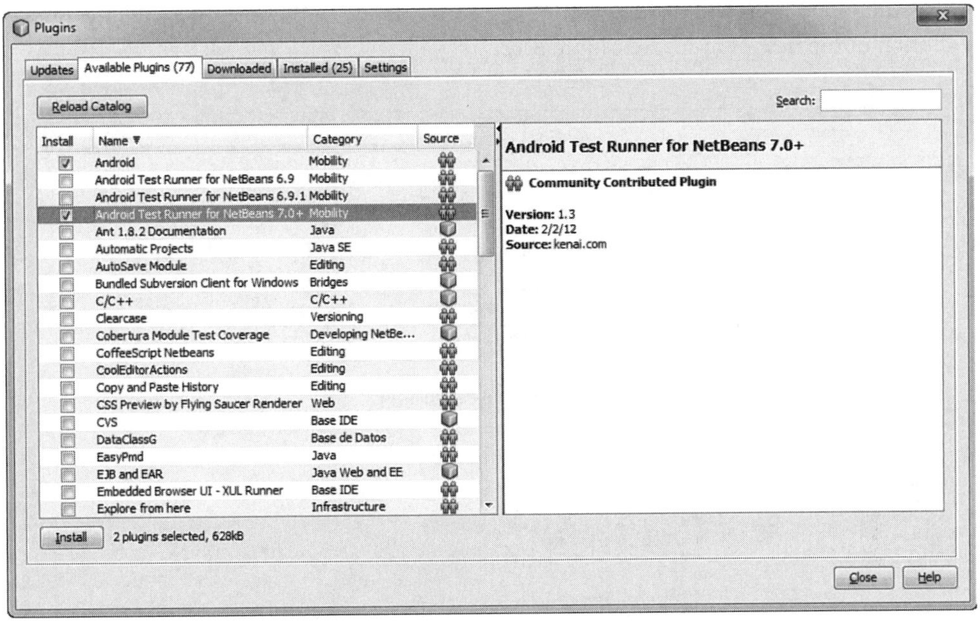

FIGURE 3.10
The list of Available Plug-ins (from all sources).

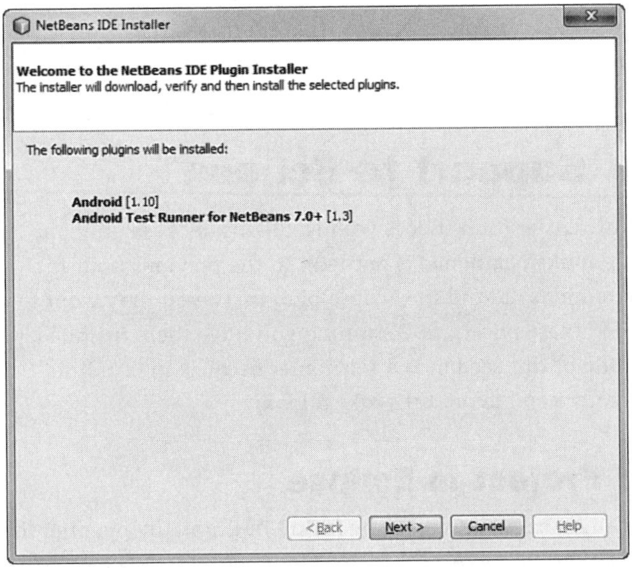

FIGURE 3.11
Preparing to install the Android plug-in for NetBeans.

The new NBAndroid plug-in will be installed. When complete, go to the Installed tab to verify the installation of the new plug-in. See Figure 3.12.

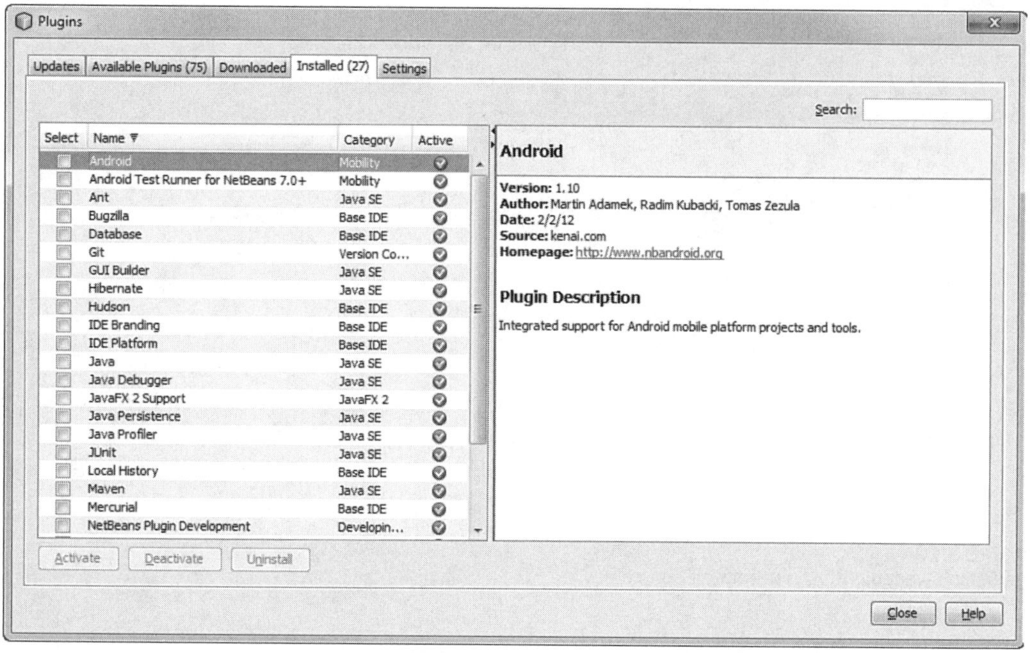

FIGURE 3.12
The Android plug-in now appears in the Installed list.

Adding Android SDK Support to Eclipse

The Android SDK plugs into Eclipse a little easier than it does with NetBeans because only one install is required (and no separate plug-in like *NBAndroid* is needed). In the previous hour is a tutorial on installing the Android Development Kit and the Eclipse plug-in, so you may want to refer to Hour 2 if you haven't yet installed these packages. Assuming you have them installed, Eclipse is ready to go. In that case, the title of this section is a misnomer because the Android SDK does not need to be added—it's already good to go. Let's take a look.

Creating a New Android Project in Eclipse

If you finished installing the files in the previous hour, verify the install in Eclipse by opening the Window menu, shown in Figure 3.13. You should see Android SDK Manager and AVD Manager to verify that Eclipse recognizes the new Android packages.

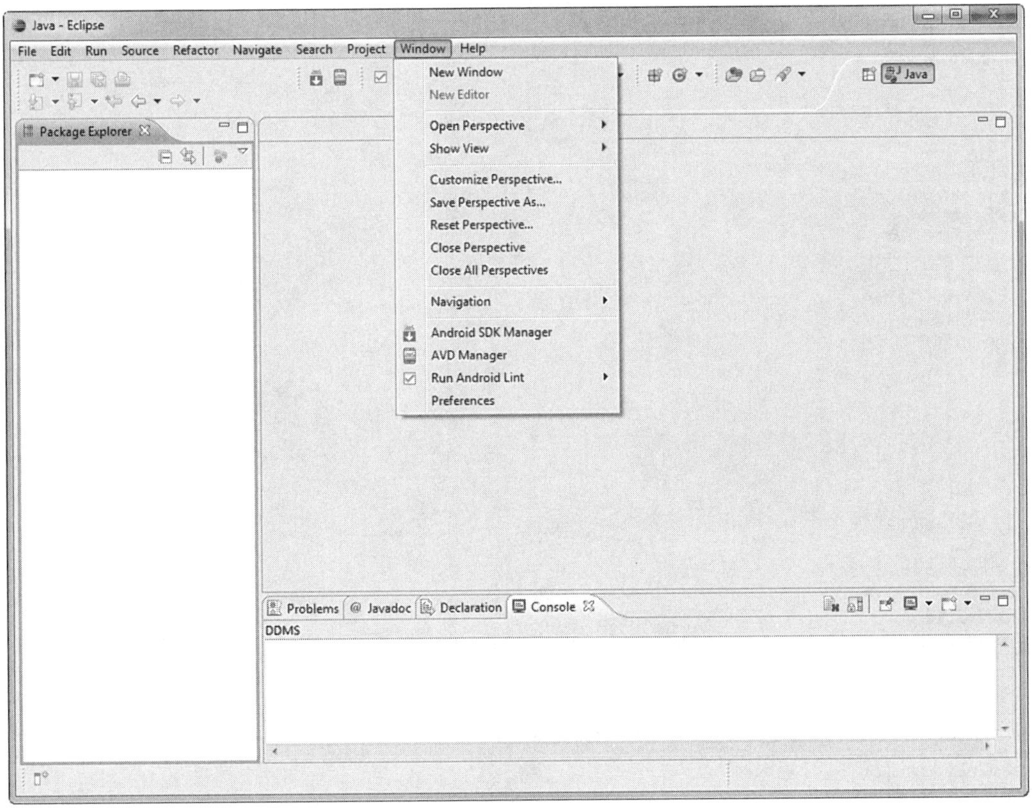

FIGURE 3.13
The Window menu in Eclipse shows the Android SDK tools.

Now, open the File menu and choose New, Project. You should see a new Android group, as shown in Figure 3.14. Choose Android Project from the options shown and click Next.

The New Android Project dialog appears next, as shown in Figure 3.15. Enter a name for the project and choose either the default location or enter a new location for the project files.

The next dialog, shown in Figure 3.16, allows you to choose the Android SDK target (because multiple Android SDK versions may be installed to support various OS release levels). In the example shown, Android 4.0.3 was automatically checked. If you have more than one SDK installed, you may choose from among them.

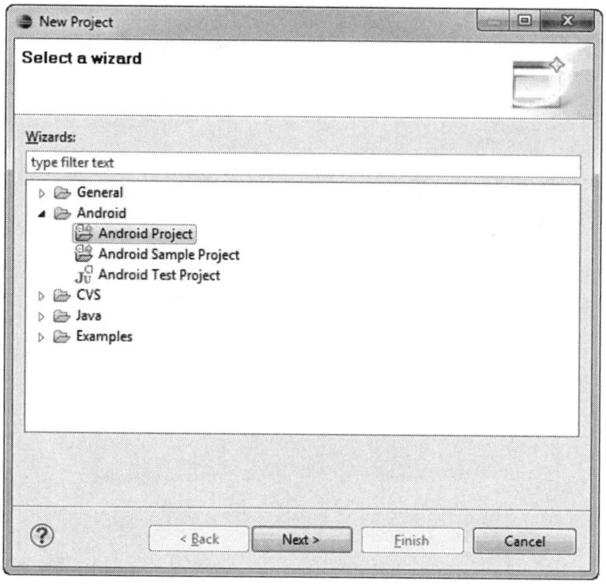

FIGURE 3.14
Creating a new Android project in Eclipse using the New Project dialog.

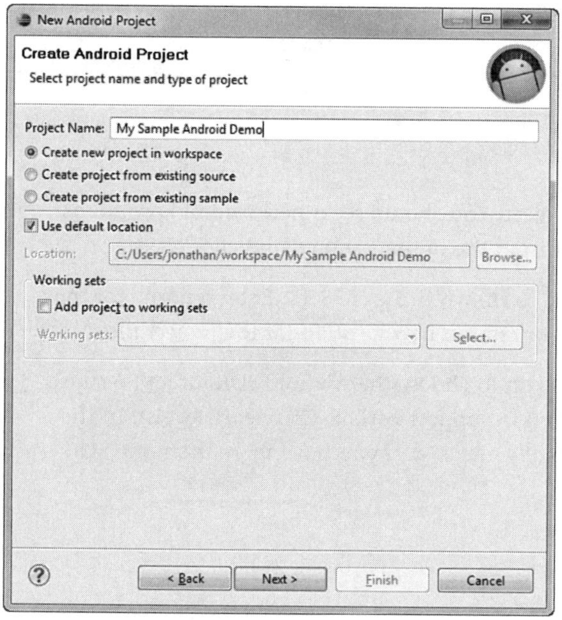

FIGURE 3.15
Entering the new project details.

FIGURE 3.16
Verifying the Build Target for the new project.

The next dialog that comes up in the New Android Project Wizard, shown in Figure 3.17, will look familiar because you dealt with this information earlier in the NetBeans project: the Package Name and Activity. These will make a little more sense in the next hour when you see the names in the source code. For now, you may change the values as needed. Because this is only a configuration tutorial and you aren't writing any real Android code just yet, the values are not that important. But, as was the case with NetBeans, you must enter at least two words separated by a period into the Package Name field.

There are a *lot* of files created for a new project. Take a look at Figure 3.18, which shows the newly created project. In Package Explorer (on the left side of the IDE) you will see a folder called `src`, and then `my.project` (the package name), which contains the source code file called `MySampleAndroidDemoActivity.java`. This is similar to the files in the NetBeans project.

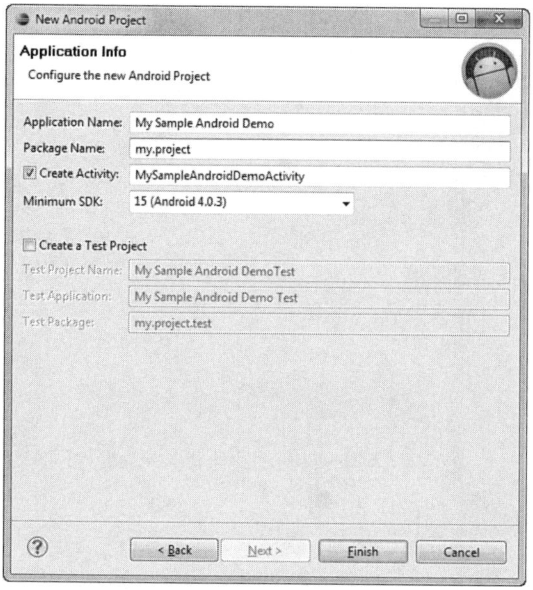

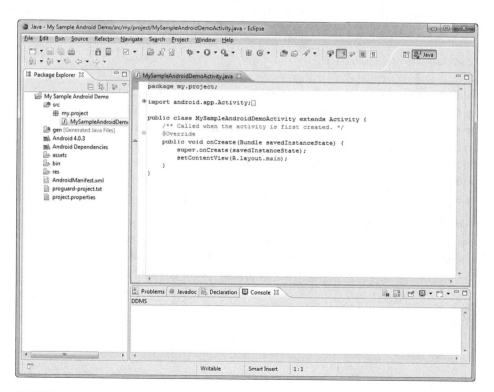

FIGURE 3.17
Entering the Application Info fields.

FIGURE 3.18
The new Android project has been created.

Choosing an Android Build Target

To build and run an Android project in Eclipse, open up the Window menu and choose Preferences. This brings up a dialog called Preferences, shown in Figure 3.19. In the list of preference groups, choose Android to show the Android preferences. Use the Browse button to choose the Android SDK location. This may be in `C:\Program Files\Android`, or it may be in My Documents, or elsewhere—it depends on where you chose to install the SDK according to the steps. Next, choose the target from the list (Android 4.0.3 in this case).

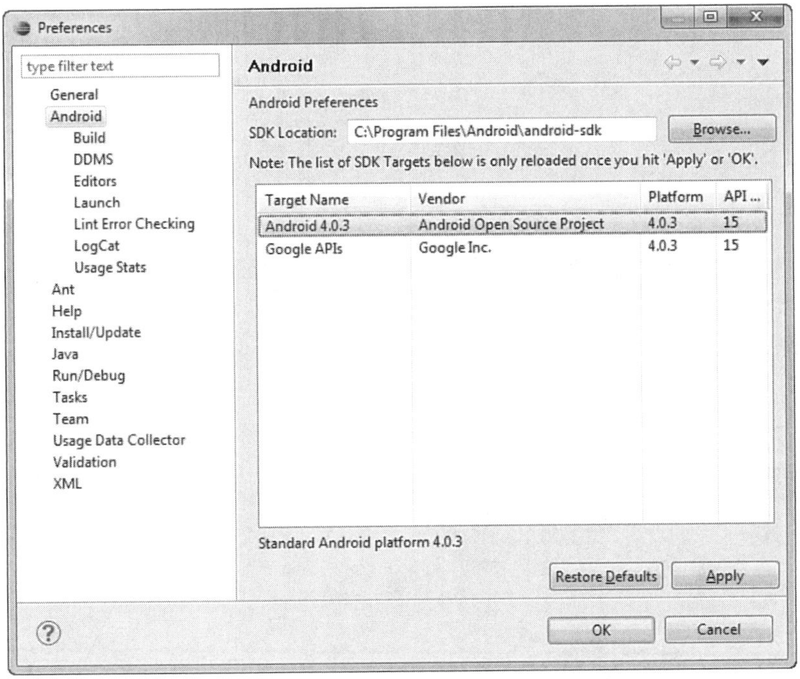

FIGURE 3.19
Setting the Android SDK location and choosing the Android build target.

Summary

This hour covered the additional steps needed to get started programming with the Android SDK using both NetBeans and Eclipse. By now you will have created an emulator device and installed the Android plug-ins for NetBeans and Eclipse and are ready to begin writing code! You write your first real Android project in the next hour.

Q&A

Q. How do you think Java compares to other languages frequently used for game programming, such as C++ and C#?

A. Answers will vary.

Q. If the Android SDK is the library for making apps and games on the Android platform, how does it compare with the DirectX SDK for Windows? You may need to search online for information in order to discuss this topic.

A. Answers will vary.

Workshop

Quiz

1. What is the technical name for the Android emulator?

2. Which version of the Android OS does the emulator support?

3. Which IDE uses the NBAndroid plug-in?

Answers

1. Android Virtual Device (AVD)

2. All versions (that have been installed).

3. NetBeans

Activities

▶ The Android SDK includes libraries written in Java that interface with a lower-level interface written in C++. It is possible to write C++ code and compile it to run on Android, with Java as a bridge. What is this C++ library called, and how does it work? You may need to do a cursory search online for "android C++ library."

HOUR 4
Creating Your First Android Program

What You'll Learn in This Hour:

▶ Creating a new Android project
▶ Configuring the NBAndroid plug-in for NetBeans
▶ Compiling and running programs in the emulator
▶ Writing a "Hello, Android!" program
▶ Comparing the Emulator to an Android Device

In this hour you will write your first Android program. The previous hours should have helped you get your NetBeans and Eclipse development environments up and running with the Android SDK. You should have also used the Android Virtual Device Manager to create an Android emulator device. Now it's time to write some code. Finally! In this hour, you learn how to build and run an Android program, targeting both the emulator and a physical Android device. Because NetBeans is more difficult to use than Eclipse, this hour spends a little extra time on that IDE, whereas Eclipse is already configured (as per the previous hour) and requires no extra steps.

Creating a New Android Project

Open the File menu in NetBeans and choose New Project or use the New Project icon on the toolbar as shown in Figure 4.1.

The New Project dialog appears, as shown in Figure 4.2. In the Categories list, you should see Android as one of the options. Select it. On the right pane you should see the Android projects available via the NBAndroid plug-in that you installed in Hour 3, "Configuring NetBeans and Eclipse with the Android SDK." Choose Android Project and click Next.

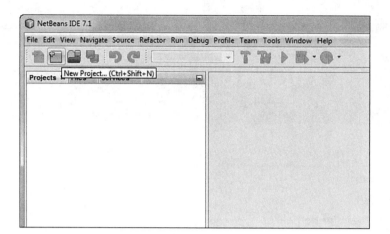

FIGURE 4.1
Preparing to create a new project in NetBeans.

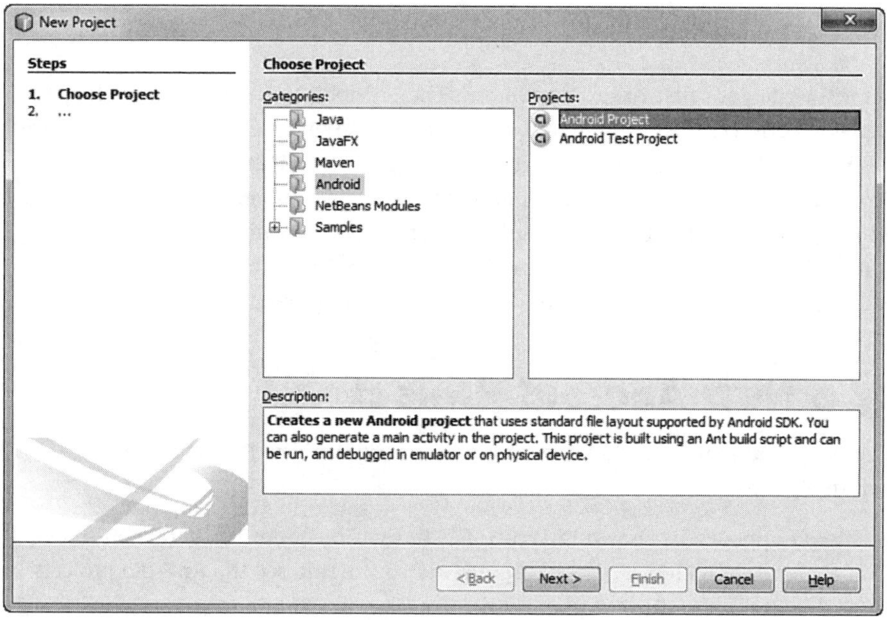

FIGURE 4.2
The New Project dialog with the Android category selected.

The New Android Application dialog, shown in Figure 4.3, is rather complex with a lot of fields. First, enter a new name using the Project Name field. Next, choose the Project Location using the Browse button. Then, if it isn't checked already, check Set as Main Project.

Before continuing with the new project, we have to configure the NBAndroid plug-in. This is very easy and we'll do it next.

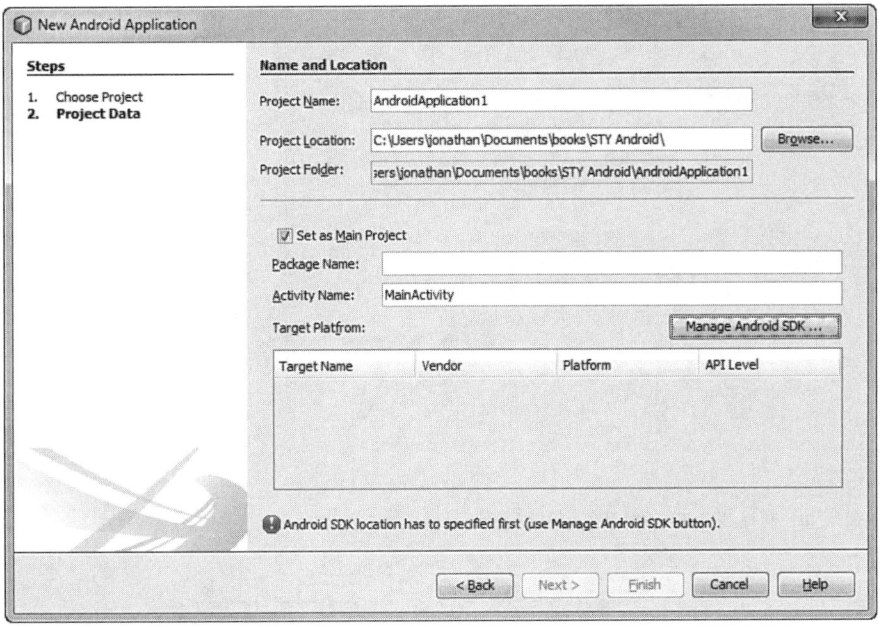

FIGURE 4.3
The New Android Application dialog.

Configuring the NBAndroid Plug-in

Click the Manage Android SDK button to bring up the Options dialog (Figure 4.4). If the SDK location is not already filled in, you will need to tell the NBAndroid plug-in where the Android SDK is located on your hard drive. The default location under Windows is shown in the figure: `C:\Program Files\Android\android-sdk`. It will look a bit different if you are using the Mac OS X or Linux version of NetBeans. After browsing for the Android SDK location, click OK to close this dialog and save the setting. This returns you to the New Android Application dialog.

When you return to the New Android Application dialog, shown in Figure 4.5, note that the Target Platform table has two entries, one of which is the all-important Android 4.0.3 item. The NBAndroid plug-in found and added these SDKs to its list. If you see more than just the few items shown here, which is very likely on some development PCs, be sure to look for the Android item and not one of the others (such as one of the Google APIs).

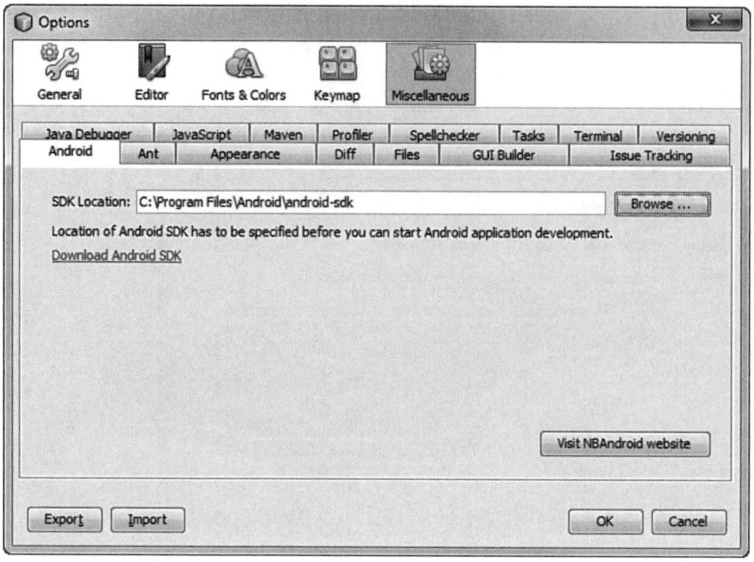

FIGURE 4.4
The NBAndroid plug-in option is found under the Android tab.

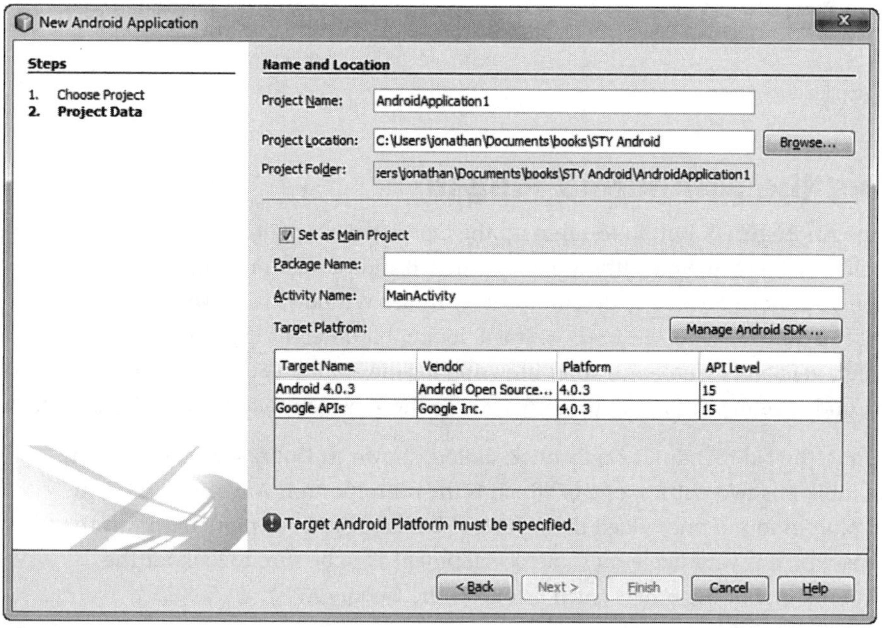

FIGURE 4.5
The SDKs have been added to the Target Platform table.

Completing the New Project Settings

If desired, change the name of the project to something other than AndroidApplication1.

If you haven't already, select the Android 4.0.x target in the Target Platform table. This tells the plug-in which SDK to use when compiling your Android code.

Enter a value into both the Package Name and Activity Name fields. MainActivity is usually filled in to the Activity Name field for you, so you need to choose only a package name.

The package name must contain *at least* two words separated by a period. For example: `john.doe`. But it's better to use the program name along with another word that identifies you as the developer. For example, I entered `jharbour.android.HelloAndroid`.

The package name does not need to be complicated—just unique. If you will *never* be deploying your program to the Android Market, then the name isn't important at all, and you can use any name that fits the format. Just note, however, that you can have only one app installed on your Android device using that unique name (including the emulator), and the package name is the internal app name. For example, if you use the same name for all your test projects (while working through this book), that is the only app you will see on the device (or emulator), which will be replaced each time you build and deploy the project.

When complete, your project properties might resemble that shown in Figure 4.6, for example.

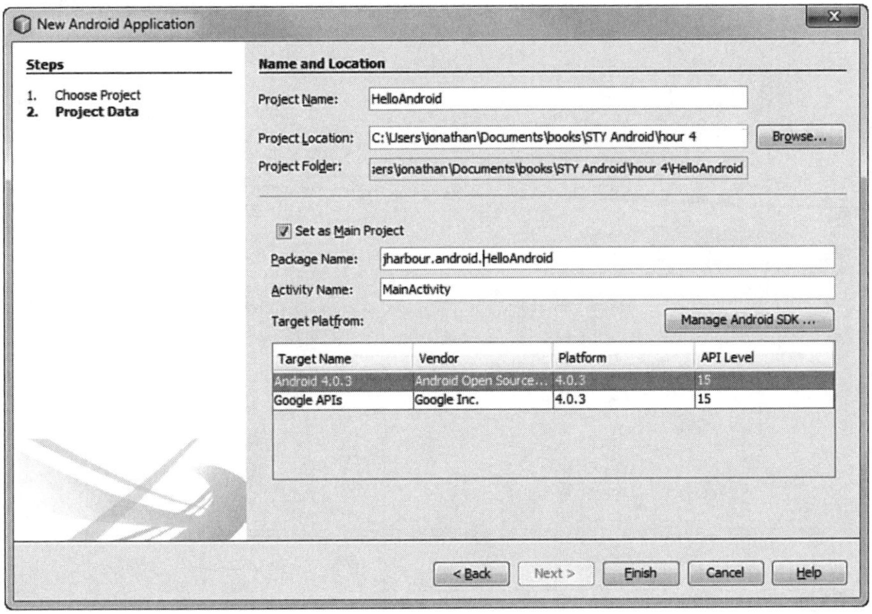

FIGURE 4.6
Entering values into the new project's property fields.

BY THE WAY

The process for creating a new project in Eclipse is so similar to the process in NetBeans that we'll forgo a duplicate tutorial. Eclipse tends to be easier to use. The tutorials in these first four hours should help you get up to speed in whichever IDE you are using. In later hours, we will be using Eclipse exclusively. Our early emphasis on NetBeans (the more difficult to use IDE) is for the benefit of a reader using either one.

Building the New Project

We're going to do a quick test build and run the new project to see if the Android SDK is working in NetBeans. You can use the hammer icon on the toolbar to compile the project or use Run, Build Project, shown in Figure 4.7.

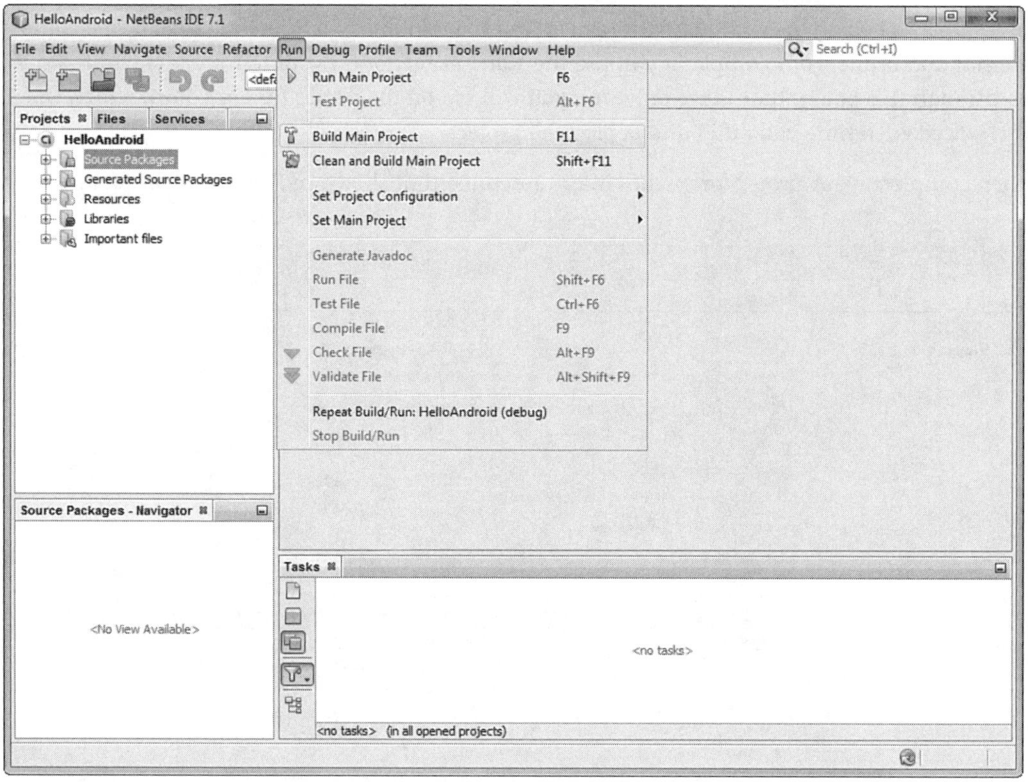

FIGURE 4.7
Using the Run, Build Project menu option for a quick test build.

Opening the Output Window

It's hard to tell whether the code compiled successfully without seeing the progress of the compiler. At the bottom of NetBeans, a progress bar and status message will display the progress of the compile, but I find this inadequate. I prefer to see what the compiler is doing. To view the output window, open the Window menu and choose Output, Output, as shown in Figure 4.8.

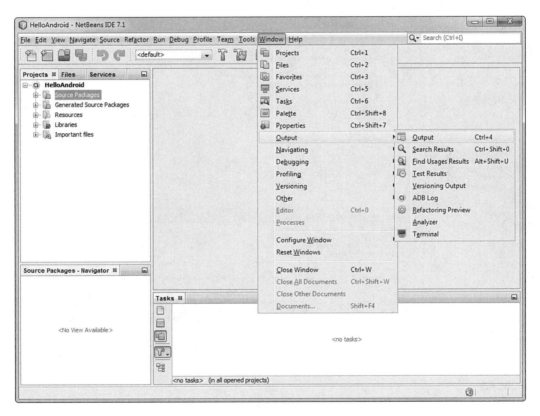

FIGURE 4.8
Opening the Output window to see the build progress.

The Output window appears. At the bottom in green text is the message BUILD SUCCESSFUL. That's what I like to see—details! Also, at this time, if you want to see the source code, look in the Project Manager (upper left), and expand Source Packages, *your package name*, MainActivity. java. Double-click the file to open it in the editor, as shown in Figure 4.9.

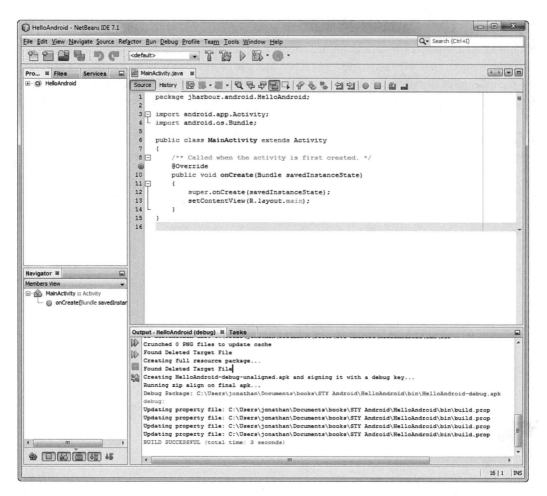

FIGURE 4.9
The Output window shows the steps taken by the compiler to build the project.

Running the Program in the Emulator

You do not absolutely *have* to build first before running the program. You can just press the little green arrow icon on the toolbar to run the program. If it needs to be compiled first (based on file save time), it will compile first. Another way to run the program is by opening the Run menu and choosing Run Project, as shown in Figure 4.10.

You should have created an emulator device using the AVD Manager back in Hour 3, "Configuring NetBeans and Eclipse with the Android SDK." If you skipped that step, now might be a good time to return to that hour to learn about the options available in the Android emulator.

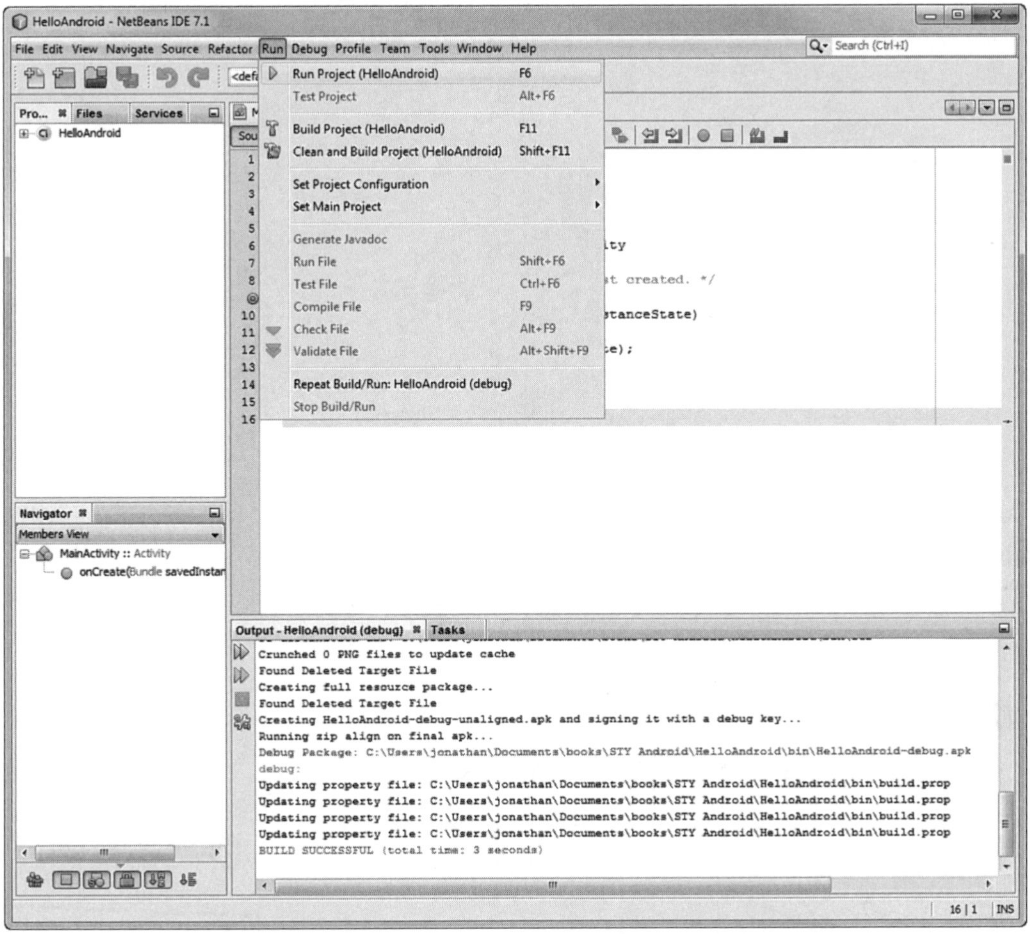

FIGURE 4.10
Using the Run, Run Project menu option to run the program.

If the emulator is not already running, the dialog shown in Figure 4.11 appears, showing no running devices and one device in the bottom list.

The emulator takes a *very* long time to start up! You will want to keep the emulator running while working on your Android code. After the emulator is running, you don't need to wait for it to start up every time you compile and run your programs. If the emulator is already running, you can select it from the upper list, shown in Figure 4.12.

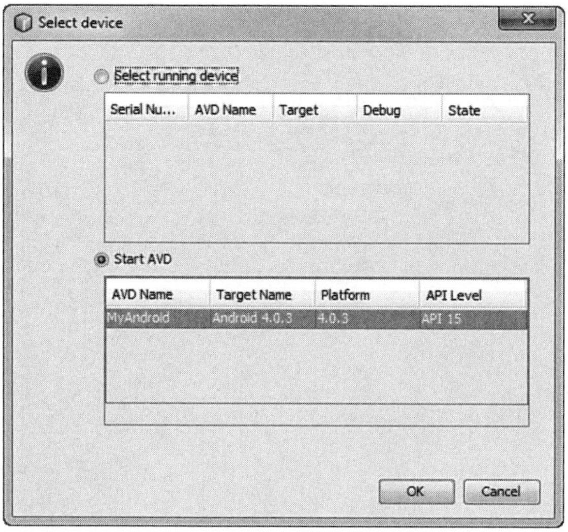

FIGURE 4.11
Choosing the emulator target for the program.

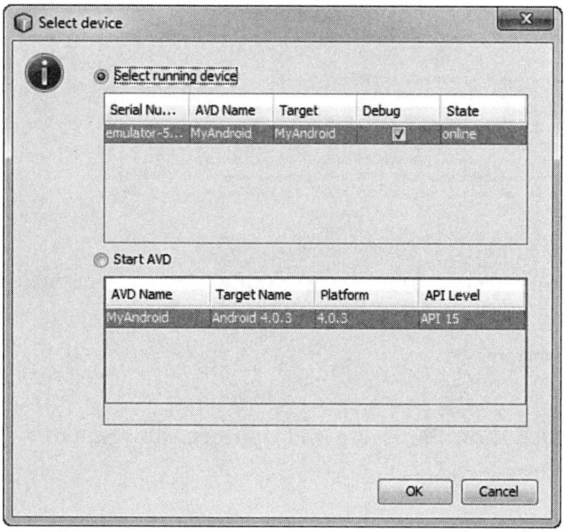

FIGURE 4.12
Selecting an emulator device that is already running.

When running a new instance of the emulator, the OS is loaded, which takes an unpleasantly long time (Figure 4.13). For this reason, you should be sure to keep the emulator window running while doing your programming. After it is loaded, the emulator responds quickly to the Run command.

FIGURE 4.13
New instances of the emulator start up rather slowly.

The OS also starts up just like a physical Android 4.0 device, including the startup lock (Figure 4.14). Slide the lock to the right to unlock the device before attempting to run your program, or the emulator won't run it (because it's locked!).

FIGURE 4.14
The Android screen starts in locked mode.

Although we asked NetBeans to run the project and then waited for the emulator to start up, it does not proceed to run after the startup process is over some time later (see Figure 4.15). This happens because NetBeans launches the run command and does not wait for a response—it just goes back into normal editing mode.

FIGURE 4.15
The Android home screen.

After reaching the Android home screen, you will need to rerun the project again. The result is shown in Figure 4.16. This program doesn't have any functional code yet, so all we see is the blank program screen come up with the title at the top.

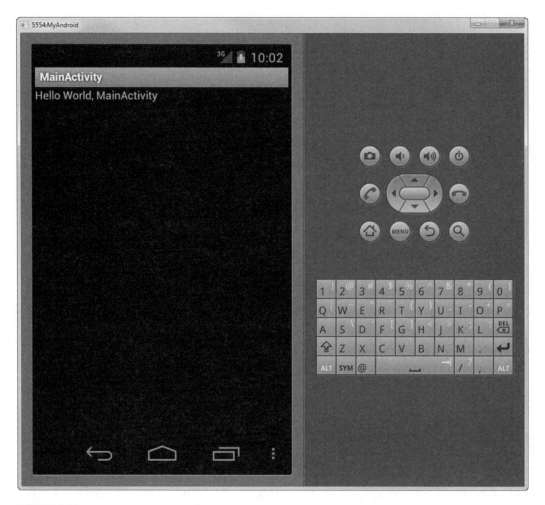

FIGURE 4.16
This program doesn't do anything yet, but it does run!

Editing the "Hello, Android!" Program

Modify the source code for the program so that it looks like Figure 4.17. Do you see the new
`import` line? It imports the `android.widget` library, which contains user interface controls like
`TextView`. This isn't game programming with a pixel buffer by any means, but we have to start
somewhere, and this is an easy way to test the tools and SDKs.

```
package jharbour.android.HelloAndroid;

import android.app.Activity;
```

```
import android.os.Bundle;
import android.widget.*;

public class MainActivity extends Activity
{
    /** Called when the activity is first created. */
    @Override
    public void onCreate(Bundle savedInstanceState)
    {
        super.onCreate(savedInstanceState);
        TextView tv = new TextView(this);
        tv.setText("Hello, Android!");
        setContentView(tv);
    }
}
```

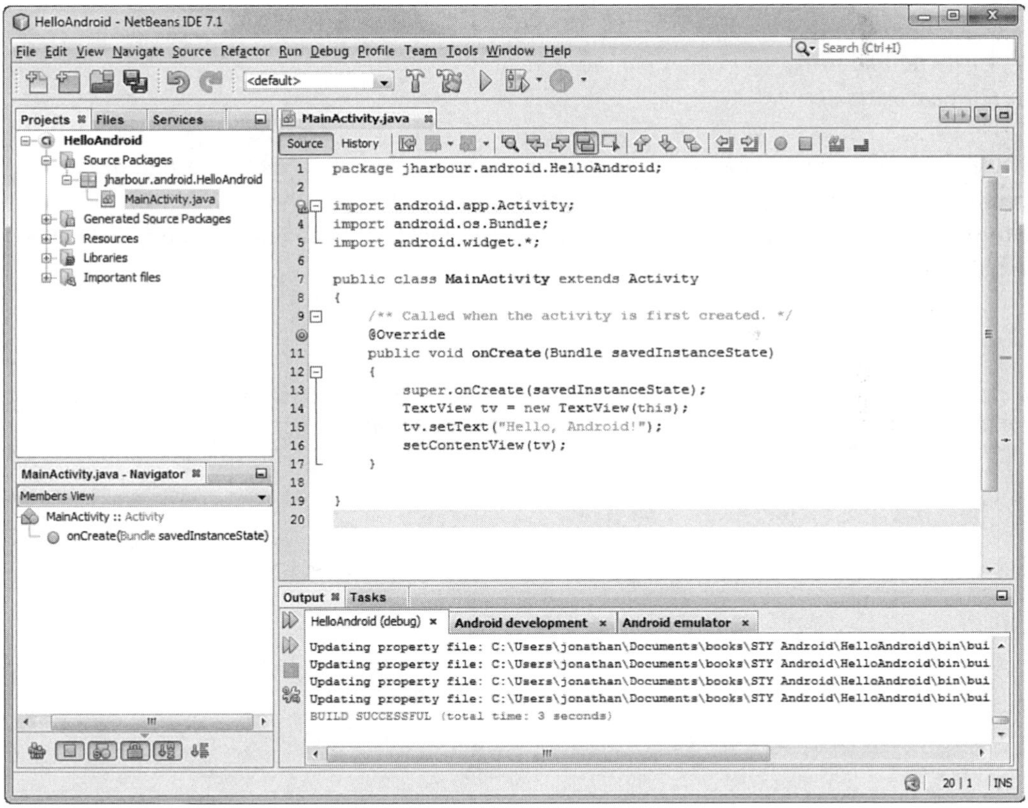

FIGURE 4.17
The newly modified "Hello, Android!" program.

Now, go ahead and build the project again (hammer icon). You can just run it without building if you prefer, but it would be helpful to get familiar with both the build and run options in NetBeans. The build icon on the toolbar looks like a hammer. The run icon on the toolbar looks like a green arrow. It is helpful to build first while getting familiar with a new editor and compiler.

Try clicking the hammer icon to build the project.

If you see the message "BUILD SUCCESSFUL" at the bottom of the Output window, you will know the program compiled and is ready to run.

Press the run icon (green arrow) to launch the program. But, before doing this, open the emulator to make sure it is ready to run. The Android OS will go to sleep if you leave it alone too long. Running the program produces the result shown in Figure 4.18. It's not too different from the previous run, except for this change:

```
Hello World, MainActivity
```

has been replaced with

```
Hello, Android!
```

The difference between the two lines of output is not important. What matters is that our program runs! It has taken quite a few steps to get the Android SDK set up with NetBeans correctly, so this is verification. What's next? Now we can begin pursuing game programming topics like graphics and user input.

BY THE WAY

To close a program without shutting down the emulator, click the small Return soft button at the bottom of the Android screen (the one that looks like a curved arrow).

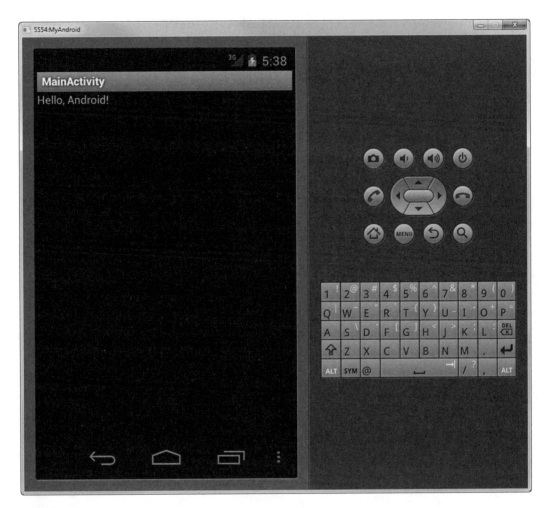

FIGURE 4.18
The program will print a text message using a TextView widget.

Comparing the Emulator to an Android Device

The emulator allows you to test your programs on different variations of the Android OS and different screen resolutions, but limitations exist to the emulator (formally known as Android Virtual Device, or AVD). The emulator is sluggish even on high-end development PCs. At this time, a high-end machine will have something like a 6-core processor (or two such processors on a server motherboard) and 8GB or more of RAM. An AVD is usually configured with 512MB or 1GB of RAM. Figure 4.19 shows the AVD configuration dialog (note the Device RAM Size field at the bottom of the Hardware list). By the way, 512MB is not enough RAM for an AVD using WSVGA mode (1024×600). With this much RAM, the emulator will be unstable and pop up error messages; 1GB of RAM is a better choice when using HD resolutions.

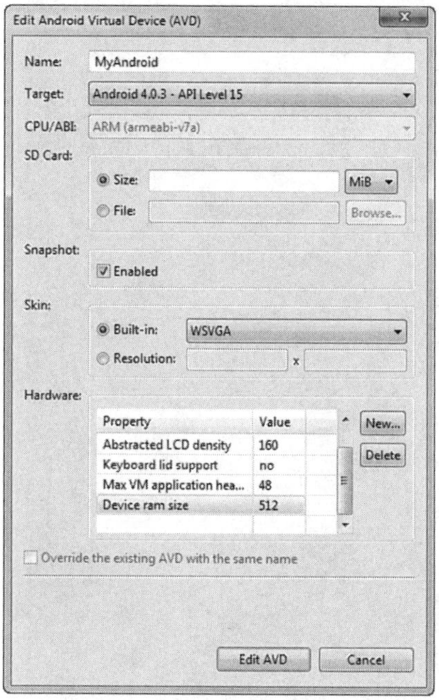

FIGURE 4.19
Changing the device RAM size setting for an AVD.

AVD Limitations

The Android SDK documentation makes this suggestion: "When building a mobile application, it's important that you always test your application on a real device before releasing it to users." This is self-evident after using the emulator for a while. Figure 4.20 shows an AVD simulating a WSVGA (1024×600) device—a low-resolution Android Tablet device. The HD tablet screen is called WXGA800 (1280×800).

DID YOU KNOW

It's interesting that 1280×800 is a multiple of 320×200, a very old MS-DOS video game resolution that was commonly used in games back in the 1990s.

An AVD is helpful for quick tests of appearance but woefully slow for serious long-term application or game development. In short, it will be very frustrating to use for very long if you haven't noticed already. If you are an indie developer, one Android device will serve you well for debugging and testing your code. If your project has some good funding, it will be useful to test your builds on several target devices. In other words, the AVD emulator is a limited support tool, not intended to be used full-time for serious development.

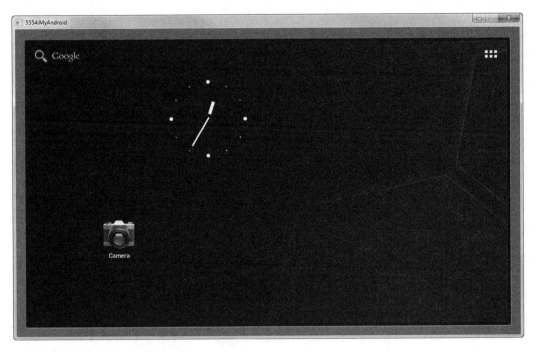

FIGURE 4.20
This AVD emulator simulates the WSVGA screen (1024×600) of a tablet.

Installing the Android Debug Bridge Device Driver

To run your code on a physical Android device, you will need to install a device driver called Android Debug Bridge, or ADB. This driver is more than just a USB device driver—by plugging your Android device into your system, it should come up as a generic memory device, where you can peruse the file system. The special ADB driver allows your system to support code debugging on the device.

WATCH OUT

By plugging the device into your system via USB, you expose the file system. This is one way that some Android users are able to gain administrator access to their devices, which is one step toward replacing the core Android OS with a new version. By rooting your Android, you usually lose support from the manufacturer for software updates and may not be able to access the Google Play (Android Market) system.

You can choose from many Android devices in the market for development. But be aware of the version of the Android OS some devices use because some cannot be upgraded. It is possible to "root" most Android devices, but by doing so you lose access to the manufacturer's support updates and possibly the Android Market as well (apps, games, and media available for sale). Rooting is fun for experimentation, but I prefer to have an unmodified Android device that more closely mirrors the experience the end user will have with my games.

BY THE WAY

If you are using Mac OS X or Linux for your Android development, go to this web page for instructions on configuring the system: http://developer.android.com/guide/developing/device.html.

First, to run code on a physical Android device (not the emulator), you must enable USB debugging on the device. This is done in the Settings on your Android Device. Go into Settings, Developer options. From here, enable the USB debugging option, shown in Figure 4.21. When you do this, your development system should detect the new device and attempt to install a driver.

Usually, on the PC side, the driver install will fail, so you will need to download a driver for it to work. Go to this web page to download the USB debug device driver: http://developer.android.com/sdk/oem-usb.html. Here are the steps for installing the USB driver for debugging under Windows 7.

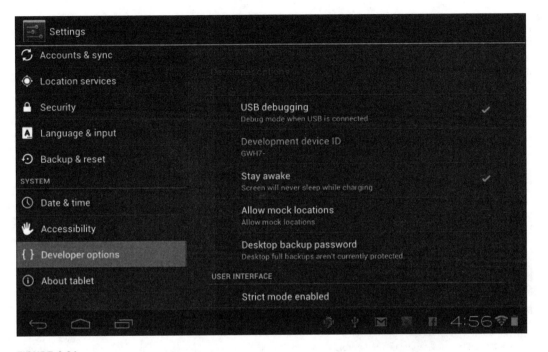

FIGURE 4.21
Enabling USB debugging on the Android device.

TRY IT YOURSELF ▼

1. Connect your Android device to the PC using a USB cable.

2. Right-click Computer on the desktop and select Manage.

3. Select Device Manager in the left pane.

4. Locate and expand Other Devices in the right pane.

5. Right-click the device name, such as AT1SO (for a Toshiba) or Nexus S (for a Samsung), and select Update Driver Software, as shown in Figure 4.22.

6. The Update Driver Software dialog will come up.

7. Select Browse my computer for driver software and click Next.

8. Click Browse and locate the USB driver folder. The Google USB Driver is located in `<sdk>\ extras\google\usb_driver`. From here, choose either amd64 or i386, as needed.

9. Click OK and then Next to install the driver.

   If these steps fail, you will want to locate the USB "ADB" driver for your specific Android device, and Google search will likely help. After completing the device driver install, the Android device will show up in the Device Manager, as shown in Figure 4.23.

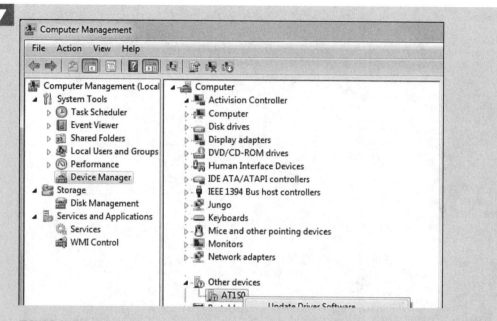

FIGURE 4.22
Updating the USB device driver for Android device debugging.

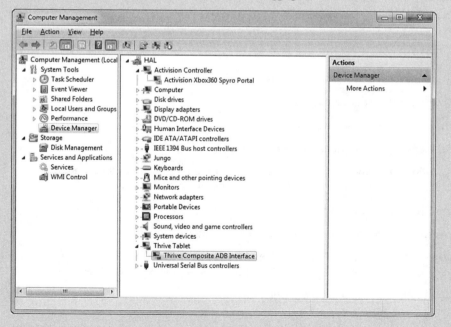

FIGURE 4.23
The Android device ADB driver has been installed.

Running Code on an Android Device

After you have your Android device connected to your development system, you can run code on the ADB. We'll use the example created earlier in the hour.

To run a program on your Android device, it must be built with the same version of the Android OS. Some devices support Android 4.0 or 4.1, and some do not. Some devices can be upgraded, and some cannot. The majority of the game code you are learning about in this book will also run on older Android OS devices, so it's not *absolutely* essential to create projects targeting SDK 4 (ICS or Jelly Bean or later). To maximize sales potential, you really do want to support older devices whenever possible. Although the OS features have improved since 3.2, the core SDK features we're concerned about for a video game have not undergone significant changes. So, you should be able to target 3.2, 4.0, 4,1, or later—although it may not be realistic to try to support versions prior to 3.2.

For the example in this hour, I have a Toshiba Thrive 7" tablet running OS 4.0.4. If you refer back to Hour 1 and the section titled "History of the Platform," you will find that this version was known by the name of Ice Cream Sandwich. The previous version was called Honeycomb. It is a good idea to support these older OSs! Fortunately, the larger Android device manufacturers are releasing updates to their older models fairly consistently now. So, for instance, while the Toshiba Thrive used for testing this book's examples originally shipped with 3.2 Honeycomb, it was updated to 4.0 Ice Cream Sandwich with a Toshiba update.

The very popular Amazon Kindle Fire runs Android 2.1 Eclair. That's pretty dated for a device launched in the fourth quarter of 2011. But Amazon has sold millions of these Kindle Fire devices, and those are millions of potential customers for your games. And just to show how quickly this platform is evolving, the newer Kindle Fire HD already ships with 4.0 ICS—not even a year after the first Kindle Fire hit the market. It is because of this rapid evolution that developers tend to use the code names rather than version numbers (Honeycomb, Ice Cream Sandwich, and so on).

So, let's test this "Hello, Android!" example on the Toshiba Thrive running 4.0 ICS. To change the target for a project in Eclipse, right-click the project name in Package Explorer and choose Properties. This brings up the dialog shown in Figure 4.24.

Select the Android option from the list of property groups on the left to show the Android options. Here you can see that 3.2 Honeycomb and 4.0 Ice Cream Sandwich are available. You can install these two and more if you want to target additional devices. If your code uses new features in a later version of the OS, be prepared to deal with any changes to get your code to compile on older versions. Fortunately, Android is only a scant three years old at the time of this writing, so compatibility is not a big issue (yet).

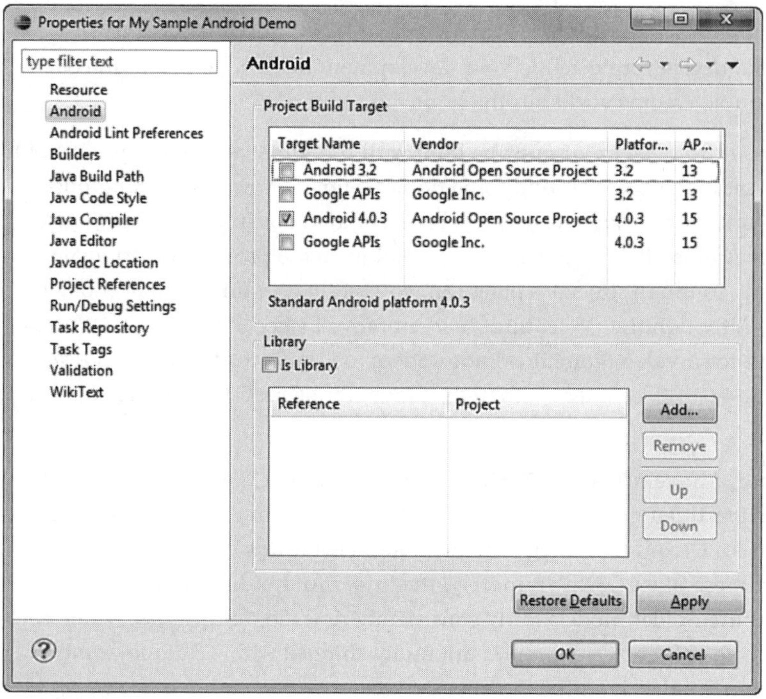

FIGURE 4.24
Changing the target Android OS version for a project in Eclipse.

DID YOU KNOW

If you want to target multiple Android versions (a good idea!), use the Android SDK Manager to download additional versions of the SDK to target each version.

Assuming the project is configured to build with an SDK that matches the OS on the target, you can run the project on the device. The Run command in Eclipse brings up the Android Device Chooser dialog shown in Figure 4.25. If you run into an API-level error, you can change the API level in the manifest file (AndroidManifest.xml).

The sample program is shown running on the physical Android device in Figure 4.26.

BY THE WAY

If you want to get screenshots from your Android device, look in the Android SDK install folder (usually in `C:\Program Files\android\android-sdk` on Windows systems) for a folder called tools, within which is a program called Dalvik Debug Monitor. Launch it by running the ddms.bat batch file. Use the Device menu or press Ctrl+S to take a screenshot. Or from within Eclipse, use the DDMS Perspective to gain access to the device.

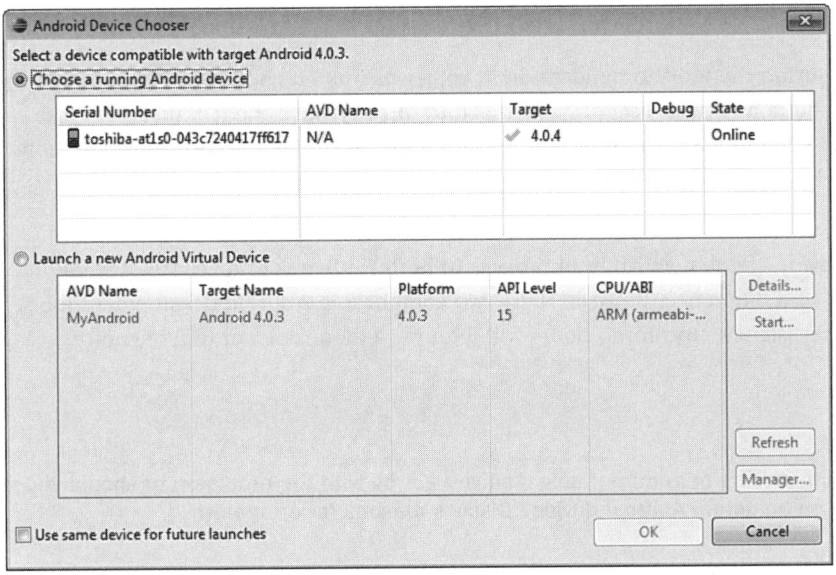

FIGURE 4.25
Choosing a run target with the Android Device Chooser dialog.

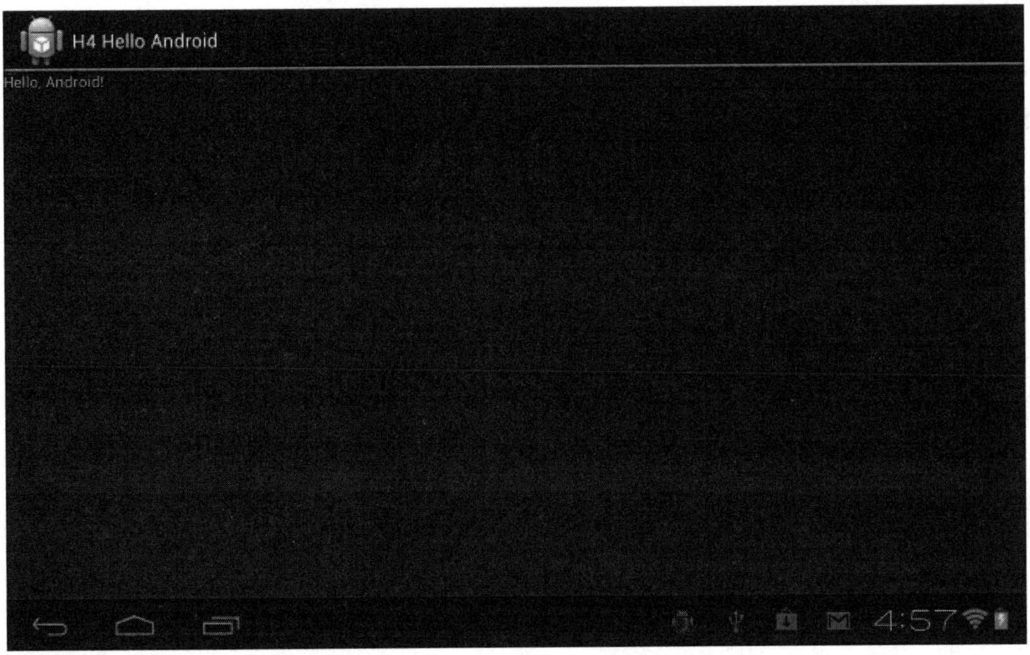

FIGURE 4.26
The sample program is now running on an Android device.

Summary

Installing and configuring the tools to build Android code was quite a challenge. Admittedly, it goes much faster if you're a regular user of NetBeans and already have the JDK installed. Just adding the Android SDK and NBAndroid plug-in is fairly quick if that is the case. Now you have a fully working development environment and can proceed to the next hour to start writing game code!

You have learned how to create new Android projects in both NetBeans and Eclipse. It is helpful to point out features and differences between these two comparable Android development tools, but for the sake of consistency, upcoming hours will feature NetBeans as our tool of choice.

Q&A

Q. When developing an app or game for sale, can you get by with the emulator, or should you test your code on an actual Android device? Discuss reasons for or against.

A. Answers will vary.

Q. Because there are so many devices in circulation running various versions of the Android OS, what approach should you take regarding compatibility?

A. Answers will vary.

Workshop

Quiz

1. What is the name of the program used to manage the Android emulator?
2. What is the base class for every Android program?
3. What software makes it possible to run programs on an Android device via USB?

Answers

1. AVD Manager
2. Activity
3. Android Device Bridge (ADB)

Activities

▶ Did you save the URL to the Android SDK documentation? If not, do a Google search to locate the most up-to-date location. Look for the list of version changes made with each new version of the SDK, from 1 to 18 (the latest version at the time of this writing). Are there significant differences among the versions from 13 on up to the latest? (13 targeted Honeycomb). Consider what would be a good target for you to use in your projects.

PART II

Android Hardware

Getting Started with Graphics

What You'll Learn in This Hour:

▶ How the `Activity` class works.

▶ How to print text to the screen using `TextView`.

▶ How to create a custom `View`.

▶ How to draw graphics using `Canvas`.

The `Canvas` class is a Java class in the Android SDK with features (that is, functions or methods) for drawing. You can draw all sorts of shapes and images using the `Canvas` class. We are going to study this class and learn how to use it for drawing graphics as an important first step on the path of programming games on the Android platform. This is the primary way to draw in Android. We'll spend most of our attention on `Canvas`. Because this is the first hour on graphics programming, but we have not covered the basics of making an interactive Android application, this hour also briefly discusses the `Activity` class and shows how to create a more complete example of an application.

Understanding the Activity Class

An Android program is based on the `Activity` class, which extends (or inherits from) `ApplicationContext`. Before digging into the graphics system, you need to first learn about the `Activity` class and how it works. You may want to see the `Activity` class as the main program or base class of an Android program. Activity works very much within the structure of the Java platform, but for the sake of comparison, its purpose is similar to that of `main()` in a Mac OS X application, or `WinMain()` in a Windows application (written in the C++ language). Although `Activity` is not a function—it is a Java *class*—the comparison should be helpful.

`Activity` is our base application class.

In Microsoft's XNA Game Studio, the base application class is called `Game` (`Microsoft.Xna.Framework.Game` to be precise) and is written in the C# language. C# shares many design similarities with Java, so it is no surprise that Android and XNA work in a similar way (in contrast to a C++ program).

As the main application class, `Activity` has many constants, fields, and methods used by an application. For instance, `Activity.setTitle()` is used to change the program title (which appears at the top of the screen when the program runs). You might recall in the "Hello, Android!" example in the previous hour, the title was `MainActivity`. This is the default name of the `Activity` subclass, and we can change the default title from within `onCreate()` like so:

```
this.setTitle("My New Program Title");
```

An Android game, however, will not need most of the application services. For a game, we are mainly concerned about gaining access to the display screen and drawing! We will not need user interface controls and events normally associated with an application because a game runs in a frame buffer—a buffer of memory reserved for the screen or window, used for drawing and rendering graphics.

Here is the definition for the `Activity` class showing its overridable methods:

```
public class Activity extends ApplicationContext {
    protected void onCreate(Bundle savedInstanceState);
    protected void onStart();
    protected void onRestart();
    protected void onResume();
    protected void onPause();
    protected void onStop();
    protected void onDestroy();
}
```

The `Activity` class methods may be used in your own programs. You do not need to use every one, only those you want to override. If you do not include one of these methods in your program, Android will call the default behavior by calling the method in the parent `Activity` class.

- ▶ onCreate()
- ▶ onDestroy()
- ▶ onStart()
- ▶ onStop()
- ▶ onResume()
- ▶ onPause()

Program Lifetime

An Android program is called an *activity* and is based on the `Activity` class. An activity has a certain lifetime that takes place in between calls to `onCreate()` and `onDestroy()`. These methods are called automatically, like events. When you define them in your own program, you override their default behavior. `onCreate()` is called when the program first starts up, and `onDestroy()` is called before the program ends. This is a good point in the program to initialize variables.

When programming a game, you will want to create objects in `onCreate()` and destroy your game objects (such as sprites, textures, sounds, and so on) in `onDestroy()`. By doing so, you are writing good code that cleans up after itself. It is always best to destroy objects you have created, even if the Java garbage collector cleans up memory for you. Not freeing objects from memory may be a source of erroneous bugs in the future.

Visible Lifetime

A program or activity's visible lifetime represents the state of the program when the user can see and interact with the program.

Immediately after `onCreate()` returns, `onStart()` is called. This happens after the program window is created and appears on the Android screen. This stage of the program is called the visible lifetime because it represents the state where the program is visible to the user. The end of the visible lifetime happens when `onStop()` is called.

`onStart()` and `onStop()` can be called by Android multiple times while the program is running, depending on whether the program is visible to the user.

Foreground Lifetime

A program or activity's foreground lifetime begins with `onResume()` and ends with `onPause()`. These events can happen multiple times during the run of a program. The program will be paused when the device goes to sleep or the program is minimized while another app takes the focus.

Testing the Activity States

We're going to create a program to demonstrate the `Activity` states and then reuse the project for the `Canvas` demo coming up later this hour. Because the previous hour was concerned with configuring the development tools, I will show you again how to create a new Android project, but it will be a bit simpler this time with everything installed and set up already. We'll use NetBeans one last time before permanently shifting gears and using Eclipse afterward. The process of creating a new project in Eclipse is very similar to these steps.

Creating a New Project

We're going to create a new project. First, use the File menu and choose New Project, as shown in Figure 5.1.

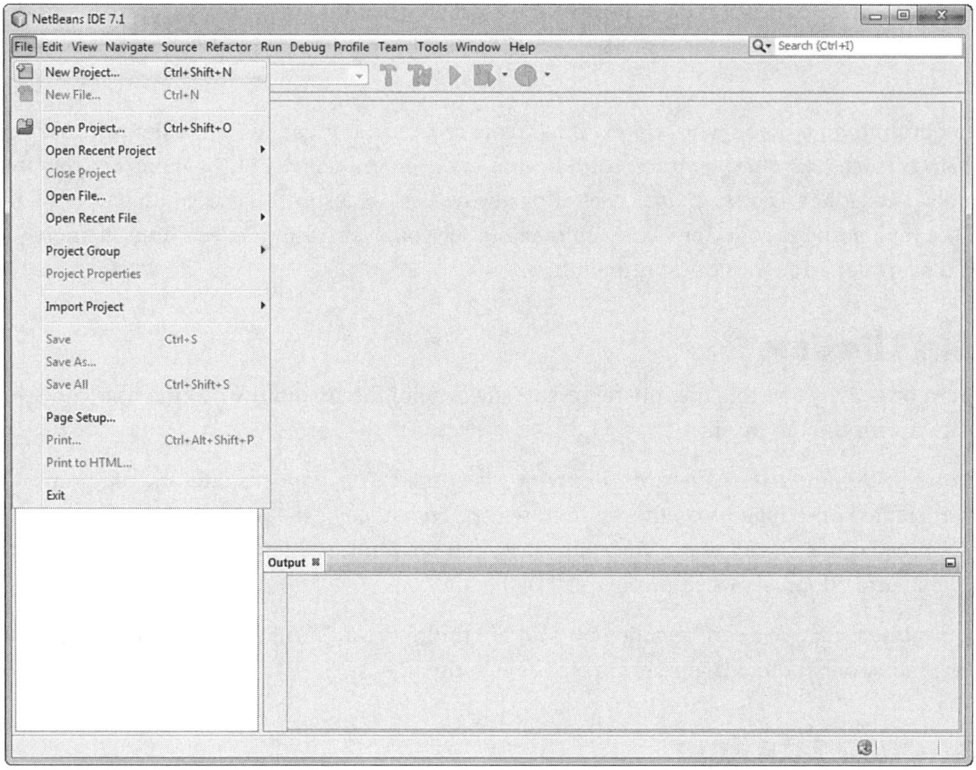

FIGURE 5.1
Preparing to create a new project.

Next, the New Project dialog comes up, shown in Figure 5.2. Choose Android from the Categories list and choose Android Project from the Projects list.

Next, you'll see the New Android Application dialog, shown in Figure 5.3. This dialog is part of the NBAndroid plug-in that added support for the Android SDK to NetBeans. In Eclipse, you will find a similar Android "wizard" dialog that is part of the Android Development Tools (ADT) package. Although Eclipse is a bit easier to use, one thing I like a little more in NetBeans is how it shows every step in the Output window (whereas Eclipse tends to hide everything but failure notices). In NetBeans, I also somewhat prefer the hammer-shaped Build icon in the toolbar. The build step is done automatically when you run the project, but as an older coder, I have become accustomed to building before running, and it's just a habit.

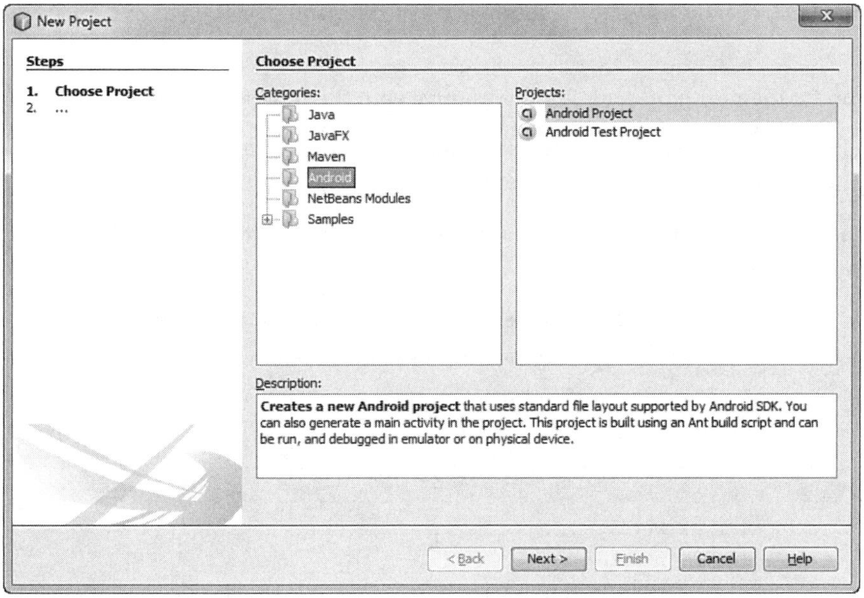

FIGURE 5.2
The New Project dialog.

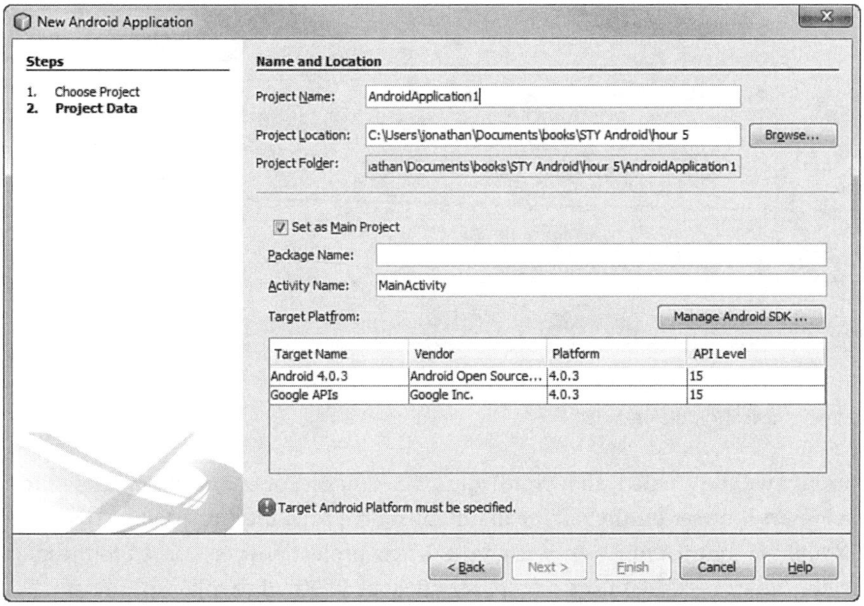

FIGURE 5.3
The New Android Application dialog.

In the Project Name field, enter a name for your project. I recommend using `Create Canvas Demo` as the name.

Choose the location for the new project on your hard drive with the Browse button.

You will need to choose a Target Platform. The list should look like the one in the figure, with "Android 4.0.x" and "Google APIs" or a similar item. Choose "Android 4.0.x."

Enter a value in the Package Name field. Remember, this must be two words separated by a period, such as `canvas.demo`.

Enter the value for the Activity Name. This will be the name of the main class in your program that inherits from Activity. The default value is `MainActivity`.

The completed project configuration is shown in Figure 5.4.

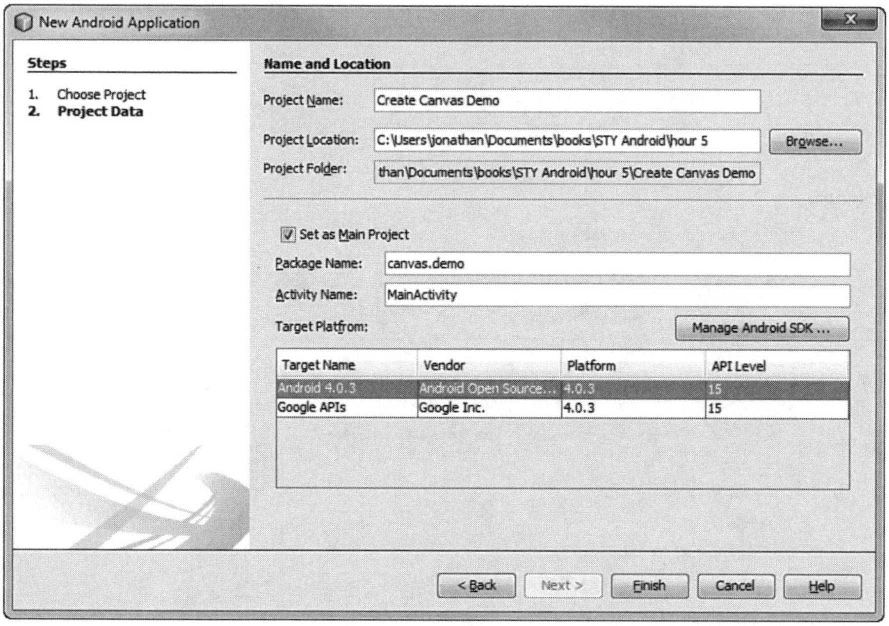

FIGURE 5.4
Filling in the New Android Application dialog fields.

At this point, the project will be created, shown in Figure 5.5. You can open the source code file by browsing in the Project Browser on the left for the main source code file (`MainActivity.` `java` by default). You'll see that it's fairly easy to create a new project now compared to the steps required in the previous hour because of the configuration steps you had to take with a new installation of the Android SDK.

You will find the source code file under Source Packages in the Project Browser.

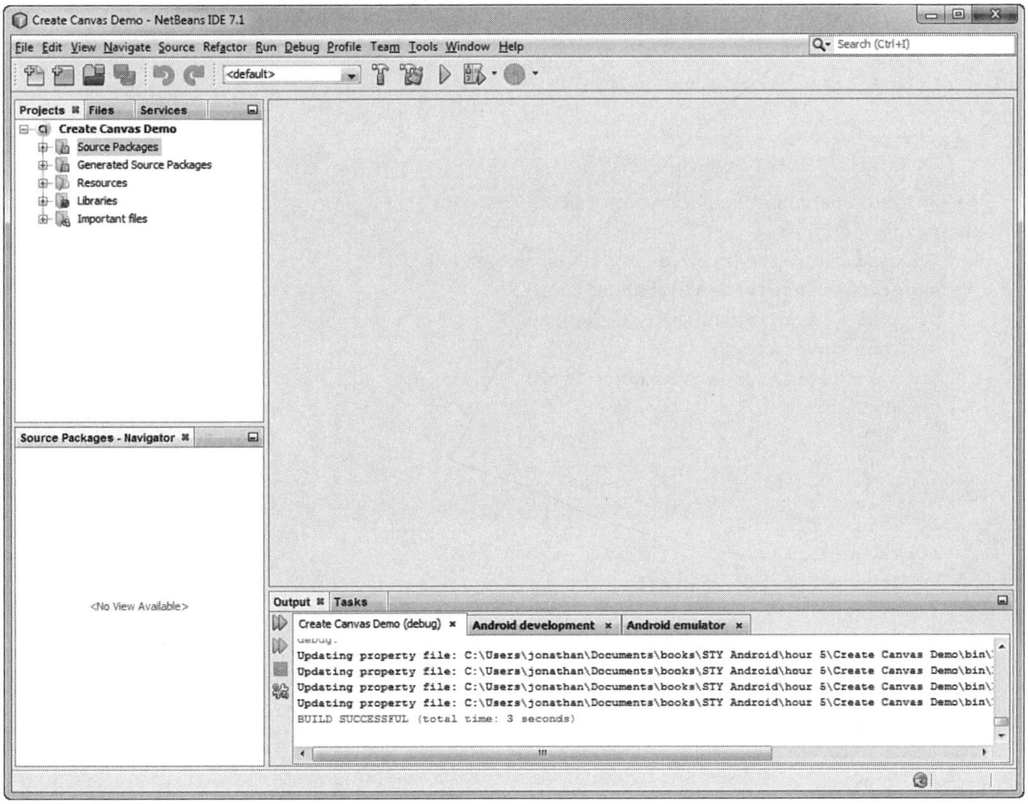

FIGURE 5.5
The new project has been created.

Source Code

Here is the source code for the program that will eventually be called the Create Canvas Demo program. This is the source code listing for the program at this early stage. The purpose of this example is to show how to use the Activity event methods discussed earlier (onCreate(), onStart(), and so on).

To help illustrate the process flow, this program prints out a message from each method, appended to a TextView (which you first saw in the previous hour as a means to print text). In the code listing, note that some lines have been highlighted in bold. These are extremely important lines. In each overridden method, the parent class method (that is, super) *must* be called. If you forget to call the parent method, the program will crash with an exception error.

```
package canvas.demo;
import android.app.Activity;
import android.os.Bundle;
import android.widget.*;

public class MainActivity extends Activity
{
    android.widget.TextView tv;

    /** Called when the activity is first created. */
    @Override
    public void onCreate(Bundle savedInstanceState) {
        super.onCreate(savedInstanceState);
        tv = new TextView(this);
        setContentView(tv);
        this.setTitle("Create Canvas Demo");
        tv.setText("Now in onCreate()\n");
    }

    @Override
    public void onStart() {
        super.onStart();
        tv.append("Now in onStart()\n");
    }

    @Override
    public void onPause() {
        super.onPause();
        tv.append("Now in onPause()\n");
    }

    @Override
    public void onResume() {
        super.onResume();
        tv.append("Now in onResume()\n");
    }

    @Override
    public void onStop() {
        super.onStop();
        tv.append("Now in onStop()\n");
    }

    @Override
    public void onRestart() {
        super.onRestart();
        tv.append("Now in onRestart()\n");
    }
```

```
    @Override
    public void onDestroy() {
        super.onDestroy();
        tv.append("Now in onDestroy()\n");
    }
}
```

Running the program produces the output shown in Figure 5.6. Take note of the order of the methods called when this program is run. The first method called when the program starts is onCreate(), as expected. This is followed by onStart(), onResume(), and onPause().

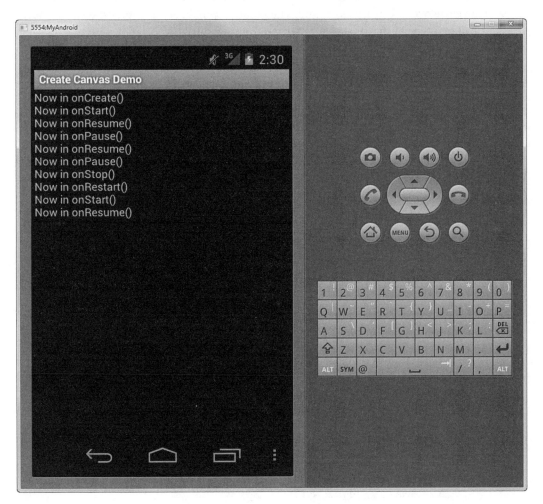

FIGURE 5.6
An early version showing the flow of the program.

There are several repeat calls to `onResume()` and `onPause()` in the figure. These extra calls are a result of my testing the program's ability to pause and resume by doing various things in the Android emulator (such as clicking the Home button and then switching back to the Create Canvas Demo program using the Running Apps button).

World's Simplest Android Graphics Demo

Now, you can create a new project or modify the last one for this new program. I tend to reuse a project when working on simple examples. Following is an extremely simple graphics demo that draws a blue circle over a white background. The program produces the output shown in Figure 5.7. Go ahead and type in this program, replacing the code currently in the `MainActivity`. `java` file with this all-new code. When done, run the program by pressing F6.

```
package canvas.demo;
import android.app.Activity;
import android.content.Context;
import android.graphics.Canvas;
import android.graphics.Color;
import android.graphics.Paint;
import android.os.Bundle;
import android.view.View;

public class MainActivity extends Activity {

    @Override public void onCreate(Bundle savedInstanceState) {
        super.onCreate(savedInstanceState);
        this.setTitle("Create Canvas Demo");
        setContentView(new DrawView(this));
    }

    public class DrawView extends View {

        public DrawView(Context context) {
            super(context);
        }

        @Override public void onDraw(Canvas canvas) {
            super.onDraw(canvas);

            //fill the screen with white
            Paint paint = new Paint();
            paint.setAntiAlias(true);
            canvas.drawColor(Color.WHITE);
```

```
        //draw a blue circle
        paint.setColor(Color.BLUE);
        canvas.drawCircle(100, 100, 50, paint);
    }
  } //DrawView
} //MainActivity
```

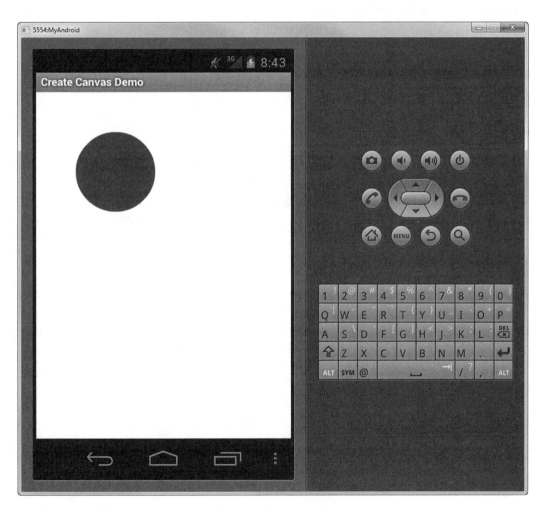

FIGURE 5.7
Your first graphics demo features a blue circle over a white background.

Dissecting the First Graphics Demo

This is a very useful example because it shows—as a snapshot—a complete graphics example in a single source code listing. Many of the examples included with the Android SDK (such as the Lunar Lander demo) are quite large, with dependent classes. I like to see a simple example that is about as irreducible as possible when learning a new system for the first time.

First up is the code for the package and import statements.

```
package canvas.demo;
import android.app.Activity;
import android.content.Context;
import android.graphics.Canvas;
import android.graphics.Color;
import android.graphics.Paint;
import android.os.Bundle;
import android.view.View;
```

This section is *very* important! But the import statements are not—strictly speaking—completely necessary. Does that sound like a contradiction? The thing is, you *can* get by without these imports, but it makes the rest of the program clunky. For instance, without importing `android.app.Activity`, the class definition line for `MainActivity` (coming up shortly) would necessarily look like this:

```
public class MainActivity extends android.app.Activity {
```

If you don't mind writing a *lot* more code in your program, you can forgo the use of the import lines. But it's usually better to use the imports to increase your productivity.

Next we come to the `MainActivity` class definition and its `onCreate()` method. This is *all* the code in the `MainActivity` class. There really is no more code for the main class! The key is in the calling of `setContentView()`. Here, a new instance of the `DrawView` class is simultaneously created and passed to set up a new custom view for the program.

```
public class MainActivity extends Activity {

    @Override public void onCreate(Bundle savedInstanceState) {
        super.onCreate(savedInstanceState);
        this.setTitle("Create Canvas Demo");
        setContentView(new DrawView(this));
    }
}
```

The next section of code invokes a *new class definition*. The new class is called `DrawView`, and it's coming up next. This `DrawView` class is defined inside `MainActivity`. When the source code for a game grows large, you might want to define your `View` subclass in its own separate source file. But it's easier to see what's going on in this simple example by nesting the classes together.

The DrawView class is defined and its constructor method is also shown here.

```
public class DrawView extends View {

    public DrawView(Context context) {
        super(context);
    }
```

The real functionality of this program is coming up now in the onDraw() method (which comes from android.view.View). Now we can finally see some graphics code! There is a class called android.graphics.Paint that has attributes and methods for drawing shapes in different colors to a Canvas.

Note that the Canvas is passed to onDraw() as a parameter—this is crucial to our little demo, for the Canvas is where the output goes.

Two things happen here. First, the screen is cleared in white using Canvas.drawColor() (which fills the screen with a color). Next, a blue filled circle is drawn using Canvas.drawCircle(). The circle is drawn at location (100,100) with a radius of 50 (which gives the circle a diameter or width of 100 total pixels).

```
@Override public void onDraw(Canvas canvas) {
    super.onDraw(canvas);

    //fill the screen with white
    Paint paint = new Paint();
    paint.setAntiAlias(true);
    canvas.drawColor(Color.WHITE);

    //draw a blue circle
    paint.setColor(Color.BLUE);
    canvas.drawCircle(100, 100, 50, paint);
}
```

The last two lines of the program contain closing brackets to conclude both the DrawView and MainActivity classes.

```
    } //DrawView
} //MainActivity
```

After we've seen the program running in the emulator, we will now run it on a physical device. If you need help configuring your system to debug on your Android phone or tablet, refer to the previous hour where that was explained in detail. At this point, you should be up and running with your preferred Android device. Here in Figure 5.8 is a screenshot of the program running on a real Android device. I'm sure you'll agree that there is a qualitative improvement in the output over the emulator's output. Not only was it a hassle to sort out the resolution issues (which are needlessly complicated and in dire need of improvement), but examples run much faster on a real device.

FIGURE 5.8
The Create Canvas Demo running on an Android device.

Introducing Canvas and View

The `Canvas` class is a Java class in the Android SDK that you can use for basic graphics shapes and advanced bitmaps with animation (using special techniques we'll cover in a later hour). `Canvas` is part of the Android SDK and is available for use in your game code without any special requirements. We can use `Canvas` with an output `View` to draw graphics to the screen. In simple examples like the Create Canvas Demo program, we can use the `Paint` class to create an object with graphics methods, and this is essentially what `Canvas` uses for output when invoked directly. We will spend a considerable amount of time on all these subjects in the next hour and in quite a few hours to come!

Summary

You are making some good progress with Android! Now that all the challenging issues regarding configuration and setup have been resolved, its much easier to delve into the code. The first four hours were devoted to getting the development environments set up so that you could write, compile, and run Android code. You learned how to target both emulator devices and physical devices (via USB cable). Now, beginning with this hour, you are writing code to do graphics. This is really good progress in a short time. We have been taking it slowly up to this point. But from this page forward, we will be going at a much accelerated pace and writing a *lot more code*!

Q&A

Q. Why are the `onCreate()` and `onDestroy()` methods of the `Activity` class important to a game programmer?

A. They are called at the start and end of a program, respectively; as such, they represent a good time to create and destroy objects in memory, respectively.

Q. In the program example create in this hour, why does the `DrawView` class inherit from `View`?

A. The `View` class must be implemented, not instantiated (that is, created as an object with a variable name).

Workshop

Quiz

1. What is the name of the class that must be inherited from to render output to the Android screen via its `onDraw()` method?

2. What is the name of the class that features properties and methods for drawing shapes in various colors?

3. What Canvas method fills the screen with a solid color?

Answers

1. `android.view.View`

2. `android.graphics.Canvas`

3. `Canvas.drawColor()`

Activities

There are plenty of additional graphics methods in the `Canvas` class! Try experimenting with a different shape, such as a line.

Drawing Basic Shapes and Text

What You'll Learn in This Hour:

▸ How to draw shapes using `Canvas`

▸ How to print text using `Canvas`

▸ How to change draw settings with `Paint`

▸ How to write Javadoc code comments

In this hour you learn more about `Canvas` and `View` and about the many methods available for drawing shapes and text.

Drawing Basic Vector Shapes

As you saw in the previous hour, you can draw to the Android screen using `Canvas` and `View`. We take a look at most of the `Canvas` drawing methods here. Although you might not consider vector shapes useful, they can be handy for in-game editors, for highlighting game objects, for underlining or boxing areas, and even for simple games.

Drawing Circles

Because you have already seen a circle drawn in the previous hour, let's start with circles again this hour before moving on to other shapes and techniques. We will learn about the features of the `Paint` class along the way. The `Canvas.drawCircle()` method is used to draw circles:

```
public void drawCircle (float cx, float cy, float radius, Paint paint)
```

Drawing Lines

The `Canvas` class has a method called `drawLine()` that will draw a single line, and a method called `drawLines()` that will draw several lines passed in an array. We will focus on the single line drawing method, which has this syntax:

```
public void drawLine (float startX, float startY, float stopX,
float stopY, Paint paint)
```

Drawing Boxes

Just for fun, let's see how to derive our own box-drawing method by using `Canvas.drawLine()`. Call the new method `drawBox()`:

```
public void drawBox( Canvas canvas, Point p1, Point p2, Paint paint ) {
    canvas.drawLine( p1.x, p1.y, p2.x, p1.y, paint);
    canvas.drawLine( p2.x, p1.y, p2.x, p2.y+1, paint);
    canvas.drawLine( p1.x, p1.y, p1.x, p2.y, paint);
    canvas.drawLine( p1.x, p2.y, p2.x+1, p2.y+1, paint);
}
```

To make the new method even more interesting, we can write some overloaded versions that take the two `Point` parameters in more convenient forms:

```
public void drawBox( Canvas canvas, float x1, float y1, float x2,
float y2, Paint paint ) {
    drawBox( canvas, (int)x1, (int)y1, (int)x2, (int)y2, paint );
}

public void drawBox( Canvas canvas, int x1, int y1, int x2, int y2,
Paint paint) {
    drawBox( canvas, new Point(x1,y1), new Point(x2,y2), paint );
}
```

There is just one problem: `Canvas` already provides a `drawRect()` method with several over-loads already! Alas, we might as well use the built-in method instead. "Why bring it up, then?" you may ask.

There is a good lesson in this: Always study a new SDK or library before spending time writing your own methods that might already have been done. Many features in the Java namespaces will most likely solve any programming problem you're likely to run into. `Canvas` has all the basic methods you will need to do vector graphics for various purposes.

One common need for vectors is to highlight game objects, such as units, in a real-time strategy (RTS) game, where you can use the mouse to drag a box around several units to select them. Here is `Canvas.drawRect()`:

```
public void drawRect (float left, float top, float right, float bottom,
Paint paint)
```

Drawing Rounded Rectangles

A variation of the rectangle is also available in our trusty `Canvas` class, but this new version has *rounded corners*! We can draw this new shape using a method called `Canvas.drawRoundRect()`:

```
public void drawRoundRect (RectF rect, float rx, float ry, Paint paint)
```

The `float rx` and `float ry` parameters specify the radius of the quarter-circle used to draw the rounded corners. This shape is very pleasing and may be preferable to a solid square rectangle in some cases. For instance, if you are making a graphical user interface (GUI) for your game, rounded rectangles look especially nice as buttons and window borders.

Drawing Triangles

We can derive more shapes with the basic `Canvas.drawLine()` method, such as triangles. This is a fairly easy shape to draw, although it requires three points rather than two, as was the case with `drawBox()` (which we might say is now *deprecated*, to borrow a popular Java term). Although the code listing in the previous hour contained the complete set of `import` statements you'll need at this stage, we're skipping ahead a bit without covering every single line of code here. Note that the usual `import` lines are still needed. In the case of the `Canvas` methods, be sure to use `import android.graphics.*`. All of the complete examples will have this line, so you may refer to the listings for reference.

```
public void drawTriangle( Canvas canvas, int x1,int y1, int x2,int y2,
int x3,int y3, Paint paint ) {
    drawTriangle(canvas, new Point(x1,y1), new Point(x2,y2),
        new Point(x3,y3), paint);
}

public void drawTriangle( Canvas canvas, Point p1, Point p2,
Point p3, Paint paint ) {
    canvas.drawLine(p1.x,p1.y,p2.x,p2.y, paint);
    canvas.drawLine(p2.x,p2.y,p3.x,p3.y, paint);
    canvas.drawLine(p3.x,p3.y,p1.x,p1.y, paint);
}
```

Changing the Style: Stroke and Fill

Some basic shapes can be drawn either as an outline or border (stroked) or filled in with a color (filled). The stroke constant is `Style.STROKE`, and the filled constant is `Style.FILL`. You can set the draw style with a `Paint` object. `Paint.setStyle()` and `Paint.setColor()` work in tandem to draw shapes with any color or draw style you specify. For instance, the following sets the draw color to green and style to filled:

```
paint.setColor( Color.GREEN );
paint.setStyle( Style.FILL );
```

Basic Graphics Demo

You have seen several shapes that can be drawn with the `Canvas` class, so what we need to do now is see them in action in a real example. See Figure 6.1.

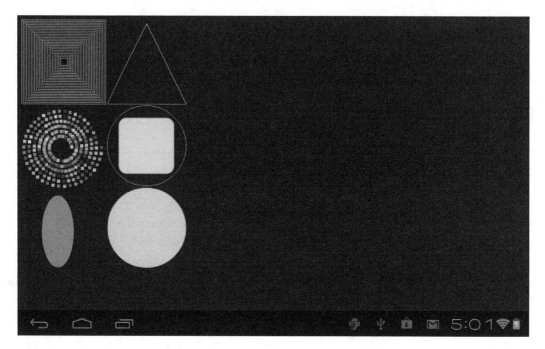

FIGURE 6.1
The Basic Graphics Demo shows off the `Canvas` drawing capabilities.

```java
package android.program;

import android.os.Bundle;
import android.app.Activity;
import android.content.Context;
import android.util.*;
import java.util.Random;
import android.graphics.*;
import android.graphics.Paint.Style;
import android.view.*;

public class Main extends Activity  {

    @Override public void onCreate(Bundle savedInstanceState) {
        super.onCreate(savedInstanceState);
        requestWindowFeature(Window.FEATURE_NO_TITLE);
        setContentView(new DrawView(this));
    }
```

```java
public class DrawView extends View {
    Random rand = new Random();

    public DrawView(Context context) {
        super(context);
        DisplayMetrics metrics = new DisplayMetrics();
        getWindowManager().getDefaultDisplay().getMetrics(metrics);
    }

    @Override public void onDraw(Canvas canvas) {
        super.onDraw(canvas);
        float px, py;

        //create a paint object
        Paint paint = new Paint();
        paint.setAntiAlias( true );
        paint.setColor( Color.WHITE );

        //clear the screen with dark blue
        canvas.drawColor( Color.rgb(0,0,80) );

        //draw some boxes
        for (int n=0; n<100; n+=4) {
            drawBox( canvas, 10+n, 10+n, 220-n, 220-n, paint );
        }

        //draw a yellow triangle
        paint.setColor( Color.YELLOW );
        drawTriangle( canvas, 225,220, 325,20, 425,220, paint );

        //draw small boxes in the path of a circle
        float radius=100f;
        float loops=6.0f;
        for (double angle = 0.0; angle < 2*Math.PI*loops; angle += 0.15){
            px = (float)(110 + Math.cos(angle) * radius);
            py = (float)(330 + Math.sin(angle) * radius);
            radius -= 0.3f;
            paint.setColor( Color.rgb(rand.nextInt(256),
                rand.nextInt(256), rand.nextInt(256)) );
            canvas.drawRect( px-4, py-4, px+4, py+4, paint );
        }

        //draw a circle outline
        paint.setColor( Color.CYAN );
        paint.setStyle( Style.STROKE );
        canvas.drawCircle( 325, 325, 100, paint );
```

```
        paint.setStyle( Style.FILL );
        canvas.drawRoundRect( new RectF(325-70,325-70,325+70,325+70),
            20, 20, paint );

        //draw a filled circle
        paint.setColor( Color.GREEN );
        paint.setStyle( Style.FILL );
        canvas.drawCircle( 325, 530, 100, paint );

        //draw a filled oval
        paint.setColor( Color.RED );
        canvas.drawOval(new RectF(60,450,140,630), paint);
    }

    public void drawBox( Canvas canvas, float x1, float y1, float x2,
    float y2, Paint paint ){
        drawBox( canvas, (int)x1, (int)y1, (int)x2, (int)y2, paint );
    }

    public void drawBox( Canvas canvas, int x1, int y1, int x2,
    int y2, Paint paint) {
        drawBox( canvas, new Point(x1,y1), new Point(x2,y2), paint );
    }

    public void drawBox( Canvas canvas, Point p1, Point p2,
    Paint paint ) {
        canvas.drawLine( p1.x, p1.y, p2.x, p1.y, paint);
        canvas.drawLine( p2.x, p1.y, p2.x, p2.y+1, paint);
        canvas.drawLine( p1.x, p1.y, p1.x, p2.y, paint);
        canvas.drawLine( p1.x, p2.y, p2.x+1, p2.y+1, paint);
    }

    public void drawTriangle( Canvas canvas, int x1,int y1, int x2,
    int y2, int x3,int y3, Paint paint ) {
        drawTriangle(canvas, new Point(x1,y1), new Point(x2,y2),
            new Point(x3,y3), paint);
    }

    public void drawTriangle( Canvas canvas, Point p1, Point p2,
    Point p3, Paint paint ) {
        canvas.drawLine(p1.x,p1.y,p2.x,p2.y, paint);
        canvas.drawLine(p2.x,p2.y,p3.x,p3.y, paint);
        canvas.drawLine(p3.x,p3.y,p1.x,p1.y, paint);
    }
  }
}
```

Drawing Text

Canvas can also draw text based on fonts. You can specify the text output style using a `Paint` object. Our base `Canvas` method for drawing text is `Canvas.drawText()`, with several over-loads. Our base `Paint` method for setting the text *size* is `Paint.setTextSize()`, which accepts any font point size, typically from 8 point (tiny) to 72 points (huge). You can also use `Paint.setColor()` to set the color used to draw the text characters, in the same way that color affects the other `Canvas` graphics primitives.

Following is a short example of the text output features. In Figure 6.2, the output is shown in portrait mode, whereas in Figure 6.3, it is shown in landscape mode. This is a good example that you may want to consider. In portrait mode there appears to be plenty of room on the screen on the lower half. But, as you can clearly see, in landscape mode the text paragraph reaches down to the bottom of the screen. This is a problem for a game. Like the preferred full-screen setting with no title bar, some settings are better for a game. You'll learn to get around this potential problem by disabling the screen autorotate feature in code.

FIGURE 6.2
Demonstration of text output in portrait mode.

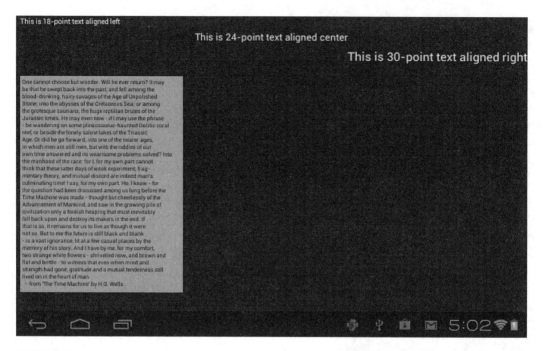

FIGURE 6.3
Demonstration of text output in landscape mode.

```
package android.program;

import android.app.Activity;
import android.os.Bundle;
import android.content.Context;
import android.util.*;
import android.graphics.*;
import android.graphics.Paint.*;
import android.view.*;

public class Main extends Activity {

    @Override public void onCreate(Bundle savedInstanceState) {
        super.onCreate(savedInstanceState);
        requestWindowFeature(Window.FEATURE_NO_TITLE);
        setContentView(new DrawView(this));
    }

    public class DrawView extends View {
```

```
public DrawView(Context context) {
    super(context);
    DisplayMetrics metrics = new DisplayMetrics();
    getWindowManager().getDefaultDisplay().getMetrics(metrics);
}

@Override public void onDraw(Canvas canvas) {
    super.onDraw(canvas);
    float px, py;

    //create a paint object
    Paint paint = new Paint();
    paint.setAntiAlias( true );
    paint.setColor( Color.WHITE );

    //clear the screen with dark red
      canvas.drawColor( Color.rgb(30,0,0) );

      paint.setTextSize(18);
      paint.setTextAlign(Align.LEFT);
      canvas.drawText("This is 18-point text aligned left", 10, 20,
          paint);

      paint.setTextAlign(Align.CENTER);
      paint.setTextSize(24);
      canvas.drawText("This is 24-point text aligned center",
          canvas.getWidth()/2, 60, paint);

      paint.setTextAlign(Align.RIGHT);
      paint.setTextSize(30);
      canvas.drawText("This is 30-point text aligned right",
          canvas.getWidth(), 110, paint);

      paint.setStyle(Style.FILL);
      paint.setColor(Color.rgb(140, 160, 130));
      canvas.drawRect(new Rect(10,150,420,690), paint);

      String text =
      "One cannot choose but wonder. Will he ever return? It may\n" +
      "be that he swept back into the past, and fell among the\n" +
      "blood-drinking, hairy savages of the Age of Unpolished\n" +
      "Stone; into the abysses of the Cretaceous Sea; or among\n" +
      "the grotesque saurians, the huge reptilian brutes of the\n" +
      "Jurassic times. He may even now - if I may use the phrase\n" +
      "- be wandering on some plesiosaurus-haunted Oolitic coral\n" +
      "reef, or beside the lonely saline lakes of the Triassic\n" +
      "Age. Or did he go forward, into one of the nearer ages,\n" +
      "in which men are still men, but with the riddles of our\n" +
```

```
            "own time answered and its wearisome problems solved? Into\n" +
            "the manhood of the race: for I, for my own part cannot\n" +
            "think that these latter days of weak experiment, frag-\n" +
            "mentary theory, and mutual discord are indeed man's\n" +
            "culminating time! I say, for my own part. He, I know - for\n" +
            "the question had been discussed among us long before the\n" +
            "Time Machine was made - thought but cheerlessly of the\n" +
            "Advancement of Mankind, and saw in the growing pile of\n" +
            "civilization only a foolish heaping that must inevitably\n" +
            "fall back upon and destroy its makers in the end. If\n" +
            "that is so, it remains for us to live as though it were\n" +
            "not so. But to me the future is still black and blank\n" +
            "- is a vast ignorance, lit at a few casual places by the\n" +
            "memory of his story. And I have by me, for my comfort,\n" +
            "two strange white flowers - shrivelled now, and brown and\n" +
            "flat and brittle - to witness that even when mind and\n" +
            "strength had gone, gratitude and a mutual tenderness still\n" +
            "lived on in the heart of man.\n" +
            "  --from 'The Time Machine' by H.G. Wells\n";

        paint.setTextAlign(Align.LEFT);
        paint.setTextSize(14);
        paint.setColor(Color.BLACK);
        int x=15,y=170;
        char c;
        String line="";

        for (int n=0; n<text.length(); n++) {
            c = text.charAt(n);
            if (c == '\n') {
                canvas.drawText(line,x,y,paint);
                line = "";
                y += 18;
            }
            else line += c;
        }
    }
  }
}
```

WATCH OUT

Most of the examples in this book assume that they are running on fairly modern Android hardware with a high resolution. Older Android devices with a low-res screen will not render some of the examples properly. If you are developing a game for a low-resolution Android device, you may need to adjust the X,Y position of some of the graphics. For more information, see the upcoming section titled "Android Screen Densities and Resolutions."

Writing Code for Javadoc

Let's pause for a moment to discuss an important issue that will come up fairly often. The subject is code commenting. Have you ever looked at someone's source code and found it completely indecipherable? Gobbledegook? Spaghetti code? That's a bit of a problem if you need to make changes to it or if you're trying to learn a new programming technique by studying that code.

When you write self-documented code, there is no need for separate docs. That's the theory at least! Eclipse has a very nice feature that will help with writing self-documented code. If you have a method definition already written in your source code file, add a blank line above the method definition and type /** followed by Enter. This causes Eclipse to autogenerate a method comment with the parameters listed in Javadoc format. For instance, consider this method definition:

```
public void drawBox(Canvas canvas,Point p1, Point p2, Paint paint)
```

Now add a blank line above this drawBox() method and type /** as follows:

```
/**
public void drawBox(Canvas canvas,Point p1, Point p2, Paint paint)
```

When you press Enter after the /**, Eclipse autogenerates the following Javadoc code for you:

```
/**
 *
 * @param canvas
 * @param p1
 * @param p2
 * @param paint
 */
```

The first starred line above the first @param is where you type in a description for the method. Each @param should be filled in with detail. The amount of detail is up to you, but I suggest at least the data type. Here is the Javadoc comment filled in with detail along with the entire method:

```
/**
 * Draws a box
 * @param Canvas canvas
 * @param Point p1 - upper left corner
 * @param Point p2 - lower right corner
 * @param Paint paint - draw style and color
 */
public void drawBox( Canvas canvas, Point p1, Point p2,
Paint paint ) {
    canvas.drawLine( p1.x, p1.y, p2.x, p1.y, paint);
    canvas.drawLine( p2.x, p1.y, p2.x, p2.y+1, paint);
```

```
    canvas.drawLine( p1.x, p1.y, p1.x, p2.y, paint);
    canvas.drawLine( p1.x, p2.y, p2.x+1, p2.y+1, paint);
}
```

This may seem like a lot of extra work on your part. It is especially time consuming when you make changes to a method while refining and debugging your code. So, you may want to hold off on doing *too much* documenting until you are satisfied that a method is finished (or nearly so).

You will now see how all this extra work pays off while writing a game. Suppose we're making a vector graphics game like one of the classic arcade games (Asteroids, perhaps). For such a game, you will likely need to call your `drawBox()` method quite a bit. In fact, this method could be used in a bitmap-based 2D game or even a 3D game—for instance, to highlight objects that the player has selected.

BY THE WAY

Javadoc does not work well with method definitions that take up multiple lines, although we *must* wrap some long lines to fit properly on a printed page. In source files, you will want to leave all parameters on a single line for the Javadoc parser to work correctly. Otherwise, there will be odd artifacts in the scanned parameter list.

Use the mouse cursor in the Eclipse editor to "mouse over" a call to `drawBox()`. A Javadoc help pop-up appears, showing the details of the method! Pressing F2 at this point will cause the pop-up to solidify and give you some options (see Figure 6.4). One option is the @ Javadoc icon that will bring up the method definition in the Javadoc window for further reference. The parameter data types are also hyperlinked to their @ Javadoc references.

This is obviously not a big concern for a small game, let alone one used for learning purposes (such as the examples in this book). But if you get into the habit of quickly using the autogenerate feature and further get into the habit of adding details about each new Method you write, you will write cleaner code with less opportunity for bugs to sneak in.

Android Screen Densities and Resolutions

Android programs do not actually draw using resolutions defined in pixels, the way lower-level graphics routines do. Android programs use a concept known as *pixel density* or more precisely, *density-independent pixel* (dp for short). This is because of the variety of devices built around the Android OS, with widely varying screen sizes and resolutions. It might take some adjustment if you are more accustomed to working with pixels under a 2D graphics API or SDK. It is helpful to think of the "DP" measurement in terms of how large an image appears on a typical PC monitor.

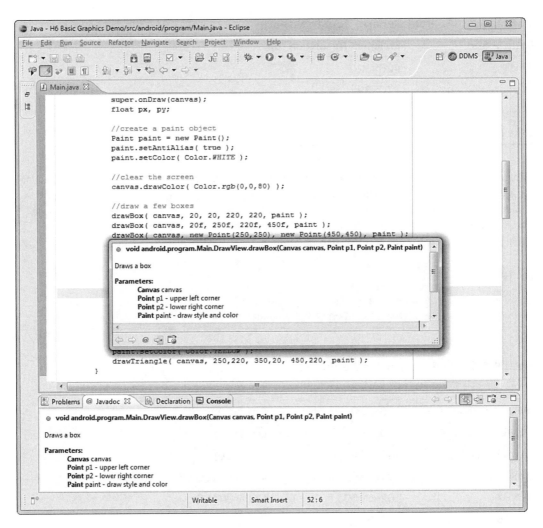

FIGURE 6.4
Testing a self-documented method with the Javadoc feature in Eclipse.

An Android device with a very high density LCD might have a resolution of 1280×800 on a tiny screen of only 3"×4"! That's extremely high density, but it is possible. On such a screen, pixels have less meaning in terms of planning for a user interface or a game. Four generalized screen sizes are standard on the Android platform, as listed in Table 6.1.

TABLE 6.1   Android General Screen Sizes

General Size	Minimum Resolution (dp)
Small	426×320
Normal	470×320
Large	640×480
Extra Large	960×720

Because Google leaves it up to the Android device manufacturers to use any resolution they wish for a device without hindrance from the OS, there is no standard, only a generalization. This is a disadvantage for developers, but at least we can count on these general standards. If a device has a very peculiar screen resolution, a game will be scaled to fit (as a worst-case scenario). Table 6.2 lists the most common screen definitions.

BY THE WAY

In the AVD Manager you can change the Skin property, which defines the size of the emulator window—and thus the screen resolution of the emulator.

TABLE 6.2   Android Screen Definitions

Mode	Resolution	Density
QVGA	240×320	Low (120)
WQVGA400	240×400	Low (120)
WQVGA432	240×432	Low (120)
HVGA	320×480	Medium (160)
WSVGA	1024×600	Medium (160)
WVGA800	480×800	High (240)
WVGA854	480×854	High (240)
WXGA720	720×1280	High (320)
WXGA800	1280×800	Medium (160)

We can detect the screen settings using a class called `DisplayMetrics` and the drawing `Canvas` object passed as a parameter to the `onDraw()` method. We are especially interested in the screen resolution (which comes from `Canvas`) and the screen density (from `DisplayMetrics`).

Because you will most likely want to test your game on several devices, it is recommended that you create a new AVD for each type of device you want to test and then start up whichever one you want to test. Using the AVD, it takes a lot of patience to put up with its slow speed of operation. If possible, you will want to develop and test your code on a real Android device via USB cable.

The two most common modes for Android Tablets (such as the Samsung Galaxy Tab or Toshiba Thrive) are WSVGA and WXGA800. Take a look at Figure 6.5 for the output from our Screen Resolution Demo program running in portrait orientation or mode, while Figure 6.6 shows the output in landscape mode. Note how easy it is to read the text when it's presented in black over a white background. This is a good idea when you want to communicate information to a player.

```
Density: 1.3312501
Scaled density: 1.3312501
Density dpi: 213
Width: 800
Height: 1216
X dpi: 216.74667
Y dpi: 225.77777
```

FIGURE 6.5
The Screen Resolution Demo displays the screen properties.

The tendency for a programmer is often to display text and information in a light over dark color theme. I think this is because programmers and engineers think of the LCD hardware when writing code, and the pixels are naturally *black* when they're *turned off*. So, we tend to think of *on* or *lit* as better than *off* or *unlit*. This is a geeky engineering thing! Any good designer will tell you to consider the end user. At any rate, I tend to display text more often in dark over light for the aforementioned aesthetic reasons, as well as this ancillary reason: Such figures are much more readable in a printed book.

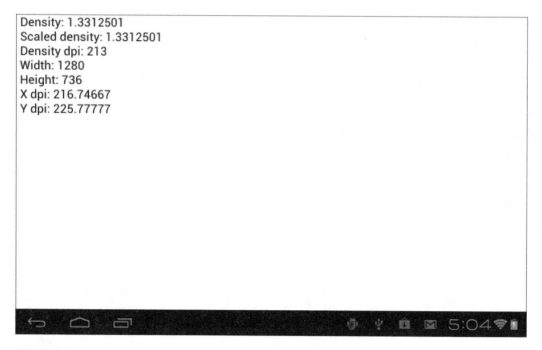

FIGURE 6.6
The same program running in landscape orientation/mode.

```
package android.program;

import android.app.Activity;
import android.os.Bundle;
import android.content.Context;
import android.util.*;
import android.graphics.*;
import android.view.*;

public class MyProgram extends Activity {

    @Override public void onCreate(Bundle savedInstanceState) {
        super.onCreate(savedInstanceState);
        requestWindowFeature(Window.FEATURE_NO_TITLE);
        getWindow().setFlags(WindowManager.LayoutParams.FLAG_FULLSCREEN,
                    WindowManager.LayoutParams.FLAG_FULLSCREEN);
        setContentView(new DrawView(this));
    }

    public class DrawView extends View {
        DisplayMetrics dm;
```

```java
public DrawView(Context context) {
    super(context);
    dm = new DisplayMetrics();
    getWindowManager().getDefaultDisplay().getMetrics(dm);
}

@Override public void onDraw(Canvas canvas) {
    super.onDraw(canvas);

    //fill screen with white
    canvas.drawRGB(255,255,255);

    //set text format and color
    Paint paint = new Paint();
    paint.setColor(Color.BLACK);
    paint.setTextSize(30f);

    //get canvas resolution
    int width = canvas.getWidth();
    int height = canvas.getHeight();

    //print out screen details
    int x=10,y=30,step=36;
    canvas.drawText("Density: " + dm.density,x,y,paint);
    y+=step;
    canvas.drawText("Scaled density: " + dm.scaledDensity,x,y,paint);
    y+=step;
    canvas.drawText("Density dpi: " + dm.densityDpi,x,y,paint);
    y+=step;
    canvas.drawText("Width: " + width,x,y,paint); y+=step;
    canvas.drawText("Height: " + height,x,y,paint); y+=step;
    canvas.drawText("X dpi: " + dm.xdpi,x,y,paint); y+=step;
    canvas.drawText("Y dpi: " + dm.ydpi,x,y,paint); y+=step;
    }
  }
}
```

Summary

This hour provided a quick introduction to the graphics features of the Canvas, which you should now feel fairly comfortable using for basic graphics output. In the next few hours, you will learn more advanced features, such as bitmaps, back buffers, sprites, and animation. It's also about time to make your first Android game, so that will be an important goal in the very next hour.

Q&A

Q. Screen resolutions are a real finicky problem for Android developers. What do you suggest as a solution to the problem of trying to support a dozen or more resolutions in your game code? Discuss possible solutions.

A. Answers will vary. One possible answer involves using a standard resolution for the game and then scaling the output to any final screen resolution.

Q. The `Paint` class allows you to change the size of text fonts. How might you adjust the font size so that it looks uniform on any resolution?

A. This question *might* use the same answer as the previous question, but the discussion should revolve around ways to adjust the font size dynamically.

Workshop

Quiz

1. Which class makes it possible to draw shapes on the Android screen?

2. What are the two most common landscape-oriented screen resolutions used by Android tablets?

3. Which class can provide the screen resolution when `Canvas` is not available (that is, while in some method other than `onDraw()`)?

Answers

1. `Canvas`

2. WSVGA and WXGA800

3. `DisplayMetrics`

Activities

The difference between QVGA (240×360) and WXGA854 (480×854) is *huge*. Suppose you are targeting two Android devices with these two resolutions, and you have to support both with the same source code. Disregarding the preceding Q&A question, what class or method will you specifically use to solve this problem?

Loading and Drawing Images

What You'll Learn in This Hour:

▶ How to draw with a custom back buffer

▶ How to add a bitmap file asset to the project

▶ How to load a bitmap asset into memory

▶ How to draw a bitmap image

Double-Buffered Drawing

While getting started learning about bitmap programming with the Android SDK (namely, the Canvas class), it will be helpful to see a practical use for a bitmap and a purposefully created Canvas of our own. Normally, we use the Canvas parameter that is automatically passed to the onDraw() method, so there is no need to create one. But to use a secondary or *back* buffer for drawing, you will need to learn how to create a Canvas and a Bitmap at runtime. This is a helpful way to get introduced to bitmap programming, and it's extremely practical, as well.

Double buffering is a technique in which a copy or *buffer* of the "screen" is kept in memory, and all graphics drawing takes place on that memory buffer, which is then drawn to the screen all at once, once per frame. The advantage to this technique is performance—drawing to the screen is often slower than drawing to a bitmap in memory, and that slowdown often results in noticeable flicker on the screen. You will have an opportunity to explore real-time screen updates in the next hour when we get into the Runnable interface and worker threads. Until then, the examples will continue to be of the "run once" variety.

Creating a Memory Bitmap

You will need to create a Bitmap object to represent the "surface" for the memory screen buffer. The actual screen, as represented in video memory, is called the *frame buffer* or *front buffer*. A secondary screen, such as the one we are planning to create, is called a *back buffer*.

To use `Bitmap`, you have to import the `android.graphics.Bitmap` namespace. Some programmers may dislike the practice, but for quicker results while learning, I recommend including the entire android.graphics namespace by using this line:

```
import andriod.graphics.*;
```

Declaring a new Bitmap variable goes like this:

```
Bitmap bufferBitmap;
```

Creating the new object is done using a static method called `Bitmap.createBitmap()`, with parameters for the width, height, and color depth. Here is an example:

```
bufferBitmap = Bitmap.createBitmap( 600, 500, Bitmap.Config.ARGB_8888);
```

DID YOU KNOW

The resolution of this `Bitmap` is 600 by 500, but you can specify any size you want using these two parameters in the call to `Bitmap.createBitmap()`.

The third parameter, `Bitmap.Config.ARGB_8888`, specifies 32-bit color and is the normal or default constant to use. It is rare to find an Android device without support for 32-bit color, so we can assume that it is on devices running Android 4.

The new `Bitmap` variable is now ready to use. To use it for drawing, you need a `Canvas` to go with it.

Creating a Drawing Canvas

When you have a new `Bitmap` variable ready to go, you can create a new `Canvas` object based on that `Bitmap` variable (or object). Any drawing methods invoked by the resulting `Canvas` will be output onto the base `Bitmap`.

First, define the new `Canvas` variable:

```
Canvas bufferCanvas;
```

Next, create the object with a `Bitmap` as the single parameter to the constructor:

```
bufferCanvas = new Canvas(bufferBitmap);
```

The `Canvas` is now ready and will draw onto the associated `Bitmap` object. You can use any of the drawing methods found in `Canvas` that we have studied over the past two hours, such as `Canvas.drawCircle()`.

Using the Back Buffer

The Buffered Graphics Demo program demonstrates how to use a back buffer for graphics output by filling a `Bitmap` with circles and then drawing the custom buffer to the screen with a single call to `Canvas.drawBitmap()`. Figure 7.1 shows the output. We will revisit this example again in the next hour and show it running within a loop. Presently, because the screen refreshes only once, it is not very apparent how a back buffer helps with performance and quality. But with a loop and timing, you can see the results in real-time, and then it will make more sense.

FIGURE 7.1
The Buffered Graphics Demo uses a back buffer for drawing.

```
package android.program;
import java.util.Random;
import android.app.Activity;
import android.content.Context;
import android.graphics.*;
import android.os.Bundle;
import android.util.*;
import android.view.*;

public class Main extends Activity {
```

```java
@Override public void onCreate(Bundle savedInstanceState) {
    super.onCreate(savedInstanceState);
    requestWindowFeature(Window.FEATURE_NO_TITLE);
    setContentView(new DrawView(this));
}

public class DrawView extends View {
    Bitmap bufferBitmap;
    Canvas bufferCanvas;
    Point screenSize;
    Random rand = new Random();

    public DrawView(Context context) {
        super(context);

        //get the screen size before the main canvas is ready
        DisplayMetrics metrics = new DisplayMetrics();
        getWindowManager().getDefaultDisplay().getMetrics( metrics );
        screenSize = new Point( metrics.widthPixels-20,
            metrics.heightPixels-20 );

        //create the back buffer
        bufferBitmap = Bitmap.createBitmap( screenSize.x, screenSize.y,
            Bitmap.Config.ARGB_8888);
        bufferCanvas = new Canvas(bufferBitmap);
    }


    @Override public void onDraw(Canvas canvas) {
        super.onDraw(canvas);

        //fill the back buffer with graphics
        drawOnBuffer();

        //copy the back buffer to the screen
        canvas.drawBitmap(bufferBitmap, 0, 0, new Paint());
    }

    public void drawOnBuffer() {
        Paint paint = new Paint();
        paint.setAntiAlias(true);

        //clear the buffer with color
        bufferCanvas.drawColor(Color.WHITE);

        //draw random circles
        for (int n=0; n<500; n++) {
            //make a random color
```

```
            int r = rand.nextInt(256);
            int g = rand.nextInt(256);
            int b = rand.nextInt(256);
            paint.setColor(Color.rgb(r, g, b));

            //make a random position and radius
            int x = rand.nextInt(bufferCanvas.getWidth());
            int y = rand.nextInt(bufferCanvas.getHeight());
            int radius = rand.nextInt(100) + 20;

            //draw one circle
            bufferCanvas.drawCircle( x, y, radius, paint);
        }
    }
  }
}
```

Loading a Bitmap File

The Android SDK supports several bitmap file formats that can be loaded and used as the source for game graphics. Here are the bitmap formats supported in Android 4.0:

- JPEG
- GIF
- PNG
- BMP
- WEBP

Among these five bitmap formats, the only one that is suitable for game development is the PNG format, which is an acronym for Portable Network Graphics. The reason why PNG is the only suitable format for use in a game is that it is a lossless format with support for 32-bit color. Lossless means the pixels are preserved exactly when saved. You could very well use any of the other four formats for a game, but PNG alone (among those listed) supports an alpha channel, which is essential for transparency.

There are several steps to loading a bitmap file in an Android program. We'll go over each step and then show a complete example at the end.

Adding a Bitmap Asset

Media files that you want to use in a game are treated as *assets*. Another word that you might see often is *resource*. We want to load a bitmap file and draw it on our Android device. Before continuing, you will need a bitmap file to draw. Any bitmap file will do, as long as it's in a supported format (with one of the file extensions previously listed). If a file you want to draw is not in a supported format, you can convert the image from one format to another with a graphic editor.

I use GIMP (http://getgimp.com). I like that it's open source and free, but more so that it is powerful and easy to learn. You may use any graphic editor, although some do not support all the features you will need for working with game graphics. A graphic editor program must, at the very least, support the capability to create and edit an alpha channel in a 32-bit image. Most graphic editors *do* support this. Microsoft Paint (which comes with Windows) does *not*, so it is not a good candidate for editing game images. If you do not like or have access to GIMP, you might try Paint.NET (http://www.getpaint.net). Commercial graphic editors also work, including Photoshop, Paint Shop Pro, and CorelDRAW, among others.

The file we're going to use for this tutorial on loading bitmaps is shown in Figure 7.2. It is the image of a castle, created by Reiner Prokein (http://www.reinerstileset.de), who offers game artwork such as this for free.

FIGURE 7.2
The castle.png bitmap file used in this example.

In the Android project, you should see a folder called Assets. The files and folders of a project are found in Package Explorer in Eclipse. To add an asset file to the project, drag the file into the Eclipse GUI, and Eclipse will take care of the import. When you drop in the file, Eclipse brings up the File Operation confirmation dialog shown in Figure 7.3.

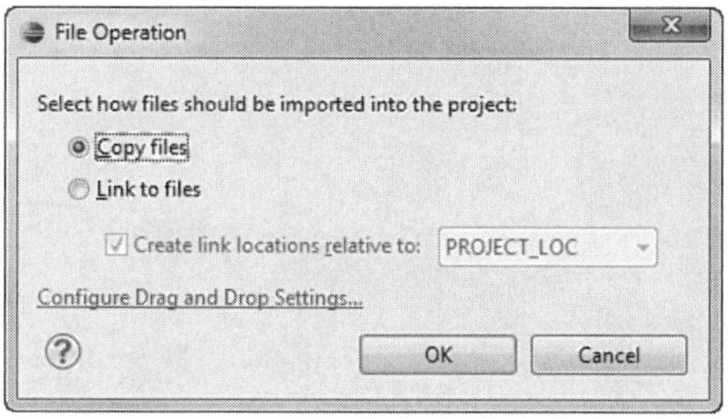

FIGURE 7.3
The File Operation dialog comes up when you add an asset file to the project.

This dialog gives you the option of having Eclipse copy the file into the project or just linking to it at its original location. Normally, you will want to use the Copy option. After the file has been added to the project, Eclipse automatically compiles the file as a resource in the Android package, and you can load it by name without any special techniques. (You'll learn how to load a file from this location in a moment). When the file has been added, it will appear as shown in Figure 7.4.

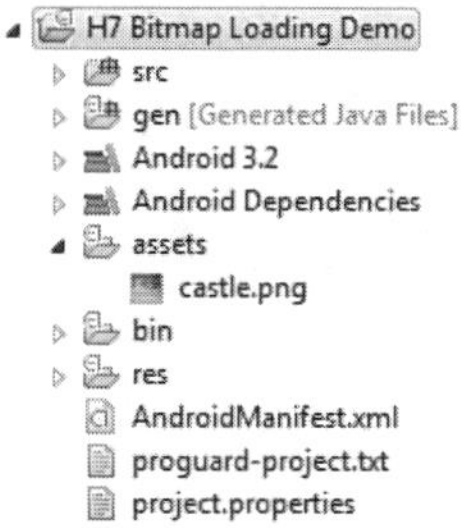

FIGURE 7.4
The castle.png file has been added to the assets folder in the project.

If you want to see the file properties for an asset (such as its location in disk), right-click the file and choose Properties from the context menu. The properties dialog is shown in Figure 7.5.

Using `AssetManager`

A class called `android.content.res.AssetManager` is used to load assets for a game, including bitmap files. You will need an `AssetManager` object to load the assets for a game from the compiled resources in the Android application package. You can get access to the assets from the `View` constructor's single parameter: `Context`. When you create a subclass of `View`, as we have done in several examples already, you gain access to the `Context` parameter. It is in this constructor that we want to load the assets for a game, anyway, so here is how the object is obtained:

```
AssetManager assets = context.getAssets();
```

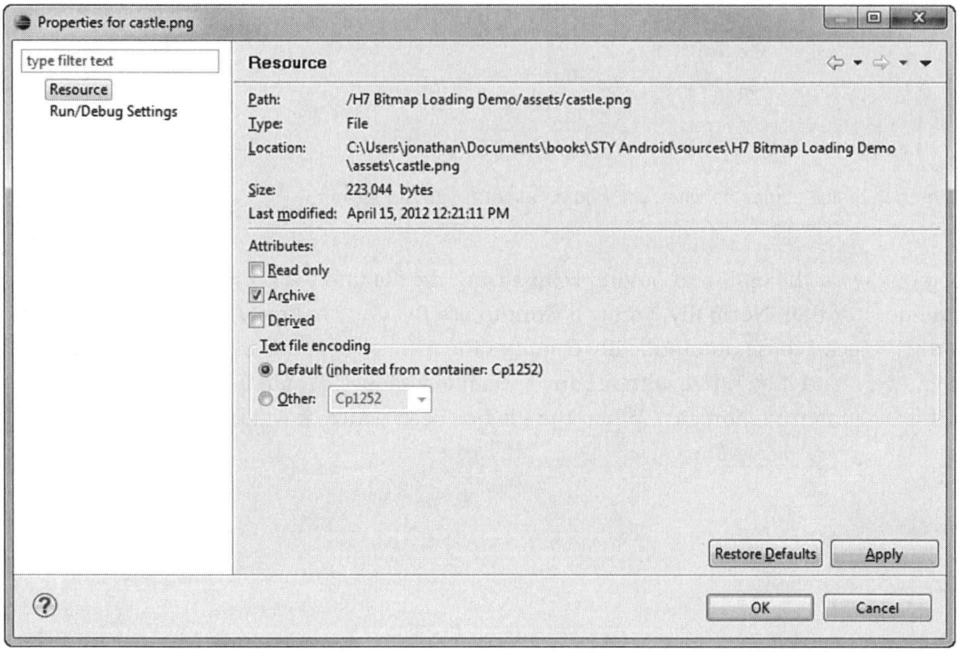

FIGURE 7.5
The file properties for the castle.png bitmap file.

Using `InputStream`

The next step to loading an image is to create an object of type `java.io.InputStream` and set it to receive data from a method from our `AssetManager` object (which was called `assets`). `AssetManager.open()` accepts a parameter containing the name of your bitmap file resource.

```
InputStream istream = assets.open("castle.png");
```

Using `BitmapFactory`

Now that you have an input stream of data from the source asset file (castle.png in this case), you will use the `BitmapFactory.decodeStream()` method to read the data in and return it as a `Bitmap`. This is the last step. If the source file is valid, the result will be a `Bitmap` ready to draw.

Before reading the file stream, though, we need to tell `BitmapFactory` how to decode the bitmap into the desired color depth (if necessary). This takes any source image and ensures it is in the appropriate format for your game. You can do this using the `BitmapFactory.Options` class:

```
BitmapFactory.Options options = new BitmapFactory.Options();
```

After creating the `options` object, you can set the preferred image format to 32-bit with the constant `Bitmap.Config.ARGB_8888`, like so:

```
options.inPreferredConfig = Bitmap.Config.ARGB_8888;
```

Now we are ready to use the `BitmapFactory` class to decode the bitmap data into the desired format. Note in the following line that the return value is a `Bitmap` object.

```
castle = BitmapFactory.decodeStream(istream,null,options);
```

Closing the In

Beco w, we can close it by calling `istream.close()`. skipped, or the input file will be left in an

ode

 throw an exception error, so we have h any such exceptions. When dealing n asset file to be named wrong or not has been debugged and is ready for t. Nevertheless, we have to trap exceplete bitmap file loading code with error

```
.Options();
_88;
_ream,null,options);
} catc
    e.    _ackTrace();
}
```

Drawing a Bitmap

The next step, drawing the bitmap, is extremely easy. Android offers us additional features for drawing a bitmap with special effects (like scaling) that we will explore later. For now, let's just start off with simple, basic bitmap drawing code.

`Canvas.drawBitmap()` has several overloads, but the one you will want to use for starters draws the whole bitmap to the target location on the screen:

```
public void drawBitmap (Bitmap bitmap, float left, float top, Paint paint)
```

The first parameter is the source bitmap. Then you specify the left (X) and top (Y) position. Next, supply an optional `Paint` parameter. If you don't want to use the `Paint` parameter, just pass `null`.

You can draw it by using the code we used already to load the castle bitmap:

```
canvas.drawBitmap(castle, 20, 20, null);
```

The program example in the resource file for this hour is called *Bitmap Loading Demo,* if you want to load and run it directly. The program output is shown in Figure 7.6. As you can see, a problem exists with the transparency of the image. This particular castle.png image has no alpha channel, so the background color is showing up in the rendered scene.

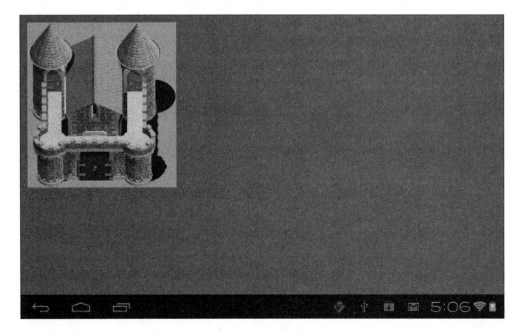

FIGURE 7.6
The castle.png image is drawing without transparency.

Creating an Alpha Channel for Transparency

Using your favorite graphic editor, open up the image you want to convert to 32-bit color with an alpha channel. This short tutorial will show you how to do it using GIMP. The steps will be *very similar* using other graphic editors.

TRY IT YOURSELF ▼

1. First, find the Color Select tool in your graphic editor's tool palette. Figure 7.7 shows the tool's location in GIMP 2.4. If you have a newer version of GIMP or a different graphic editor, the tool should still be similar in function and these instructions will still apply—just adapt to the tool you're using.

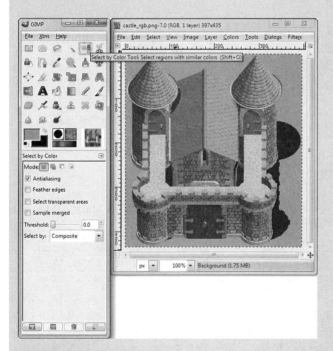

FIGURE 7.7
Using the Color Select tool to highlight the background pixels of the image.

2. Next, using the Color Select tool, click one of the background pixels of the image. Although it is not visible on the printed page, the background color of this image is magenta with an RGB value of (255,0,255). We're going to convert this into a transparent mask using an alpha channel. Figure 7.8 shows that GIMP has highlighted the background (note the dashed line around the border of the castle's pixels).

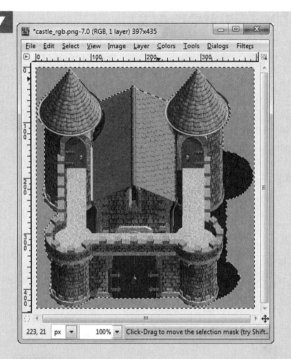

FIGURE 7.8
Highlighting the background pixels using the Select Color tool.

3. Next, with the background pixels selected, use the Layer menu and choose Mask, Add Layer Mask from the menu, as shown in Figure 7.9.

4. This menu choice brings up the Add Layer Mask dialog shown in Figure 7.10. Choose the option called Selection so that that new layer is based on the selected pixels. Use the Invert Mask option to reverse the selection for the mask (so that the castle's pixels are chosen instead of the background's pixels).

5. The previous step should have added a mask to the image, which will have the effect of hiding or *masking* the background pixels. The final step is to apply the mask, which will result in the addition of an alpha channel to the image. Use the Layer menu again, choose Mask, and then Apply Layer Mask. See Figure 7.11.

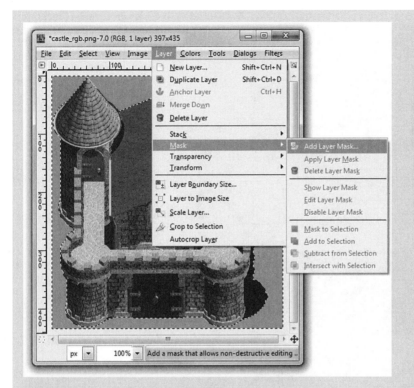

FIGURE 7.9
Preparing to add a new layer mask.

FIGURE 7.10
The Add Layer Mask dialog.

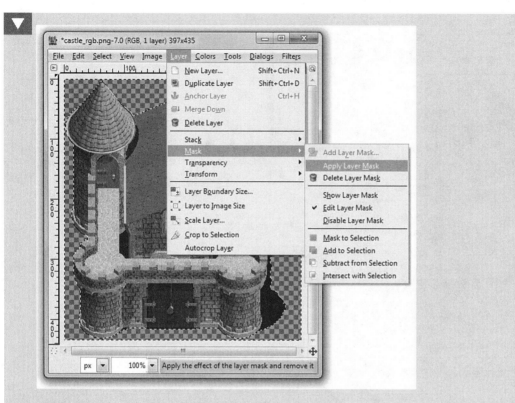

FIGURE 7.11
Applying the layer mask results in the addition of an alpha channel.

The image now has an alpha channel! Save it as a PNG file so that the Android SDK can load it as a 32-bit image with transparency intact. Save the file before continuing. You can follow these basic steps for all other artwork you intend to use in your Android games.

BY THE WAY

When you edit an image used in a game, be sure to copy it into the project again. If you find that you're doing a lot of editing of images, you might want to use the Link option instead of the Copy option when adding the file to the assets folder of the project. This way, changes made to the source image (outside of the project) will be used without requiring the extra step of dragging the file over again. You might set up a special folder for the artwork in your game. Don't worry, Eclipse will still compile the asset files into the package for deployment.

Finished Example

For the sake of completion, we'll see a finished example of the source code that loads and draws a bitmap from a file. The final result, using the 32-bit RGBA version of the castle image with a transparency mask in the alpha channel, is shown in Figure 7.12.

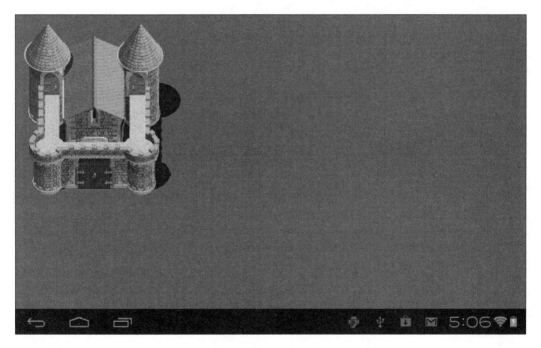

FIGURE 7.12
The Bitmap Loading Demo program drawing the castle with transparency.

```
package android.program;

import java.io.*;
import android.app.Activity;
import android.content.Context;
import android.content.res.AssetManager;
import android.graphics.*;
import android.os.Bundle;
import android.view.*;

public class Main extends Activity {

    @Override public void onCreate(Bundle savedInstanceState) {
        super.onCreate(savedInstanceState);
```

```
        requestWindowFeature(Window.FEATURE_NO_TITLE);
        setContentView(new DrawView(this));
    }

    public class DrawView extends View {
        Bitmap castle = null;

        public DrawView(Context context) {
            super(context);
            try {
                AssetManager assets = context.getAssets();
                InputStream istream = assets.open("castle.png");
                BitmapFactory.Options options = new BitmapFactory.Options();
                options.inPreferredConfig = Bitmap.Config.ARGB_8888;
                castle = BitmapFactory.decodeStream(istream,null,options);
                istream.close();
            } catch (IOException e) {
                e.printStackTrace();
            }
        }

        @Override public void onDraw(Canvas canvas) {
            super.onDraw(canvas);
            canvas.drawColor(Color.rgb(85,107,47));
            canvas.drawBitmap(castle, 20, 20, null);
        }
    }
}
```

Summary

Bitmaps are essential for any serious game development effort on any platform. Now you have
the tools and know-how to load and draw bitmaps with the Android SDK, so you're ready to
start doing some more serious work on this platform. In the next few hours, you will learn to do
real-time animation!

Q&A

Q. The back buffer program example introduced an interesting new concept for Android graphics. Given the performance of the examples in this hour, do you think that double buffering
is necessary? Discuss the pros and cons.

A. Answers will vary.

Q. Adding bitmap assets to a project seems fairly seamless, but in a large game project with several members contributing, how should the assets be managed? Should the programmer drag and drop images into the project as they are updated by the artist? Given what you now know about how Eclipse manages assets in an Android project, how would you tackle this issue?

A. Answers will vary.

Workshop

Quiz

1. What is the class used to work with bitmap images in memory?

2. What class gives access to bitmap files in the assets folder of a project by providing an input stream?

3. What class is used to decode the input stream from a bitmap file, converting it into a bitmap image in memory?

Answers

1. `Bitmap`

2. `AssetManager`

3. `BitmapFactory`

Activities

There seems to be a lot of code required to load a bitmap file into memory. Try writing your own method that encapsulates all this functionality, making it possible to load a bitmap with only a single method call.

Bringing Your Game to Life with Looping

What You'll Learn in This Hour:

▶ How to create a threaded game loop

▶ Using the `Runnable` interface

▶ Using the `Thread` class

▶ Drawing from the new game loop

This hour shows how to create a loop for a game that gives it real-time capabilities not tied in to the GUI methods (such as `onDraw()`) for the game's display. To detach drawing from the GUI, you learn how to create components that can draw without being directly tied to the `onDraw()` event method. While exploring this new capability, you also get a glimpse at bitmap frame animation, bitmap scaling, and timing.

Creating a Threaded Game Loop

In the past few hours you have seen several examples that draw shapes and bitmaps to the Android screen. The problem with these examples is that nothing actually *happens* after the initial drawing code is finished. Nothing moves or changes in any way. If you'll recall the Bitmap Loading Demo and Buffered Graphics Demo programs from Hour 7, "Loading and Drawing Images," these programs extended `Activity` and `View` to run and draw, respectively, but there was no "engine" or "pump," so to speak, driving the program to do anything more than once. These programs were designed to draw something one time and then stop with no more activity.

Reviewing Nonthreaded Code

Here again is the core code from the Bitmap Loading Demo program presented in the previous hour, with all the "functional" code removed, leaving just the core structure of the program:

```
public class Main extends Activity {
    @Override public void onCreate(Bundle savedInstanceState) {
        super.onCreate(savedInstanceState);
```

```
        setContentView(new DrawView(this));
    }
    public class DrawView extends View {
        public DrawView(Context context) {
            super(context);
        }
        @Override public void onDraw(Canvas canvas) {
            super.onDraw(canvas);
        }
    }
}
```

Do you see why this program runs only once and then stops? Although Android OS continues to display the program window until you manually close it (with the Back or Home soft buttons), the program is essentially finished running. Now, it is possible for onDraw() to be called again and for the screen to redraw itself. That is a GUI event, after all. We can also cause onDraw() to run manually by calling invalidate() to redraw the screen. All this method does is cause onDraw() to be called again.

The problem is, where would we call invalidate()? There is no *running* code here, just one place where the program starts up (the DrawView() constructor) and one place where drawing occurs (onDraw()), which happens only once. There's no repeating loop. To make a real-time game that animates, draws, updates, and responds to user input, we must have a game loop!

BY THE WAY

Although it is possible to make a game using the GUI event onDraw() with a running thread, that is actually more work than what you'll learn to do later in this hour. Stay tuned!

Writing Threaded Code

Java provides an easy way to add a threaded method to our program, via an interface class called Runnable. By implementing Runnable, we can give any class a real-time "pump" or loop. Technically, all Runnable does is call a function once. That's a key thing to remember—it is called only *once*. The looping part is up to *you*!

This runnable method is called run(). When you implement Runnable, you gain access to this run() method. Presto, instant game loop! All you have to do is add a while loop to the method to keep the thread running. And it's important to allow the thread to exit when the program is done. Furthermore, we need to make sure the program behaves nicely when it's minimized. To that end, we'll revisit some more of the Activity events.

At this point, we might add Runnable support to the program shown earlier to give it a game loop. The only problem is, the old Context parameter is passed to onDraw() but not to the threaded `run()` method. We could probably create a global pointer to the `Context` passed to `onDraw()`, but that's a bit dangerous because `Context` could change if the program is minimized and brought back into focus again. No, a global will not solve that particular problem. What we need is to gain access to the screen from the thread and then just ignore the old `onDraw()` entirely. It will not be used again after we make the shift to a threaded game loop!

To add threading support to the `DrawView` class, add `implements Runnable` to the class definition, like so:

```
public class DrawView extends SurfaceView implements Runnable
```

This new class definition for `DrawView` is also crafty in one additional sense: It features a different base class. Instead of extending `View`, it extends `SurfaceView`. We'll learn about this change shortly.

Next, you will need a variable used to manage the thread:

```
Thread gameloop = null;
```

In the `resume()` method (yet to be shown), we will create the `Thread` object and start it running. Note that this will be repeatedly called anytime the app is minimized/refocused:

```
gameloop = new Thread(this);
gameloop.start();
```

Next, in the upcoming `pause()` method, we'll write a `while` loop that waits for the app to respond again by repeatedly calling `Thread.join()`.

```
while (true) {
    try {
        gameloop.join();
    }
    catch (InterruptedException e) { }
}
```

Finally, the last thing we'll do to enable threading is write the `run()` method. Within this method, we'll have a `while` loop that continues running essentially forever (until the app shuts down).

To illustrate the threading code, a complete example is presented later this hour. But first, we need to learn about the `SurfaceHolder` class.

DID YOU KNOW

The `Main` class we've been defining as an `Activity`-based class can be made into a reusable `Game` class after you've finished writing the threaded game loop and new drawing system. Food for thought!

Drawing Without `onDraw()`

In the previous examples, we have used `onDraw()` to do graphics output, drawing vector shapes and bitmaps. That works well for an app with GUI controls (button, listbox, and so on), but it does not work well for a game that requires a real-time loop and high-speed screen refresh. So, we need to work on a new technique to draw without relying on the `Context` parameter. Now that we have a `run()` method (thanks to the threading code via `Runnable`), we can do real-time, but we lose the `Context` parameter and have to find a new one. To help visualize the way these classes are used, Figure 8.1 shows a diagram of the current system we have used in past examples.

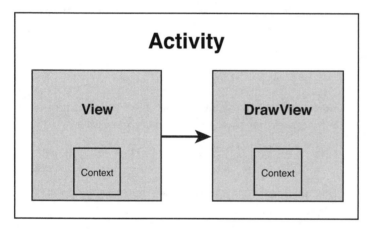

FIGURE 8.1
Inheriting from the `View` class.

First, we make a change to the base class. Previously, it was `View`. To gain access to the screen and built-in `Canvas` object, we will use a variation of `View` called `SurfaceView`. This new base class gives access to a method called `getHolder()`.

Next, you need to declare a `SurfaceHolder` variable. I called mine `surface`:

```
SurfaceHolder surface;
```

Actually, that's the *only* thing you need, not just the first, because it has a built-in `Context`! To create the `surface` object, use the inherent `getHolder()`:

```
surface = getHolder();
```

When you're ready to draw something, which will happen in the `run()` method now, you grab a pointer to the `Canvas` using `SurfaceHolder.lockCanvas()` and then release it after drawing by calling `SurfaceHolder.unlockCanvasAndPost()`.

```
Canvas canvas = surface.lockCanvas();
// draw, draw, draw...
surface.unlockCanvasAndPost(canvas);
```

That's all there is to it; no other steps are required—because this `canvas` object draws right onto the screen. We're getting access to the screen by locking the canvas, then doing our drawing, and then unlocking the canvas again. Just be sure not to leave the canvas in a locked state. This approach to drawing is very common, shared by Direct3D and OpenGL and most other SDKs and APIs. You can differentiate between a rendering system from an SDK and an "event" type system using a GUI typically because in the latter, drawing is done inside some sort of "draw" type event (such as `onDraw()`), while a rendering system gives you control over when drawing occurs. In the case of Android's `SurfaceHolder`, that process begins when you call `lockCanvas()` and finish with `unlockCanvasAndPost()`. The "post" part of that method name literally means "put it on the screen."

WATCH OUT

Always be sure to call `lockCanvas()` and `unlockCanvasAndPost()` in pairs. If you fail to lock and unlock the screen inside a thread, the stack will fill up quickly, leading to a blank screen and a program crash!

This new approach is illustrated in Figure 8.2.

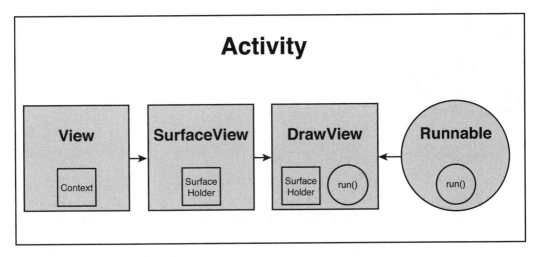

FIGURE 8.2
The new technique adds non-GUI drawing and threading.

The Runnable Animation Demo

We need to see a complete example that shows how to use Runnable, Thread, and the run() method along with the new SurfaceHolder class. The example in this hour brings all these things together and goes *one further*—this example also does animation! Let's see how it works.

Animating a Walking Character

When you have learned how to draw a bitmap, you already have what you need to do frame animation. To assist with animation, we will borrow some high quality artwork from an artist by the name of Reiner Prokein. Reiner operates a website at www.reinerstileset.de, where he makes available his huge collection of *free* game art. That's right, *royalty free*, as a gift to fellow game developers. The site has scores of fully animated characters, monsters, dragons, and buildings in great variety, with primarily an RPG slant. Figure 8.3 shows one frame of the character we're going to use. This is one of eight frames showing the character walking to the right (east). There are animation sets of this character also walking in other directions, ready to be plugged into your own games.

FIGURE 8.3
The first frame of the animated character.

Later, we'll cover new techniques for doing animation, but at this early stage this is the easiest way to demonstrate animation at a very easy level. Each frame is loaded individually, with the images stored in bitmap files named knight1.png, knight2.png, and so on until knight8.png, the last image. To add these files to the project, drag them all onto the project GUI so that they appear as shown in Figure 8.4.

FIGURE 8.4
All eight bitmap files for the animated character are dropped into the project.

The bitmaps are loaded into an array declared as

```
Bitmap knight[];
```

and instantiated with

```
knight = new Bitmap[8];
```

The code to load each file in the animation set is done using a `for` loop. For each index in the loop, the filename is built and passed to the `InputStream` object as a `String`. Then, the same `BitmapFactory` code we've seen before is used to load the file.

```
for (int n=0; n<8; n++) {
    String filename = "knight" + Integer.toString(n+1) + ".png";
    InputStream istream = assets.open(filename);
    knight[n] = BitmapFactory.decodeStream(istream,null,options);
    istream.close();
}
```

The `knight` array is indexed using a global called `frame`, which is incremented in the `run()` method:

```
frame++;
if (frame > 7) frame = 0;
```

Then, to draw the appropriate frame of the `knight` array, use `frame` as the index when calling `drawBitmap()`, like so:

```
canvas.drawBitmap(knight[frame], 0, 0, null);
```

Project Source Code

The complete project source code is included here for reference. Because we cover so many new things in this one hour, the example helps to illustrate how the new threading and drawing techniques work to produce an animated character on the Android screen. Figure 8.5 shows the program output. There's no purpose for drawing the image three times, successively larger, other than to show the animation more clearly.

FIGURE 8.5
The finished Runnable Animation Demo program.

Because the resolution is so high, you can't fully appreciate the quality of the artwork at its native size. To scale the images, we can use a variation (overload) of `drawBitmap()` that accepts a destination `Rect` parameter specifying the size of the image. Now, finally, here is the complete source code, fully commented for reference.

```
package android.program;
import java.io.*;
import android.app.Activity;
import android.content.Context;
import android.content.res.AssetManager;
import android.graphics.*;
import android.os.Bundle;
import android.view.*;
```

```
public class Main extends Activity {
/************************************************************
| This portion of code represents the "outer" main program.
| Events here are passed on to the drawing sub-class.
*/
    //define the drawing sub-class object
    DrawView drawView;

    //onCreate is called any time the program resumes
    @Override public void onCreate(Bundle savedInstanceState) {
        super.onCreate(savedInstanceState);
        requestWindowFeature(Window.FEATURE_NO_TITLE);

        //create the drawing object
        drawView = new DrawView(this);
        setContentView(drawView);
    }

    //handle resume/focus events
    @Override public void onResume() {
        super.onResume();
        //pass the resume event on to the sub-class
        drawView.resume();
    }

    //handle pause/minimize events
    @Override public void onPause() {
        super.onPause();
        //pass the pause event on to the sub-class
        drawView.pause();
    }
/*
| End of "outer" main program code.
*******************************/

/************************************************************
| This code represents the new DrawView subclass which handles
| the real-time loop, updates, and drawing, i.e. the game code.
| Note that this class now implements Runnable to give it a
| threaded loop.
*/
    public class DrawView extends SurfaceView implements Runnable {
        //define the game loop thread
        Thread gameloop = null;

        //define the surface holder
        SurfaceHolder surface;
```

```
//define the running variable
volatile boolean running = false;

//the asset manager handles resource loading
AssetManager assets = null;
BitmapFactory.Options options = null;
Bitmap knight[];
int frame = 0;

//this is the DrawView class constructor
public DrawView(Context context) {
    super(context);

    //get the SurfaceHolder object to supply a context
    surface = getHolder();

    //create the asset manager object
    assets = context.getAssets();

    //set bitmap color depth option
    options = new BitmapFactory.Options();
    options.inPreferredConfig = Bitmap.Config.ARGB_8888;

    //create the bitmap array for animation
    knight = new Bitmap[8];

    //load the knight bitmaps
    try {
        for (int n=0; n<8; n++) {
            String filename = "knight"+Integer.toString(n+1)+".png";
            InputStream istream = assets.open(filename);
            knight[n] = BitmapFactory.decodeStream(istream,null,
                options);
            istream.close();
        }
    } catch (IOException e) {
        e.printStackTrace();
    }
}

//custom resume method called by outer class
public void resume() {
    running = true;
    gameloop = new Thread(this);
    gameloop.start();
}
```

```java
//custom pause method called by outer class
public void pause() {
    running = false;
    while (true) {
        try {
            //just keep doing this until app has focus
            gameloop.join();
        }
        catch (InterruptedException e) { }
    }
}

//this is the threaded method
@Override public void run() {

    //this is the game loop!
    while (running) {

        //make sure surface is usable (it's asynchronous)
        if (!surface.getSurface().isValid())
            continue;

        //request the drawing canvas
        Canvas canvas = surface.lockCanvas();

        /**
            We should really make sure canvas is not null
            here before continuing, but if canvas is invalid
            then the game will cease anyway.
         **/

        //draw one frame of animation from the knight array
        canvas.drawColor(Color.rgb(85,107,47));
        canvas.drawBitmap(knight[frame], 0, 0, null);

        //draw the knight scaled larger
        Rect dest = new Rect(100,0,300,200);
        canvas.drawBitmap(knight[frame], null, dest, null);

        //draw the knight scaled REALLY BIG!
        dest = new Rect(200,0,800,600);
        canvas.drawBitmap(knight[frame], null, dest, null);

        //release the canvas
        surface.unlockCanvasAndPost(canvas);
```

```
            //go to the next frame of animation
            frame++;
            if (frame > 7) frame = 0;

            try {
                //slow down the animation
                Thread.sleep(50);
            }
            catch(InterruptedException e) {
                e.printStackTrace();
            }
        }
    }
}
/*
| End of DrawView sub-class code.
*******************************/
} //Main
```

WATCH OUT

Here is a caveat to be aware of when using Eclipse. In some installations, the default Java compiler is set to 1.5. But the Android code requires Java 1.6 or later. To change or verify the version in Eclipse, go to Project, Properties, Java Compiler, Compiler Compliance Level, and choose version 1.6 or later from the drop-down.

Summary

This hour has introduced some awesome new techniques that demonstrate the ability to make a real-time game with timing and animation. We can use these new techniques to design a Game class that can be easily imported. That makes it much easier to get started on new projects without going through all the steps covered so far just to get something up on the screen. I'd like to move all of this "functional" code into a new Java file and then inherit from that base Game class. We will have to revisit this idea in a future hour. Coming up next hour, you learn how to tap into the touch screen.

Q&A

Q. Making the transition to real-time introduced some interesting new challenges this hour. Now that `onDraw()` is no longer used for graphics—replaced by a thread—a workaround involving `SurfaceHolder` was used. However inconvenient this seems at first, it affords us some great new possibilities. Discuss the potential of this new technique.

A. Answers will vary.

Q. The quick blurb on animation in this hour was not meant to be a fully explained new technique, only a quick example of what's coming up in another hour. Using several bitmap files for the frames of animation might become a logistical problem. What is a better way to do animation?

A. Using a single image with frames embedded on it.

Workshop

Quiz

1. What class provides access to a `Context` at any time without using the `onDraw()` method?

2. What interface class gives a program access to a threading?

3. Which method do you use to draw a frame of animation?

Answers

1. `SurfaceHolder`

2. `Runnable`

3. `Context.drawBitmap()`

Activities

Begin searching for artwork you would like to use in a game of your own design. You may want to peruse the collection at Reiner Prokein's website, Reiner's Tileset, mentioned in this hour. You should start collecting assets for a game you would like to make for Android. Very soon, you will have the tools you need to make that game a reality.

Multi-Touch User Input

What You'll Learn in This Hour:

▶ Using single-touch input
▶ Listening for touch inputs
▶ Using multi-touch input

This hour covers the touchscreen: getting both single and multiple touch events from an Android device. Although Android supports a soft keyboard and a hardware keyboard (via Bluetooth or USB), we will concern ourselves only with touch-screen input because that is the most prevalent form of input on Android 4.0 devices.

Single-Touch Input

There are several ways to get user input on an Android device. The most common form of input on the newest devices is with a multi-touch-capable screen. Additionally, Android supports input via keyboard. The accelerometer and compass might be considered inputs as well. All devices that support Android 4.0 will have a touch screen and soft keyboard, but a Bluetooth keyboard may also be used for input. Most new games will feature touch input, although it would make sense for less interactive apps to make use of a keyboard. Because keyboard input is not going to be common in touch-enabled video games, we won't add keyboard input to our "toolbox."

"Listening" for Touch Events

To support touch input, you need to import `OnTouchListener`, a subclass below `View`, like so:

```
import android.view.View.OnTouchListener;
```

Next, a class must implement `OnTouchListener` to receive input events. The most common class to implement it will be your main `Activity` class (which we have been calling `Main` or `Game`). You could also create a custom new class designed solely to handle input, but I have found that to require some extra steps with little benefit. What we're really going for is a `Game` class that already has a lot of reusable code in it that we can use to make new games fairly easily.

In the class definition, you will need to add `implements OnTouchListener` to the class definition. Here is how we will add touch input support to an `Activity`-based program:

```
public class Game extends Activity implements OnTouchListener
```

When adding `implements OnTouchListener` to a class, that class must implement a method called `onTouch()`. Here it is:

```
@Override public boolean onTouch(View v, MotionEvent event) {
    return false;
}
```

This is the default form of `onTouch()`, which returns false. This tells the calling class (which generates `onTouch()` events for us) that it should handle the input event because we did not do anything with it ourselves (speaking as the implemented method here). When you do handle the input event and want to conclude it, return false to tell the caller that no more input processing is needed.

The `MotionEvent` parameter contains all the info we need to discern where a touch event occurred. Most touch events will be treated as a MOVE event, with an additional event when you lift your finger, generating an UP event.

Single-Touch Input Demo

The complete source code for a program that demonstrates single-touch input is listed next. Figure 9.1 shows the program with a MOVE event registered (while touching or dragging a finger across the display), and Figure 9.2 shows the program after releasing the touch.

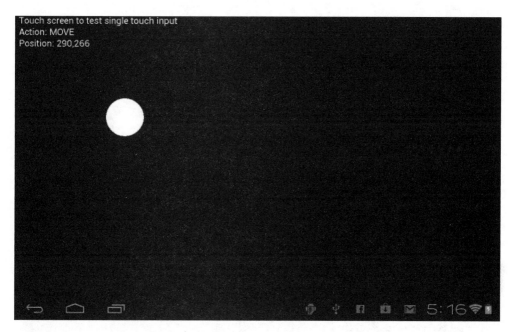

FIGURE 9.1
Single-touch input registers as a MOVE event.

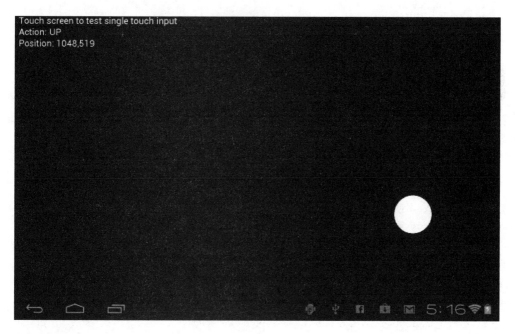

FIGURE 9.2
Releasing the single-touch input produces an UP event.

```
package android.program;
import java.io.*;
import android.app.Activity;
import android.content.Context;
import android.content.res.AssetManager;
import android.graphics.*;
import android.os.Bundle;
import android.view.*;
import android.view.View.OnTouchListener;

public class Game extends Activity implements OnTouchListener {
    DrawView drawView;

    //input variables
    Point touch = new Point(0,0);
    String inputAction = "";

    @Override public void onCreate(Bundle savedInstanceState) {
        super.onCreate(savedInstanceState);
        requestWindowFeature(Window.FEATURE_NO_TITLE);
        drawView = new DrawView(this);
        setContentView(drawView);

        //turn on touch listening
        drawView.setOnTouchListener(this);
    }

    @Override public void onResume() {
        super.onResume();
        drawView.resume();
    }

    @Override public void onPause() {
        super.onPause();
        drawView.pause();
    }

    //touch listener event
    @Override public boolean onTouch(View v, MotionEvent event) {
        switch(event.getAction()) {
            case MotionEvent.ACTION_DOWN:
                inputAction = "DOWN";
                break;
            case MotionEvent.ACTION_MOVE:
                inputAction = "MOVE";
                break;
            case MotionEvent.ACTION_UP:
                inputAction = "UP";
```

```
                break;
        }

        //remember this touch position
        touch.x = (int)event.getX();
        touch.y = (int)event.getY();

        //notify touch handler that we used it
        return true;
    }
}

public class DrawView extends SurfaceView implements Runnable
{
    //game loop thread
    Thread gameloop = null;

    //surface holder
    SurfaceHolder surface = null;

    //thread-safe running var
    volatile boolean running = false;

    //asset manager
    AssetManager assets = null;

    //constructor method
    public DrawView(Context context) {
        super(context);

        //get the SurfaceHolder object
        surface = getHolder();

        //create the asset manager
        assets = context.getAssets();
    }

    public void resume() {
        running = true;
        gameloop = new Thread(this);
        gameloop.start();
    }

    public void pause() {
        running = false;
        while (true) {
            try {
                gameloop.join();
            }
```

```
        catch (InterruptedException e) { }
    }
}

//thread run method
@Override public void run() {

    while (running) {
        if (!surface.getSurface().isValid()) continue;

        //open the canvas for drawing
        Canvas canvas = surface.lockCanvas();
        canvas.drawColor(Color.BLACK);

        //draw circle at touch position
        Paint paint = new Paint();
        paint.setColor(Color.WHITE);
        paint.setTextSize(24);
        canvas.drawText("Touch screen to test single touch input",
            10, 20, paint);
        canvas.drawText("Action: " + inputAction, 10, 50, paint);
        canvas.drawText("Position: " + touch.x + "," + touch.y,
            10, 80, paint);

        if (touch.x != 0 && touch.y != 0)
            canvas.drawCircle(touch.x, touch.y, 50, paint);

        //close the canvas
        surface.unlockCanvasAndPost(canvas);

        try {
            Thread.sleep(20);
        }
        catch(InterruptedException e) {
            e.printStackTrace();
        }
    }
}
}
```

Multi-Touch Input

The latest version of the Android SDK (at the time of this writing) allows you to tether the emulator to a physical Android device to test multi-touch functionality. This sounds like an odd suggestion, but the real benefit that the emulator affords a developer is the capability to test code on a variety of devices with different screen resolutions. Having any Android device for development, even an older one (not running the target OS version) can be a benefit. You can, for instance, run your code on the emulator running an Android 4.0 "tablet" device, while using your tethered Android phone for multi-touch. The screen resolutions do not have to match, nor does the OS version have to be the same.

The multi-touch input system is a bit convoluted, but nothing we can't handle. The way it *used to work* was by using a *pointer identifier* to represent each touch input source. Rather than return an array of input points, Android gave an identifier that was then used as an index. Fortunately, later versions of the SDK eliminated this strange behavior and switched to a simple indexed system.

Quick Example

Here is a *very quick* example that reports the position of multiple touch pointers using the log, just to give you the basic method calls at a glance. For multi-touch input, you need to iterate through each touch input, where the number of inputs is returned by `MotionEvent.getPointerCount()`. After that, you can use overloads of `getX()` and `getY()` with the index of the input to get its position.

```
@Override public boolean onTouch(View v, MotionEvent event) {
    int numPoints = event.getPointerCount();
    for (int n=0; n<numPoints; n++) {
        int x = (int)event.getX(n);
        int y = (int)event.getY(n);
        Log.d("Pointer", "Touch " + n + ": x=" + event.getX(n) +", " +
            y="+event.getY(n));
    }
    return true;
}
```

To see the output of the `Log`, you need to switch to the DDMS perspective. The normal editing environment is called the Java perspective. You should see the perspectives at the upper-right corner of the Eclipse window, as shown in Figure 9.3. This figure also shows the log output window at the bottom. You can use `Log` anytime you want to quickly display information without going through the trouble of outputting text to the screen using `Context.drawText()`. Most coders don't normally work with Eclipse in this small of a window—it was resized for the figure.

DID YOU KNOW

To test this code properly, you must use a real Android device with a multi-touch screen, even if just to tether it to the emulator.

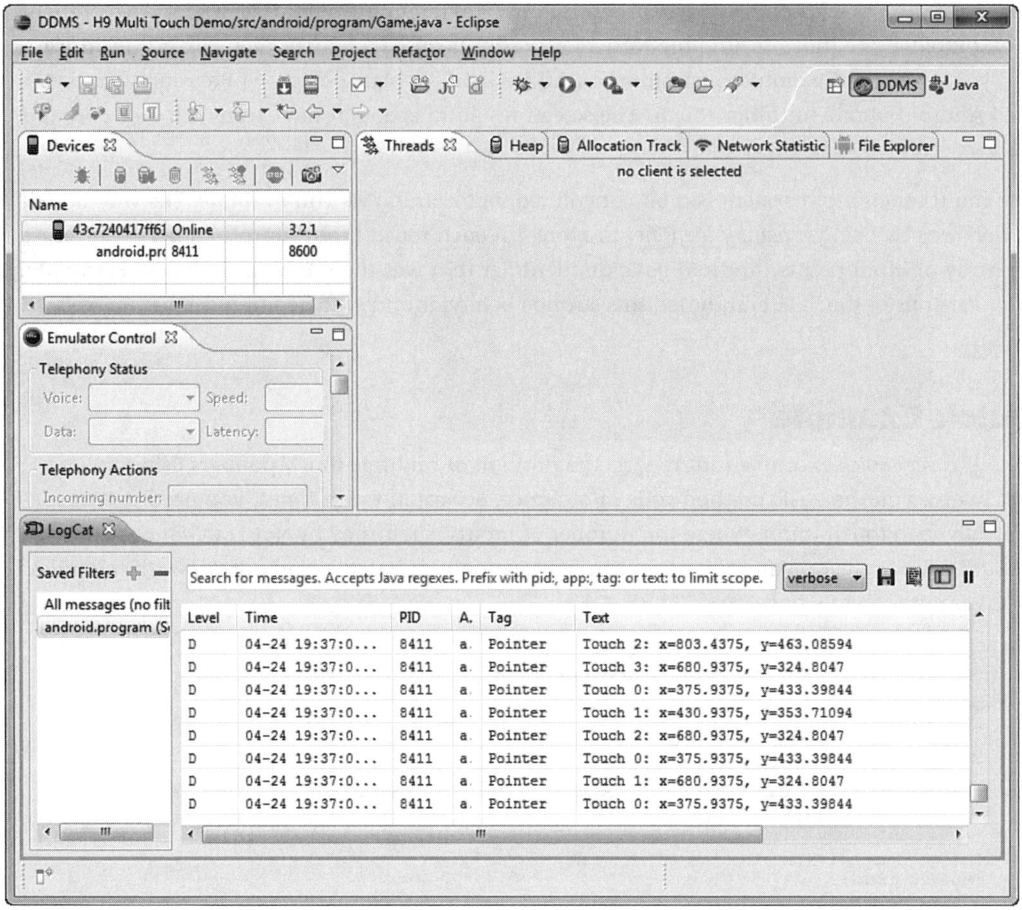

FIGURE 9.3
Viewing the Log from the DDMS perspective in Eclipse.

Encapsulating Multi-touch Input

The simple example was pretty straightforward, but we can still improve on this code by mold-
ing it into a shape that is easier to reuse, requiring less Android work, so to speak, to get input
in a game project. The quick example showed the basic data we would expect from multi-touch
input, where several points of input are reported. What we want to do is get the values from
multiple touch inputs and store those values so they can be used in any way we want during
that game loop cycle (that is, during that "frame").

First, we'll create an array to keep track of touch points:

```
Point[] points;
```

We'll assume that 5 is the maximum number of inputs. Realistically, you won't need more than this for most games. The exception might be a larger tablet with a game that supports multiple players using the same tablet. Yes, you can do that—support up to five local players—but each player would get only one input, and they could interfere with each other by using two fingers.

Next, initialize the array:

```
points = new Point[5];
for (int n=0; n<5; n++) {
    points[n] = new Point(0,0);
}
```

Now, inside the onTouch() event, we can fill the points array with touch input point values that can be used at any time. It is more efficient this way, rather than going back to the MotionEvent parameter each time. You could probably create a global copy of MotionEvent, but all you need are the points!

To ensure that we don't go out of the array's bounds, we'll get the number of touch points and adjust the total if needed. That is being handled by a global int called numPoints:

```
numPoints = event.getPointerCount();
if (numPoints > 5) numPoints = 5;
```

If an Android device supports more than five touch inputs at a time, you may want to support that device by modifying the code. This is just a quick example to show how it works!

Next, we grab the touch points out of the MotionEvent parameter:

```
for (int n=0; n<numPoints; n++) {
    points[n].x = (int)event.getX(n);
    points[n].y = (int)event.getY(n);
}
```

The Multi-touch Demo

The Multi-touch Demo is shown in Figure 9.4. This example shows how to read the touchscreen for up to five touch input points. The index number and position of each point is displayed, and a circle is drawn at each point, using a different color for each point.

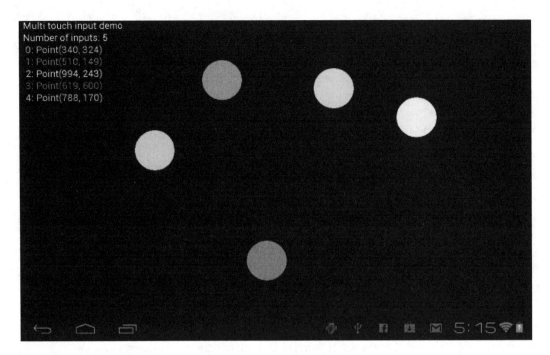

FIGURE 9.4
The Multi-touch Demo.

```
package android.program;
import android.app.Activity;
import android.content.Context;
import android.content.res.AssetManager;
import android.graphics.*;
import android.os.Bundle;
import android.view.*;
import android.view.View.OnTouchListener;

public class Game extends Activity implements OnTouchListener {
    DrawView drawView = null;
    Paint paint = null;
    Point[] points;
    int numPoints=0;

    @Override public void onCreate(Bundle savedInstanceState) {
        super.onCreate(savedInstanceState);
        requestWindowFeature(Window.FEATURE_NO_TITLE);

        //create the view object
        drawView = new DrawView(this);
        setContentView(drawView);
```

```
    //create a paint object
    paint = new Paint();
    paint.setTextSize(24);

    //turn on touch listening
    drawView.setOnTouchListener(this);

    //create the points array
    points = new Point[5];
    for (int n=0; n<5; n++) {
        points[n] = new Point(0,0);
    }
}

@Override public void onResume() {
    super.onResume();
    drawView.resume();
}

@Override public void onPause() {
    super.onPause();
    drawView.pause();
}

//touch listener event
@Override public boolean onTouch(View v, MotionEvent event) {

    //count the touch inputs
    numPoints = event.getPointerCount();
    if (numPoints > 5) numPoints = 5;

    //store the input values
    for (int n=0; n<numPoints; n++) {
        points[n].x = (int)event.getX(n);
        points[n].y = (int)event.getY(n);
    }

    return true;
}

public class DrawView extends SurfaceView implements Runnable {
    Thread gameloop = null;
    SurfaceHolder surface = null;
    volatile boolean running = false;
    AssetManager assets = null;
    int[] colors;
```

```
public DrawView(Context context) {
    super(context);
    surface = getHolder();
    assets = context.getAssets();

    //create an array of colors
    colors = new int[5];
    colors[0] = Color.GREEN;
    colors[1] = Color.MAGENTA;
    colors[2] = Color.YELLOW;
    colors[3] = Color.RED;
    colors[4] = Color.CYAN;
}

public void resume() {
    running = true;
    gameloop = new Thread(this);
    gameloop.start();
}

public void pause() {
    running = false;
    while (true) {
        try {
            gameloop.join();
        }
        catch (InterruptedException e) { }
    }
}

@Override public void run() {

    while (running) {
        if (!surface.getSurface().isValid()) continue;
        Canvas canvas = surface.lockCanvas();
        canvas.drawColor(Color.BLACK);

        paint.setColor(Color.WHITE);
        canvas.drawText("Multi touch input demo", 10, 20,
        paint);
        canvas.drawText("Number of inputs: " + numPoints,
        10, 50, paint);

        int y=80;
        for (int n=0; n<numPoints; n++) {
            paint.setColor(colors[n]);
```

```
            //display point values
            String s = " " + n + ": " + points[n].toString();
            canvas.drawText(s, 10, y, paint);
            y += 30;

            //draw a circle at each point
            if (points[n].x != 0 && points[n].y != 0)
                canvas.drawCircle(points[n].x, points[n].y,
                50, paint);
        }

        surface.unlockCanvasAndPost(canvas);

        try {
            Thread.sleep(20);
        }
        catch(InterruptedException e) {
            e.printStackTrace();
        }
    }
}
}
}
```

Summary

This hour taught you how to use the touch screen. You learned how to get single-touch input (which is similar to mouse input). You also learned how to get multiple touch input by detecting the number of touch inputs and reading the touch positions. The code to get touch input was fairly easy to write, but we could still improve on it to make it easier to use. We will keep this code handy for the game framework project coming up in a future hour.

Q&A

Q. User input is a more complex subject than it first appears to a programmer. From a design perspective, user input is *crucial* and not just a matter of getting touch coordinates. The user interface *must* be designed with *fun* in mind. The term for the study of fun in gameplay is called *Funativity*. Discuss this topic. You may want to search online references for more information.

A. Answers will vary.

Q. What types of games most benefit from single-touch input, and what types benefit most from multi-touch input? Discuss the differences among games that use the two methods. What are perhaps the most significant examples in the game market of each?

A. Answers will vary.

Workshop

Quiz

1. What is the primary interface class that gives access to touch input?

2. What method (usually called from `Activity.onCreate()`) initializes the touch input system?

3. Which event method reports touch input events?

Answers

1. `OnTouchListener`

2. `SurfaceView.setOnTouchListener()`

3. `OnTouchListener.onTouch()`

Activities

Write a pair of helper methods that encapsulate touch input for future use. Give them any name you want, but make them return the results of single touch and multiple touch inputs. You should be able to call these functions and receive back (as a return value) the coordinates, or null if no input was detected.

Hint: To make this work, some globals will need to be used.

HOUR 10
Using the Accelerometer

What You'll Learn in This Hour:

▶ About the Android sensors

▶ How to access Android sensors

▶ How to disable screen rotation

▶ How to use the accelerometer

This hour covers the broader subject of Android sensor programming, tapping into the hardware sensors included in most Android devices (smartphones and tablets). The emphasis of this hour will be on the most common sensor: the accelerometer. We'll use the code we study in this hour in the next few hours to assist with using other common Android sensors, such as the ambient light sensor, air pressure sensor, and others.

Android Sensors

Android devices may or may not come with all of the sensors supported by OS 4.0. The SDK supports the following types of sensors (which are self-explanatory):

▶ TYPE_ACCELEROMETER

▶ TYPE_AMBIENT_TEMPERATURE

▶ TYPE_GRAVITY

▶ TYPE_GYROSCOPE

▶ TYPE_LIGHT

▶ TYPE_LINEAR_ACCELERATION

▶ TYPE_MAGNETIC_FIELD

▶ TYPE_PRESSURE

- ▶ TYPE_PROXIMITY

- ▶ TYPE_RELATIVE_HUMIDITY

- ▶ TYPE_ROTATION_VECTOR

Most Android devices have an accelerometer sensor, but all the other types of sensors are optional and up to the manufacturer. Many devices will also have a compass (also called a *magnetic field* sensor).

BY THE WAY
A GPS location service is not a sensor; it is a different hardware component not part of this list.

Accessing the Sensors

Access to the accelerometer and other sensors on an Android device is provided by an interface class called android.hardware.SensorEventListener. This class must be implemented using the implements statement, in the same manner that we added support for touchscreen input. Here is an example:

```
public class Game extends Activity implements SensorEventListener
```

Just note that you will need a separate android.hardware.SensorManager variable for each individual sensor you plan to use in an Android program.

A variable is defined and then the object is created from within onCreate(). First, the definition:

```
SensorManager sensors;
```

Now, the object is created in onCreate():

```
sensors = (SensorManager)getSystemService(SENSOR_SERVICE);
```

All the device's sensors send their status changes to the program using the SensorEventListener interface class, which has two methods we have to implement:

- ▶ onSensorChanged()

- ▶ onAccuracyChanged()

Following is the definition of the onSensorChanged() method that is required to obtain input from the sensors. This one method receives all sensor events.

```
@Override public void onSensorChanged(SensorEvent event) {
    // . . .
}
```

Here is the definition of the onAccuracyChanged() method. As its name implies, this method receives notices of accuracy state changes that may occur in the sensor devices.

```
@Override public void onAccuracyChanged(Sensor arg0, int arg1) {
    // . . .
}
```

The sensor changes are reported in the SensorEvent parameter passed to onSensorChanged(), so this is the parameter we want to examine further.

WATCH OUT

Sensors will continue to function, even when the Android device is in suspend mode, until you specifically disable them during the pause event!

Disabling Screen Orientation Changes

To test the accelerometer sensor, you will have to disable the screen autorotation that changes from portrait to landscape based on how you are holding your Android device. Phones will default to portrait mode, whereas tablets will default to landscape. Many games will make sense only when running in landscape mode, which is the preferred orientation for games running on a PC or video game console. Most games are designed to run inside a specific screen boundary and cannot adapt dynamically.

Changing the screen specifications at runtime is like changing the computer hardware itself. For best performance, and best gameplay, the hardware needs to remain consistent while a game is running. As a game programmer, you have enough to do already without being concerned with hardware changing at runtime. See Figure 10.1 for an example of what happens to a game when the orientation flips from landscape to portrait.

First, import the necessary namespace:

```
import android.content.pm.ActivityInfo;
```

Add this line to onCreate() to force your Android app to stay in either landscape or portrait mode and not change:

```
setRequestedOrientation(ActivityInfo.SCREEN_ORIENTATION_LANDSCAPE);
```

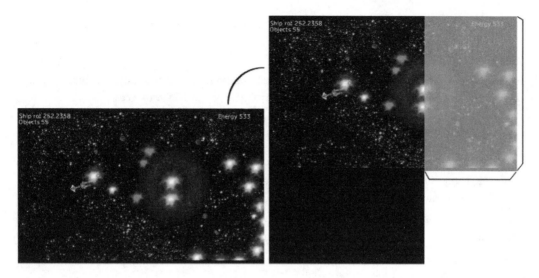

FIGURE 10.1
Screen autorotation is a serious problem for a game.

Here are the two constants that you can use:

▶ ActivityInfo.SCREEN_ORIENTATION_LANDSCAPE

▶ ActivityInfo.SCREEN_ORIENTATION_PORTRAIT

Accelerometer Initialization

We already covered the `SensorManager` object and will need to use it to create an accelerometer sensor object. This can be defined as type `android.hardware.Sensor`.

```
Sensor accel;
```

Now, assuming the `sensors` object was previously created (and therefore available), we can create the accelerometer object like so:

```
accel = sensors.getDefaultSensor(Sensor.TYPE_ACCELEROMETER);
```

WATCH OUT

It is *essential* to disable and re-enable sensor devices when the Android pauses and resumes your app or game! Failure to do so results in an exception error or a program lockup. Live sensors will also drain the battery, even if the device is suspended.

The next two steps are *crucial* to keeping the program stable. Live sensors also drain the battery—even when the device is in suspend mode.

Without these two steps, your accelerometer code will crash the program! We *must* disable the accelerometer in response to the onPause() event and reinitialize it in response to the onResume() event. Failure to do so results in a frozen program (if it doesn't crash first with an exception error).

To disable a sensor, call SensorManager.unregisterListener(). To reinitialize a sensor, call SensorManager.registerListener(). There are several versions of each method, and we'll look at the most common ones in the following code.

```
@Override public void onPause() {
    super.onPause();
    sensors.unregisterListener(this);
}

@Override public void onResume() {
    super.onResume();
    sensors.registerListener(this, accel, SensorManager.
            SENSOR_DELAY_NORMAL);
}
```

Having the register and unregister calls in place at these two crucial events in the program code results in a well-behaved program.

Accelerometer Movement

The accelerometer reports the tilting movement of the device in three axes, although we are concerned only with the two dimensions of X and Y. Tilting the device forward (away from you) results in a negative Y. Tilting backward (toward you as if to read a book) produces a positive Y. The X axis increases to the left and decreases to the right. See Figure 10.2.

All sensors report changes using the same onSensorChanged() method, and that is also the case for the accelerometer. The SensorEvent parameter has an internal sensor object with a method called getType(), and this is what we use to determine which sensor is reporting an update. Here is an example:

```
@Override public void onSensorChanged(SensorEvent event) {
    switch (event.sensor.getType()) {
    case Sensor.TYPE_ACCELEROMETER:
        //save the accelerometer motion values
        accelMotion.x = event.values[0];
        accelMotion.y = event.values[1];
        accelMotion.z = event.values[2];
        break;
    }
}
```

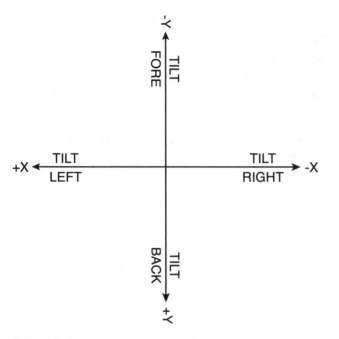

FIGURE 10.2
Accelerometer axis directions.

The `accelMotion` variable is previously defined, like so:

```
Float3 accelMotion = new Float3();
```

`Float3` is a helpful class that contains an x, y, and z, as properties that work well for storing coordinate data. Oddly enough, `Float3` is not a normal Java language support class; it's unique to the Android SDK. The actual namespace is `android.renderscript`. You may find this a useful resource with many helpful classes, such as `Float2`, among others. These are classes normally used to pass data to and from rendering scripts (so-called shader fragments), but we can use them for other purposes as well.

Incidentally, four major namespaces are used for sensor programming, so you may find this list of import lines helpful:

```
import android.hardware.Sensor;
import android.hardware.SensorEvent;
import android.hardware.SensorEventListener;
import android.hardware.SensorManager;
```

Getting a List of Available Sensors

You can detect which sensors are available using the method `SensorManager.getSensorList()`. This method returns a `List<Sensor>` containing the detected sensor objects. You can get the name of each sensor using the `Sensor.getName()` method.

To use this helper method, we'll first need a container for the returned list of sensors:

```
List<Sensor> sensorList;
```

Next, in the program's `onCreate()` method, we'll retrieve the list of sensors from our `SensorManager` object:

```
sensorList = sensors.getSensorList(Sensor.TYPE_ALL);
```

To read the names out of the list, we can create an iterator and use a while loop, like so:

```
Iterator<Sensor> iter = sensorList.iterator();
while (iter.hasNext()) {
    Sensor sensor = iter.next();
    Log.d("Sensor", sensor.getName());
}
```

On a Toshiba Thrive 7" tablet device, the following sensors were reported:

- MPL rotation vector
- MPL linear accel
- MPL gravity
- MPL Gyro
- MPL accel
- MPL magnetic field
- MPL Orientation (android deprecated format)
- Intersil is129018 Ambient Light Sensor
- Intersil is129018 Proximity sensor
- NCT1008 TEMPERATURE sensor
- Rotation Vector Sensor
- Gravity Sensor
- Linear Acceleration Sensor
- Orientation Sensor
- Corrected Gyroscope Sensor

Because this is a fairly average Android 4 tablet, we can assume that *most* Android devices at this price/quality range and higher will have a similar set of sensors. However, some Androids configured as custom devices (such as the Amazon Kindle Fire) and low-end *value* models (costing under $150) may not have as many sensors.

Complete Example

Here is the source code for a complete example that shows how to use an accelerometer. This program displays the accelerometer motion data as X, Y, and Z values, and draws a large circle that moves on the screen in response to motion. The green circle will seem to "roll" on the screen like a billiard ball on a tilting table. Also displayed is the list of sensors detected on the device. Figure 10.3 shows the output from the program.

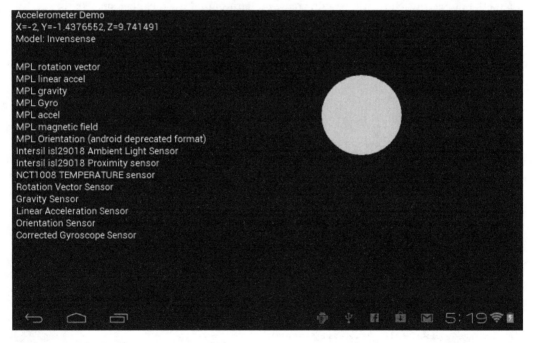

FIGURE 10.3
The Accelerometer Demo program.

```
package android.program;
import java.util.*;
import android.app.Activity;
import android.os.Bundle;
import android.content.*;
import android.content.res.*;
import android.graphics.*;
```

```
import android.view.*;
import android.content.pm.ActivityInfo;
import android.renderscript.*;
import android.hardware.Sensor;
import android.hardware.SensorEvent;
import android.hardware.SensorEventListener;
import android.hardware.SensorManager;

public class Game extends Activity implements SensorEventListener {
    DrawView drawView;
    SensorManager sensors;
    Sensor accel;
    Float3 accelMotion = new Float3();
    List<Sensor> sensorList;

    @Override public void onCreate(Bundle savedInstanceState) {
        super.onCreate(savedInstanceState);
        requestWindowFeature(Window.FEATURE_NO_TITLE);
        drawView = new DrawView(this);
        setContentView(drawView);

        //prevent orientation changes--set explictly
        setRequestedOrientation(ActivityInfo.SCREEN_ORIENTATION_LANDSCAPE);

        //initialize accelerometer
        sensors = (SensorManager)getSystemService(SENSOR_SERVICE);
        accel = sensors.getDefaultSensor(Sensor.TYPE_ACCELEROMETER);

        //get list of sensors on this device
        sensorList = sensors.getSensorList(Sensor.TYPE_ALL);
    }

    @Override public void onSensorChanged(SensorEvent event) {
        switch (event.sensor.getType()) {
        case Sensor.TYPE_ACCELEROMETER:
            //save the accelerometer motion values
            accelMotion.x = event.values[0];
            accelMotion.y = event.values[1];
            accelMotion.z = event.values[2];
            break;
        }
    }

    @Override public void onAccuracyChanged(Sensor arg0, int arg1) {
    }

    @Override public void onResume() {
        super.onResume();
```

```
    drawView.resume();
    sensors.registerListener(this, accel, SensorManager.
        SENSOR_DELAY_NORMAL);
}

@Override public void onPause() {
    super.onPause();
    drawView.pause();
    sensors.unregisterListener(this);
}

public class DrawView extends SurfaceView implements Runnable
{
    Thread gameloop = null;
    SurfaceHolder surface = null;
    volatile boolean running = false;
    AssetManager assets = null;
    Paint paint = new Paint();
    Float2 center;

    //constructor method
    public DrawView(Context context) {
        super(context);
        surface = getHolder();
        assets = context.getAssets();
    }

    public void resume() {
        running = true;
        gameloop = new Thread(this);
        gameloop.start();
    }

    public void pause() {
        running = false;
        while (true) {
            try {
                gameloop.join();
            }
            catch (InterruptedException e) { }
        }
    }

    //thread run method
    @Override public void run() {

        while (running) {
            if (!surface.getSurface().isValid()) continue;
```

```
//open the canvas for drawing
Canvas canvas = surface.lockCanvas();

//clear the screen
canvas.drawColor(Color.BLACK);

//calculate center of screen
float width = canvas.getWidth();
float height = canvas.getHeight();
center = new Float2(width/2.0f, height/2.0f);

//draw circle at center, adjusted for movement
Float2 ratio = new Float2(width/10.0f, height/10.0f);
float x = center.x - accelMotion.x * ratio.x;
float y = center.y + accelMotion.y * ratio.y;
paint.setColor(Color.GREEN);
canvas.drawCircle(x, y, 100, paint);

//display accelerometer info
paint.setColor(Color.WHITE);
paint.setTextSize(24);
canvas.drawText("Accelerometer Demo", 10, 20, paint);
String s = "X=" + Math.round(accelMotion.x) + ", Y=" +
    accelMotion.y + ", Z=" + accelMotion.z;
canvas.drawText(s, 10, 50, paint);
canvas.drawText("Model: " + accel.getVendor(), 10, 80, paint);

//parse and print out the sensor names
int texty = 150;
Iterator<Sensor> iter = sensorList.iterator();
while (iter.hasNext()) {
    Sensor sensor = iter.next();
    canvas.drawText(sensor.getName(), 10, texty, paint);
    texty += 30;
}

//close the canvas
surface.unlockCanvasAndPost(canvas);

try {
    Thread.sleep(20);
}
catch(InterruptedException e) {
    e.printStackTrace();
}
            }
        }
    }
}
```

Summary

The sensors on an Android device are a lot of fun to play around with from the programming point of view! There are so many sensors that we can tap into. Although not every Android device will support all the sensors, we can at least learn to write the code needed to read from the various sensors in preparation for a game that might use them in creative ways. In the next hour, we explore several more sensors to get a good grasp of the subject and to learn how they might be used in a real-world setting.

Q&A

Q. Some sensors are pretty much guaranteed to be present on every Android device, especially from OS 4.0 and later. Which of the sensors would you always support by default for all your games?

A. A list of sensors should be provided. There is no wrong answer.

Q. Sensor input gives a game designer some fascinating new possibilities for making an immersive game. What are some interesting game designs that could take advantage of Android sensors?

A. Answers will vary.

Workshop

Quiz

1. What class provides support for the accelerometer sensor?

2. What interface class provides access to the sensor event method?

3. What type of value does the accelerometer return for X and Y?

Answers

1. `Sensor`

2. `SensorEventListener`

3. `Float`

Activities

Do you know which sensors are available on your own personal Android device? Run the Accelerometer Demo program to find out. How does the list of detected sensors differ between your Android and the Toshiba Thrive featured earlier in the hour?

Using the Linear Acceleration and Proximity Sensors

What You'll Learn in This Hour:

▶ How to use a linear acceleration sensor

▶ How to use a proximity sensor

The previous hour introduced the sensors supported by the Android OS. Depending on the manufacturer, some Android devices will come with some sensors, and some will not, so we have to check the hardware to see if a certain sensor is available. For most game designs, advanced sensors are not needed. But a game custom-designed for a certain unique sensor, or two or three, might be very fascinating, indeed! In this hour, you learn how to use two of the advanced sensors: the linear acceleration sensor and the proximity sensor. The remaining sensors that will be studied over the next few hours include gravity, rotation, gyroscope, pressure, magnetic field, ambient light, and temperature. It almost seems like a typical Android device has enough built in to make a project robot—just add a chassis and motors because all the sensors are built in. I wouldn't be at all surprised to find roboticists using an Android for their projects.

Accessing the Linear Acceleration Sensor

The linear acceleration sensor reports the movement of the Android device in any direction with an X and Y value. This sensor is similar to the *accelerometer* in the values reported from acceleration of the device. But, whereas the accelerometer reports the tilt of the device as a continuous position (via a pair of coordinates), the linear acceleration sensor reports only short-term or "sudden" movements. Moving the device left, right, forward, or backward, and rapidly, produces a short-term value for X and Y acceleration, but those values return to 0 when the device is no longer moving. Figure 11.1 shows the X and Y values returned by the sensor based on direction of movement.

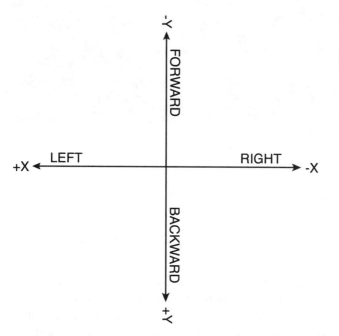

FIGURE 11.1
X and Y values reported by the linear acceleration sensor.

Acceleration does not mean movement! Acceleration is not usually continuous; it represents the increase of velocity from zero up to a certain amount. When velocity reaches the desired value, acceleration drops to zero, and the velocity continues. In space, where there is no atmosphere, an object will continue to move at a certain velocity, essentially forever, unless some counter-force slows it down. In the atmosphere, though, the air itself slows objects—as well as gravity. Firing a bullet from a gun, for instance, involves extremely high acceleration for a brief instant, and then it is "cruising" for the remainder of the time the bullet is in flight.

Initializing the Linear Acceleration Sensor

To begin using the linear acceleration sensor, you first need to create an object to gain access to the SensorManager, like you did before with the accelerometer in the previous hour. This code is shorthand; in the example, the variables are declared as public and initialized in onCreate().

```
SensorManager sensors = (SensorManager)getSystemService(SENSOR_SERVICE);
```

Next, create an object for the linear acceleration sensor:

```
Sensor linear = sensors.getDefaultSensor(Sensor.TYPE_LINEAR_ACCELERATION);
```

To use the linear acceleration sensor, no new technique is needed—just implement the same interface class as before:

```
... implements SensorEventListener
```

On Pausing and Resuming

The appropriate code should also be added to `onPause()` and `onResume()`, just as it was in the previous hour. The source code for the example shows these two methods in their entirety, so there's no need to cite them here. The important calls are as follows. When the app is paused, we call `unregisterListener()`, and when resumed, we call `registerListener()`, with the appropriate parameters. The same code will be used in all the sensor examples, so you will become familiar with it.

Reading the Sensor

Data from the sensor comes into the `onSensorChanged()` event as a `SensorEvent` parameter. There are some interesting properties in `SensorEvent` that you may want to explore, but all we really need to look at are the indexes in the `values[]` array, where `values[0]` is X and `values[1]` is Y—and these are floating point numbers.

The Linear Acceleration Demo

There's nothing better than a complete, working example to study when you're learning a new programming library. Following is the source code for an example called the Linear Acceleration Demo. The output of the program is pretty interesting, shown in Figure 11.2. The current acceleration values for both X and Y are shown as bright green (for positive) and bright red (for negative), with X going left and right, and Y going up and down (refer to Figure 11.1 for an illustration of the returned values). In addition, this program remembers the minimum and maximum values and draws them as dark red and dark green for reference.

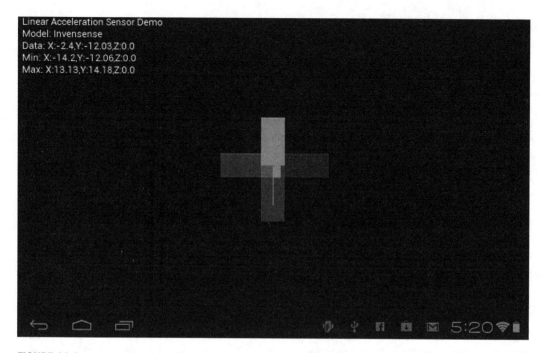

FIGURE 11.2
The Linear Acceleration Demo program.

```
package android.program;

import java.math.BigDecimal;
import android.app.Activity;
import android.os.Bundle;
import android.content.*;
import android.content.res.*;
import android.graphics.*;
import android.view.*;
import android.content.pm.ActivityInfo;
import android.renderscript.*;
import android.hardware.*;

public class Game extends Activity implements SensorEventListener {
    DrawView drawView;
    SensorManager sensors;
    Sensor linear=null;
    String title="Linear Acceleration Sensor Demo";
    Float3 data = new Float3(0,0,0);
    Float3 min = new Float3(0,0,0);
    Float3 max = new Float3(0,0,0);
```

```java
@Override public void onCreate(Bundle savedInstanceState) {
    super.onCreate(savedInstanceState);
    requestWindowFeature(Window.FEATURE_NO_TITLE);
    drawView = new DrawView(this);
    setContentView(drawView);
    setRequestedOrientation(ActivityInfo.SCREEN_ORIENTATION_LANDSCAPE);

    //initialize sensors
    sensors = (SensorManager)getSystemService(SENSOR_SERVICE);

    //try to get linear acceleration sensor
    linear = sensors.getDefaultSensor(Sensor.TYPE_LINEAR_ACCELERATION);
    if (linear==null)
        title = "ERROR: NO LINEAR ACCELERATION SENSOR WAS FOUND";
}

@Override public void onSensorChanged(SensorEvent event) {
    switch (event.sensor.getType()) {
    case Sensor.TYPE_LINEAR_ACCELERATION:

        //get X value and save limits
        data.x = event.values[0];
        if (data.x < min.x) min.x = data.x;
        if (data.x > max.x) max.x = data.x;

        //get Y value and save limits
        data.y = event.values[1];
        if (data.y < min.y) min.y = data.y;
        if (data.y > max.y) max.y = data.y;
        break;
    }
}

@Override public void onAccuracyChanged(Sensor arg0, int arg1) {
}

@Override public void onResume() {
    super.onResume();
    drawView.resume();

    //enable the sensor
    sensors.registerListener(this, linear, SensorManager.
        SENSOR_DELAY_NORMAL);
}

@Override public void onPause() {
    super.onPause();
    drawView.pause();
```

```java
        //disable the sensor
        sensors.unregisterListener(this);
    }


public class DrawView extends SurfaceView implements Runnable
{
        Thread gameloop = null;
        SurfaceHolder surface = null;
        volatile boolean running = false;
        AssetManager assets = null;
        Paint paint = new Paint();
        Float2 center;

        //constructor method
        public DrawView(Context context) {
            super(context);
            surface = getHolder();
            assets = context.getAssets();
        }

        public void resume() {
            running = true;
            gameloop = new Thread(this);
            gameloop.start();
        }

        public void pause() {
            running = false;
            while (true) {
                try {
                    gameloop.join();
                }
                catch (InterruptedException e) { }
            }
        }

        //thread run method
        @Override public void run() {

            while (running) {
                if (!surface.getSurface().isValid()) continue;

                //open the canvas for drawing
                Canvas canvas = surface.lockCanvas();

                //clear the screen
                canvas.drawColor(Color.BLACK);
```

```java
int centerx = canvas.getWidth()/2;
int centery = canvas.getHeight()/2;
int top = centery-100;
int bottom = centery+100;

paint.setColor(Color.WHITE);
canvas.drawLine(centerx, top, centerx, bottom, paint);

int minColor = Color.argb(100, 200, 0, 0);
int maxColor = Color.argb(100, 0, 200, 0);

//draw bar for -X minimum (RIGHT)
int range = (int)Math.abs(min.x)*10;
Rect rect = new Rect(centerx, centery-30, centerx+range,
        centery+30);
paint.setColor(minColor);
canvas.drawRect(rect, paint);

//draw bar for +X maximum (LEFT)
range = (int)Math.abs(max.x)*10;
rect = new Rect(centerx-range, centery-30, centerx,
        centery+30);
paint.setColor(maxColor);
canvas.drawRect(rect, paint);

//draw bar for -Y minimum (UP)
range = (int)Math.abs(min.y)*10;
rect = new Rect(centerx-30, centery-range, centerx+30,
        centery);
paint.setColor(minColor);
canvas.drawRect(rect, paint);

//draw bar for +Y maximum (DOWN)
range = (int)Math.abs(max.y)*10;
rect = new Rect(centerx-30, centery, centerx+30,
        centery+range);
paint.setColor(maxColor);
canvas.drawRect(rect, paint);

//draw bar for ACTUAL Y
range = (int)data.y*10;
if (range < 0) {
    //range is negative here
    rect = new Rect(centerx-30, centery+range, centerx+30,
            centery);
    paint.setColor(Color.RED);
}
else if (range > 0) {
```

```java
            //range is positive here
            rect = new Rect(centerx-30, centery, centerx+30,
                    centery+range);
            paint.setColor(Color.GREEN);
        }
        canvas.drawRect(rect, paint);

        //draw bar for ACTUAL X
        range = (int)data.x*10;
        if (range < 0) {
            //range is negative here
            rect = new Rect(centerx, centery-30, centerx-range,
                    centery+30);
            paint.setColor(Color.RED);
        }
        else if (range > 0) {
            //range is positive here
            rect = new Rect(centerx, centery-30, centerx-range,
                    centery+30);
            paint.setColor(Color.GREEN);
        }
        canvas.drawRect(rect, paint);

        //display sensor info
        paint.setColor(Color.WHITE);
        paint.setTextSize(24);
        canvas.drawText(title, 10, 20, paint);
        canvas.drawText("Model: " + linear.getVendor(), 10, 50,
                paint);
        canvas.drawText("Data: " + toString(data), 10, 80, paint);
        canvas.drawText("Min: " + toString(min), 10, 110, paint);
        canvas.drawText("Max: " + toString(max), 10, 140, paint);

        //close the canvas
        surface.unlockCanvasAndPost(canvas);

        try {
            Thread.sleep(20);
        }
        catch(InterruptedException e) {
            e.printStackTrace();
        }
    }
}

public String toString(int value) {
    return Integer.toString(value);
}
```

```
public String toString(Float3 value) {
    String s = "X:" + round(value.x) + "," +
        "Y:" + round(value.y) + "," +
        "Z:" + round(value.z);
    return s;
}

//round to a default 2 decimal places
public double round(double value) {
    return round(value,2);
}

//round a number to any number of decimal places
public double round(double value, int precision) {
    BigDecimal bd = new BigDecimal(value);
    BigDecimal rounded = bd.setScale(precision,
            BigDecimal.ROUND_HALF_UP);
    return rounded.doubleValue();
}
    }
}
```

Accessing the Proximity Sensor

The proximity sensor is a small light detector that is primarily used to shut off the screen when the user is talking on the phone (to save on battery consumption). Normally, the proximity sensor is located near the speaker so that it will detect when users put the phone up to their ears. On most devices, this sensor tends to be an infrared detector with a very short range of just about one inch.

```
Sensor prox=sensors.getDefaultSensor(Sensor.TYPE_PROXIMITY);
```

The key code to respond to proximity sensor events is shown here. Instead of reporting a range of values, the proximity sensor works more like a binary momentary switch—on when it's tripped, otherwise off. Some devices will simulate a proximity sensor by returning a static value, such as 4.0. Others will return a value of 1.0 for on, 0.0 for off.

```
@Override public void onSensorChanged(SensorEvent event) {
    switch (event.sensor.getType()) {
    case Sensor.TYPE_PROXIMITY:
        if (event.values[0] < prox.getMaximumRange())
            proxValue = event.values[0];
        else
            proxValue = 0.0f;
        break;
    }
}
```

The value returned by tripping this sensor is like a momentary push-on switch (like the buttons in an elevator). Wouldn't it be interesting to use this sensor for user input? How about tripping this sensor to fire a weapon or to cause a character to jump, or to engage nitrous oxide in a racing game? The possibilities are endless!

Summary

The sensor hardware that Android supports is fascinating. You learned how to use two of those sensors this hour—the linear acceleration sensor and the proximity sensor. But where is this going in terms of video game programming? That's up to the designer! As a game programmer, your job is to tap into the hardware of a system and make services available to a designer, not usually to decide which services to include or not include. If we can provide access to an acceleration sensor, maybe that will come in handy in some unique type of game.

Q&A

Q. Linear acceleration input seems very similar to accelerometer input, as far as dealing with the orientation or movement of the Android device. How might you use the linear acceleration sensor to good effect in a video game?

A. Answers should suggest some behavior like shaking the device.

Q. In what real-world scenarios do you think a linear acceleration sensor would be really helpful?

A. Answers should suggest fast-moving experiences such as sky diving or drag racing.

Workshop

Quiz

1. What `Sensor` constant do you use with the linear acceleration sensor?

2. What constant is defined for the proximity sensor?

3. What `SensorEventListener` interface *method* is not often used?

Answers

1. `Sensor.TYPE_LINEAR_ACCELERATION`

2. `Sensor.TYPE_PROXIMITY`

3. `onAccuracyChanged()`

Activities

Run the Linear Acceleration Sensor Demo, which reports the minimum and maximum acceleration values detected. See if you can find the maximum range for your own Android device. Just be careful not to fling it while doing this test! In personal tests, it was rare to see a value beyond 20 in either direction. What were your results?

Using the Gravity and Pressure Sensors

What You'll Learn in This Hour:

▶ Using the gravity sensor
▶ Using the pressure sensor

This hour continues our study of the Android sensors by examining the gravity sensor and pressure sensor, which are two of the more common sensors found in the majority of devices. These sensors might be used for some very interesting games if a creative designer were to put them to use.

Using the Gravity Sensor

The gravity sensor on Android devices reports an algorithmic value based on the linear acceleration sensor. In that regard, it is not a distinct hardware sensor but an algorithm (called a low-pass filter). However, we can still use it to get a decent report on gravity.

The gravity value returned by this sensor is a 3D vector. It represents both the direction *and* magnitude of gravity. The three values supplied by this sensor represent this vector with an x, y, and z component.

Initializing the Gravity Sensor

To initialize the gravity sensor, create a variable of type `Sensor` and initialize it with the constant `Sensor.TYPE_GRAVITY`.

```
Sensor gravity=null;
gravity = sensors.getDefaultSensor(Sensor.TYPE_GRAVITY);
if (gravity==null) {
    title = "ERROR: NO GRAVITY SENSOR WAS FOUND";
    Log.d("ERROR","Gravity sensor not found");
}
```

Reading the Gravity Sensor

To read the values reported by the gravity sensor, we use the `onSensorChanged()` event method as usual. The first three `values` array indexes provide the x, y, and z components of a 3D vector. This vector represents the direction to the gravity source (usually the center of the Earth). A `Float3` works well to record this data for later use in the program.

```
Float3 data = new Float3(0,0,0);
@Override public void onSensorChanged(SensorEvent event) {
    switch (event.sensor.getType()) {
    case Sensor.TYPE_GRAVITY:
        data.x = event.values[0];
        data.y = event.values[1];
        data.z = event.values[2];
        break;
    }
}
```

The vector makes sense only if you hold your Android device flat (on a table or in your hand) and then move it from that initial position. From this orientation, the Z axis pointing *downward* toward the Earth receives actual gravity values that correspond with known gravity. See Table 12.1 for a list of predefined gravity constants that can be used for comparison.

TABLE 12.1 **SensorManager Gravity Constants**

Constant	Value
GRAVITY_DEATH_STAR_I	3.5303614E-7
GRAVITY_EARTH	9.80665
GRAVITY_JUPITER	23.12
GRAVITY_MARS	3.71
GRAVITY_MERCURY	3.7
GRAVITY_MOON	1.6
GRAVITY_NEPTUNE	11.0
GRAVITY_PLUTO	0.6
GRAVITY_SATURN	8.96
GRAVITY_SUN	275.0
GRAVITY_THE_ISLAND	4.815162
GRAVITY_URANUS	8.69
GRAVITY_VENUS	8.87

WATCH OUT

Whenever you use the `Float2` or `Float3` class, be sure to instantiate it by passing zeroes to the constructor! Failure to initialize these values will result in an exception error if the object is ever parsed by `BigDecimal` (for rounding).

Because the value recorded by the gravity sensor is a 3D vector, you will have to convert this value to 2D screen space to visualize the vector. Screen space involves only an X and Y pair. To convert a 3D coordinate to a 2D coordinate, divide each of X and Y by Z, like so:

```
U = X / Z
V = Y / Z
```

U and V represent the resulting screen coordinate of a 3D point. This could be handy later on!

Testing the Gravity Sensor

The following program is called Gravity Sensor Demo in the included source code projects. Figure 12.1 shows the output from this program.

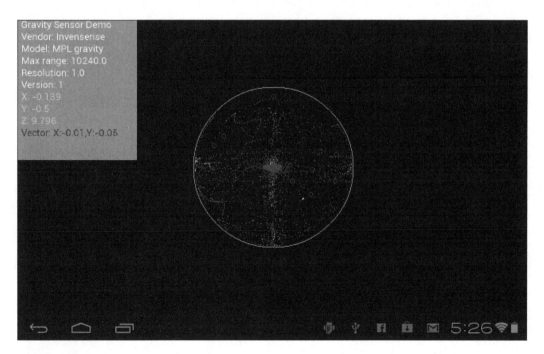

FIGURE 12.1
The Gravity Sensor Demo program graphs the gravity vector.

```java
package android.program;
import java.math.BigDecimal;
import android.app.Activity;
import android.os.Bundle;
import android.content.*;
import android.content.res.*;
import android.graphics.*;
import android.graphics.Paint.Style;
import android.util.Log;
import android.view.*;

import android.content.pm.ActivityInfo;
import android.renderscript.*;
import android.hardware.*;

public class Game extends Activity implements SensorEventListener {
    DrawView drawView;
    SensorManager sensors;
    Sensor gravity=null;
    String title="Gravity Sensor Demo";
    volatile Float3 data = new Float3(0,0,0);

    @Override public void onCreate(Bundle savedInstanceState) {
        super.onCreate(savedInstanceState);
        requestWindowFeature(Window.FEATURE_NO_TITLE);
        drawView = new DrawView(this);
        setContentView(drawView);
        setRequestedOrientation(ActivityInfo.SCREEN_ORIENTATION_LANDSCAPE);

        //initialize sensors
        sensors = (SensorManager)getSystemService(SENSOR_SERVICE);

        //try to get linear acceleration sensor
        gravity = sensors.getDefaultSensor(Sensor.TYPE_GRAVITY);
        if (gravity==null) {
            title = "ERROR: NO GRAVITY SENSOR WAS FOUND";
            Log.d("ERROR","Gravity sensor not found");
        }
    }

    @Override public void onSensorChanged(SensorEvent event) {
        switch (event.sensor.getType()) {
        case Sensor.TYPE_GRAVITY:
            data.x = event.values[0];
            data.y = event.values[1];
            data.z = event.values[2];
            break;
        }
    }
}
```

```java
@Override public void onAccuracyChanged(Sensor arg0, int arg1) {
}

@Override public void onResume() {
    super.onResume();
    drawView.resume();

    //enable the sensor
    sensors.registerListener(this, gravity,
        SensorManager.SENSOR_DELAY_NORMAL);
}

@Override public void onPause() {
    super.onPause();
    drawView.pause();

    //disable the sensor
    sensors.unregisterListener(this);
}

public class DrawView extends SurfaceView implements Runnable
{
    Thread gameloop = null;
    SurfaceHolder surface = null;
    volatile boolean running = false;
    AssetManager assets = null;
    Paint paint = new Paint();
    Float2 center = new Float2(0,0);
    Float2 screenCoords = new Float2(0,0);


    //constructor method
    public DrawView(Context context) {
        super(context);
        surface = getHolder();
        assets = context.getAssets();
    }

    public void resume() {
        running = true;
        gameloop = new Thread(this);
        gameloop.start();
    }

    public void pause() {
        running = false;
        while (true) {
            try {
```

```
            gameloop.join();
        }
        catch (InterruptedException e) { }
    }
}


//thread run method
@Override public void run() {

    while (running) {
        if (!surface.getSurface().isValid()) continue;

        //open the canvas for drawing
        Canvas canvas = surface.lockCanvas();

        //erase the text with a big gray box
        paint.setColor(Color.GRAY);
        paint.setStyle(Style.FILL_AND_STROKE);
        canvas.drawRect(new Rect(0,0,300,350), paint);

        //calculate center of screen
        center.x = canvas.getWidth()/2;
        center.y = canvas.getHeight()/2;

        //draw a plain white circle to show the boundary of the data
        paint.setColor(Color.WHITE);
        paint.setStyle(Style.STROKE);
        canvas.drawCircle(center.x, center.y, 200, paint);

        //display sensor info
        int y = 20;
        paint.setColor(Color.WHITE);
        paint.setTextSize(24);
        canvas.drawText(title, 10, y, paint); y+=30;
        canvas.drawText("Vendor: " + gravity.getVendor(),
            10, y, paint); y+=30;
        canvas.drawText("Model: " + gravity.getName(),
            10, y, paint); y+=30;
        canvas.drawText("Max range: " + gravity.getMaximumRange(),
            10, y, paint); y+=30;
        canvas.drawText("Resolution: " + gravity.getResolution(),
            10, y, paint); y+=30;
        canvas.drawText("Version: " + gravity.getVersion(),
            10, y, paint); y+=30;

        //draw raw gravity vector data to the screen with green circles
        //(not as useful as the mapped coords but still interesting)
        paint.setColor(Color.GREEN);
```

```java
        canvas.drawPoint(center.x + data.x*20, center.y + data.y*20,
            paint);
        canvas.drawText("X: " + toString(round(data.x,3)), 10, y,
            paint); y+=30;
        canvas.drawText("Y: " + toString(round(data.y,3)), 10, y,
            paint); y+=30;
        canvas.drawText("Z: " + toString(round(data.z,3)), 10, y,
            paint); y+=30;

        //convert 3D vector to 2D screen space
        screenCoords.x = data.x / data.z;
        screenCoords.y = data.y / data.z;

        //draw blue circle for vector mapped to screen
        paint.setColor(Color.BLUE);
        canvas.drawCircle(center.x + screenCoords.x, center.y +
            screenCoords.y, 5, paint);
        canvas.drawText("Vector: " + toString(screenCoords),
            10, y, paint); y+=30;

        //close the canvas
        surface.unlockCanvasAndPost(canvas);

        try {
            Thread.sleep(20);
        }
        catch(InterruptedException e) {
            e.printStackTrace();
        }
    }
}

/**
 * Helper methods section (reusable code)
 */
public String toString(int value) {
    return Integer.toString(value);
}

public String toString(float value) {
    return Float.toString(value);
}

public String toString(double value) {
    return Double.toString(value);
}

public String toString(Float2 value) {
```

```
    String s = "X:" + round(value.x) + "," +
        "Y:" + round(value.y);
    return s;
}

public String toString(Float3 value) {
    String s = "X:" + round(value.x) + "," +
        "Y:" + round(value.y) + "," +
        "Z:" + round(value.z);
    return s;
}

//round to a default 2 decimal places
public double round(double value) {
    return round(value,2);
}

//round a number to any number of decimal places
public double round(double value, int precision) {
    try {
        BigDecimal bd = new BigDecimal(value);
        BigDecimal rounded = bd.setScale(precision,
            BigDecimal.ROUND_HALF_UP);
        return rounded.doubleValue();
    }
    catch (Exception e) {
        Log.d("round",e.getMessage());
    }
    return 0;
}
/**
 * End of helper methods section
 */
    }
}
```

Using the Pressure Sensor

The pressure sensor is one of the minor sensors in the Android hardware spec that is not always implemented in every Android device. This is a "hit or miss" sensor that may be included only in specialized devices or high-end models. If there is a waterproof Android camera or watch out there, it would be really fun to write an app that reports underwater pressure!

The pressure sensor returns the atmospheric pressure level in millibars (shorthand: hPa). Only a single value is returned in values[0]. Because this sensor is often not available, we have to ensure that our code handles a null object favorably rather than allowing an exception error to occur.

Initializing the Pressure Sensor

To access the pressure sensor, declare a `Sensor` variable and initialize it using `Sensor.TYPE_PRESSURE`, being sure to check for `null` in the process.

```
Sensor pressure=null;
if (pressure==null) {
    title = "ERROR: NO PRESSURE SENSOR WAS FOUND";
    Log.d("Sensor Error","No pressure sensor was found");
}
```

Reading the Pressure Sensor

Accessing the pressure sensor change events in `onSensorChanged()` involves only looking at the `values[0]` array index.

```
float pressValue=0;
@Override public void onSensorChanged(SensorEvent event) {
    switch (event.sensor.getType()) {
    case Sensor.TYPE_PRESSURE:
        pressValue = event.values[0];
        break;
    }
}
```

BY THE WAY

If you have a particular interest in a certain sensor and want more thorough information, it can be difficult to find the appropriate Android doc with details about specific sensors. Here is the URL to the `SensorEvent` class that you'll want to peruse: http://developer.android.com/reference/android/hardware/SensorEvent.html.

Summary

This hour explained how the gravity and pressure sensors work and how to read them. There are still quite a few sensors remaining to be studied, which will be the focus of the next two hours. You will have a good grasp of the most significant Android sensors after completing these hours and will be able to use them for some of the more esoteric or specialized game design ideas.

Q&A

Q. Why do you suppose the gravity sensor returns a 3D vector instead of just a gravity *weight* value? How could this vector be useful?

A. Answers will vary.

Q. Some sensors, such as proximity and pressure, are not often included in the majority of Android devices. Why do you suppose some sensors are more useful than others, and why might a manufacturer choose one over another?

A. Answers should focus on the use of multisensor chips that include some, but not all, sensor devices.

Workshop

Quiz

1. Which `SensorEvent` properties are read to get input from the gravity sensor?

2. How do you convert a 3D vector into a 2D screen coordinate?

3. What is the approximate gravity of the Earth in meters per second squared?

Answers

1. `values[0]`, `values[1]`, and `values[2]`

2. By dividing X and Y each by Z.

3. 9.8

Activities

Modify the gravity demo program so that it displays the current gravity value as a percentage of one of the defined gravity constants (such as `GRAVITY_JUPITER`).

Creating Your Own "Tricorder"

This hour draws together the information on the Android sensors from the past two hours into one place and adds the additional sensors into a single sample program that displays all of them at once. In addition to those sensors previously covered, several new ones will be included in this final hour on sensors: gyroscope, compass, light detector, and thermometer. Using multiple sensors in one program is useful because you have seen examples with only one sensor at a time up to this point. Although it will be rare to need more than two or three sensors at once, the code presented in this hour is also helpful as an introduction to GUI programming. Each of the sensor displays is composed of its own bitmap, due to several custom classes.

Encapsulating the Android Sensors

The simple fact is that all the sensors return data via the SensorEvent.values array, and only three items of data are ever returned as an upper limit. This hardly calls for a custom class for each sensor, but for future use, it is helpful to provide these classes. Each class should provide data suitable for use in any given app or game, as appropriate. These simple examples expose the data as a Float3, which is public. When you decide how the data will be used, you should create custom accessor/mutator methods suitable for the data, with any desired conversion algorithms that will be needed.

BaseSensor

The BaseSensor class contains the properties and methods shared by all the sensors but does not have any connectivity to the Android hardware. This class handles the sensor data internally, although derived classes may present that data in specific ways (as needed).

```
public class BaseSensor {
    protected Sensor p_sensor;
    protected Float3 p_data;

    BaseSensor() {
        p_sensor = null;
        p_data = new Float3(0,0,0);
    }

    public void Update(SensorEvent event) {
        p_data.x = event.values[0];
        p_data.y = event.values[1];
        p_data.z = event.values[2];
    }

    //return the sensor object
    public Sensor getSensor() {
        return p_sensor;
    }

    public String getName() {
        return p_sensor.getName();
    }

    public String getVendor() {
        return p_sensor.getVendor();
    }

    public int getVersion() {
        return p_sensor.getVersion();
    }

    public float getResolution() {
        return p_sensor.getResolution();
    }

    public float getMaximumRange() {
        return p_sensor.getMaximumRange();
    }

    public Float3 getData() {
        return p_data;
    }
}
```

Accelerometer

The accelerometer sensor was covered previously in Hour 10, "Using the Accelerometer." The three axis values returned reflect the orientation or tilt of the device on all three axes. What is not shown here is an additional method that should be added to return the data in a format specifically suited for the accelerometer. An app or game that consumes this data would benefit from such a method. I leave it up to the reader to decide how best to present the data for each sensor class. Just note that the base `Float3 p_data` variable is used internally and visible in each derived class—so that is the place to start.

```
public class AccelerometerSensor extends BaseSensor {
    AccelerometerSensor(SensorManager sm) {
        p_sensor = sm.getDefaultSensor(Sensor.TYPE_ACCELEROMETER);
    }
    public void Update(SensorEvent event) {
        super.Update(event);
    }
}
```

Linear Acceleration

The linear acceleration sensor was covered previously in Hour 11, "Using the Linear Acceleration and Proximity Sensors." Like the accelerometer sensor, the linear acceleration sensor returns data for the three axes. But in this case, the data represents *motion* or *acceleration* in terms of the three axes. Moving the device quickly in any direction produces a result.

```
public class LinearAccelerationSensor extends BaseSensor {
    LinearAccelerationSensor(SensorManager sm) {
        p_sensor = sm.getDefaultSensor(Sensor.TYPE_LINEAR_ACCELERATION);
    }
    public void Update(SensorEvent event) {
        super.Update(event);
    }
}
```

Proximity

The proximity sensor was also covered in Hour 11. This sensor is based on the light detector (also called the ambient light sensor). The data returned by the light detector is used by the so-called proximity sensor to determine when an object is near, causing the local lighting level to drop. The proximity sensor is typically a threshold flag that reports an on/off binary value, or a fixed number for either case.

```
public class ProximitySensor extends BaseSensor {
    ProximitySensor(SensorManager sm) {
        p_sensor = sm.getDefaultSensor(Sensor.TYPE_PROXIMITY);
```

```
    }
    public void Update(SensorEvent event) {
        super.Update(event);
    }
}
```

Gravity

The gravity sensor was covered in the previous hour—Hour 12, "Using the Gravity and Pressure Sensors." This sensor returns a vector that points toward a gravity source, which will presumably always be the Earth itself.

```
public class GravitySensor extends BaseSensor {
    GravitySensor(SensorManager sm) {
        p_sensor = sm.getDefaultSensor(Sensor.TYPE_GRAVITY);
    }
    public void Update(SensorEvent event) {
        super.Update(event);
    }
}
```

Pressure

The pressure sensor, also covered in Hour 12, returns the local atmospheric pressure level. This sensor is not common in most Android devices.

```
public class PressureSensor extends BaseSensor {
    PressureSensor(SensorManager sm) {
        p_sensor = sm.getDefaultSensor(Sensor.TYPE_PRESSURE);
    }
    public void Update(SensorEvent event) {
        super.Update(event);
    }
}
```

Gyroscope

The gyroscope sensor is a new sensor that we haven't studied yet.

The gyroscope sensor reports the rate of rotation around the device's axes (X, Y, and Z). The data returned is in a format representing radians per second. A full circle is 2 × Math.Pi (3.14), or approximately 6.28. In a 360-degree circle, the value of one degree equals approximately 0.0174 radian. This is the format of the data coming out of the gyroscope sensor.

For the raw rotation speed, the radians/second reading can be found for each axis by reading the event.values array like usual (handled by the base class).

```
public class GyroscopeSensor extends BaseSensor {
    GyroscopeSensor(SensorManager sm) {
        p_sensor = sm.getDefaultSensor(Sensor.TYPE_GYROSCOPE);
    }
    public void Update(SensorEvent event) {
        super.Update(event);
    }
}
```

Compass

The magnetic field sensor is a new sensor that we haven't studied yet. The magnetic field level detected by this sensor is returned as a vector with a strength value for each of the three axes: X, Y, and Z. The values returned for each measurement are in micro Teslas (uT).

```
public class CompassSensor extends BaseSensor {
    CompassSensor(SensorManager sm) {
        p_sensor = sm.getDefaultSensor(Sensor.TYPE_MAGNETIC_FIELD);
    }
    public void Update(SensorEvent event) {
        super.Update(event);
    }
}
```

Light Detector

The ambient light sensor is a new sensor that we also haven't studied yet. Given the challenges we have faced with some of the more complex sensors, the light sensor is wonderfully simple! We need only to observe the ambient light level returned in the `SensorEvent.values[0]`.

```
public class LightSensor extends BaseSensor {
    LightSensor(SensorManager sm) {
        p_sensor = sm.getDefaultSensor(Sensor.TYPE_LIGHT);
    }
    public void Update(SensorEvent event) {
        super.Update(event);
    }
}
```

Creating the Tricorder Project

The sensors have been a hit-or-miss affair as far as support goes. Some sensors work fine, and some simply do not exist, so we have to deal with nulls (to avoid exception errors). To help illustrate how to use more than one sensor at a time, this project will present all the sensors on the screen at once (that is, the nine most common sensors). This example app shows most of the sensors on the screen at one time. The usefulness of this project is in the code that reads multiple sensors at once via the `onSensorChanged()` method. Figure 13.1 shows the output of the program.

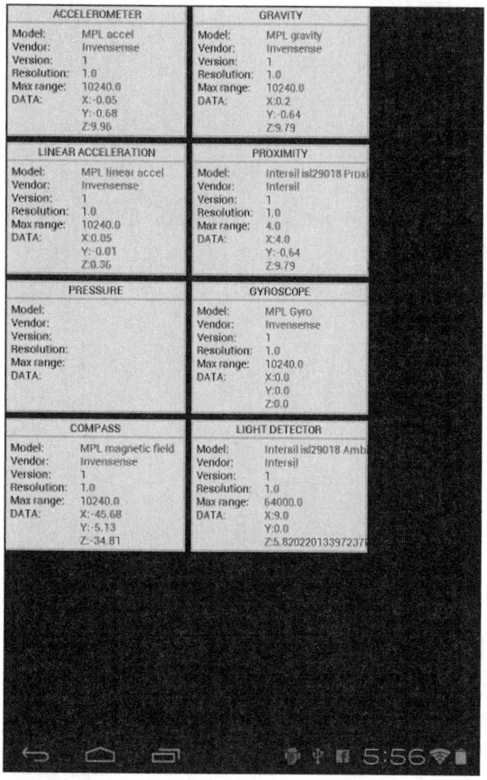

FIGURE 13.1
The so-called Tricorder Demo shows the output of multiple sensors at once.

Package and Imports

Let's start with the package and import lines.

```
package android.tricorder;
import java.math.BigDecimal;
import android.app.Activity;
import android.os.Bundle;
import android.content.*;
import android.graphics.*;
import android.graphics.Paint.Align;
import android.util.Log;
```

```
import android.view.*;
import android.content.pm.ActivityInfo;
import android.renderscript.*;
import android.hardware.*;
```

Main Class

The definition of the main program class, `Tricorder`, is next on our to-do list. This code includes the `onCreate()`, `onResume()`, and `onPause()` methods. Note that the pause and resume functionality includes calls to the sensor's object to manipulate all the sensors from a single method call.

```
public class Tricorder extends Activity {
    DrawView drawView;
    String title="";
    Sensors sensors;

    @Override public void onCreate(Bundle savedInstanceState) {
        super.onCreate(savedInstanceState);
        requestWindowFeature(Window.FEATURE_NO_TITLE);

        //must initialize sensors before view
        sensors = new Sensors();

        //initialize view
        drawView = new DrawView(this);
        setContentView(drawView);
        setRequestedOrientation(ActivityInfo.SCREEN_ORIENTATION_PORTRAIT);
    }

    @Override public void onResume() {
        super.onResume();
        drawView.resume();
        sensors.Resume();
    }

    @Override public void onPause() {
        super.onPause();
        drawView.pause();
        sensors.Pause();
    }
}
```

DrawView

The `DrawView` class is our main workhorse class for the program, implementing `Runnable` to spawn a thread and give us a usable `run()` method.

```
public class DrawView extends SurfaceView implements Runnable {
    volatile boolean running = false;
    Thread gameloop = null;
    SurfaceHolder surface = null;
    Paint paint = new Paint();
    TextPrinter text;
    SensorPanel[] panels;

    //constructor method
    public DrawView(Context context) {
        super(context);
        surface = getHolder();
        text = new TextPrinter();
        createPanels();
    }
```

Pausing and Resuming

Pausing and resuming is a fact of life on the Android platform. We can never count on our app or game to run continually until the user chooses to quit because, frankly, there is no such thing as *quitting* on Android. It's a very positive OS! These methods handle the "meat and potatoes" of the whole program—that is, the creation of the thread and resuming after the app loses and regains focus.

```
public void resume() {
    running = true;
    gameloop = new Thread(this);
    gameloop.start();
}

public void pause() {
    running = false;
    while (true) {
        try {
            gameloop.join();
        }
        catch (InterruptedException e) { }
    }
}
```

Thread Process

The thread fires off a call to run(), which literally runs once unless we put a loop inside. So, that is exactly what you'll find in the code for this method. This is the core game loop that repeatedly updates and displays the game.

```
@Override public void run() {
    while (running) {
        if (!surface.getSurface().isValid()) continue;
        Canvas canvas = surface.lockCanvas();
        updateSensors();
        drawSensors(canvas);
        surface.unlockCanvasAndPost(canvas);
        try {
            Thread.sleep(20);
        }
        catch(InterruptedException e) {
            e.printStackTrace();
        }
    }
}
```

Creating the Panels

This is a helper method called by the DrawView constructor, with the purpose of creating all the display panels for the sensors.

```
public void createPanels() {
    panels = new SensorPanel[8];

    paint.setTextSize(18);
    paint.setTextAlign(Align.CENTER);

    float y = 0;
    //create accelerometer panel
    panels[0] = new SensorPanel(300,220);
    panels[0].getCanvas().drawText("ACCELEROMETER", 150, 22, paint);
    panels[0].position = new Float2(0,y);
    panels[0].attachSensor(sensors.accelerometer);

    //create gravity panel
    panels[1] = new SensorPanel(300,220);
    panels[1].getCanvas().drawText("GRAVITY", 150, 22, paint);
    panels[1].position = new Float2(310,y);
    panels[1].attachSensor(sensors.gravity);
    y += 230;

    //create linear acceleration panel
    panels[2] = new SensorPanel(300,220);
    panels[2].getCanvas().drawText("LINEAR ACCELERATION",
            150, 22, paint);
    panels[2].position = new Float2(0,y);
    panels[2].attachSensor(sensors.linear);
```

```
//create proximity panel
panels[3] = new SensorPanel(300,220);
panels[3].getCanvas().drawText("PROXIMITY", 150, 22, paint);
panels[3].position = new Float2(310,y);
panels[3].attachSensor(sensors.proximity);
y += 230;

//create pressure panel
panels[4] = new SensorPanel(300,220);
panels[4].getCanvas().drawText("PRESSURE", 150, 22, paint);
panels[4].position = new Float2(0,y);
panels[4].attachSensor(sensors.pressure);

//create gyroscope panel
panels[5] = new SensorPanel(300,220);
panels[5].getCanvas().drawText("GYROSCOPE", 150, 22, paint);
panels[5].position = new Float2(310,y);
panels[5].attachSensor(sensors.gyroscope);
y += 230;

//create compass panel
panels[6] = new SensorPanel(300,220);
panels[6].getCanvas().drawText("COMPASS", 150, 22, paint);
panels[6].position = new Float2(0,y);
panels[6].attachSensor(sensors.compass);

//create light detector panel
panels[7] = new SensorPanel(300,220);
panels[7].getCanvas().drawText("LIGHT DETECTOR",150,22,paint);
panels[7].position = new Float2(310,y);
panels[7].attachSensor(sensors.light);
}
```

Updating the Sensors

These two methods are called from the game loop in run(). The sensor data is event-driven, so this updateSensors() method does *not* poll the sensors; its purpose is to update the *panels* that display the sensor information on the screen.

```
public void updateSensors() {
    for (int n=0; n<panels.length; n++) {
        BaseSensor sensor = panels[n].getSensor();
        if (sensor.getSensor() != null)
            updateSensor(panels[n]);
    }
}
```

```
public void updateSensor(SensorPanel panel) {
    BaseSensor sensor = panel.getSensor();
    panel.Clear();
    text.setCanvas(panel.getCanvas());
    text.setColor(Color.BLUE);
    text.Draw("" + sensor.getName(), 125, 55);
    text.Draw("" + sensor.getVendor());
    text.Draw("" + sensor.getVersion());
    text.Draw("" + sensor.getResolution());
    text.Draw("" + sensor.getMaximumRange());
    text.Draw("X:" + round(sensor.getData().x));
    text.Draw("Y:" + round(sensor.getData().y));
    text.Draw("Z:" + round(sensor.getData().z));
}
```

Drawing the Sensor Panels

The drawSensors() helper method is called from the game loop in run() to draw all the panels containing sensor information.

```
public void drawSensors(Canvas canvas) {
    Paint paint = new Paint();
    for (int n=0; n<panels.length; n++) {
        canvas.drawBitmap(panels[n].getBitmap(),
            panels[n].position.x, panels[n].position.y, paint);
    }
}
```

Helper Methods

We have used several helper methods in past hours to facilitate string conversion, and these two helpers are also very useful—rounding a floating-point number to a specified number of decimal places. We've used these two before, and they are used again in this program.

```
//round to a default 2 decimal places
public double round(double value) {
    return round(value,2);
}

//round a number to any number of decimal places
public double round(double value, int precision) {
    try {
        BigDecimal bd = new BigDecimal(value);
        BigDecimal rounded = bd.setScale(precision, BigDecimal.
                ROUND_HALF_UP);
        return rounded.doubleValue();
    }
```

```
        catch (Exception e) {
            Log.e("round","error rounding");
        }
        return 0;
    }
}
```

The `SensorPanel` Class

The `SensorPanel` class is a GUI container that is used to display the information from a single hardware sensor. Included in the display is a background color, a border color, a title, and a content area. The whole panel is drawn as a single bitmap to the screen when displayed. This class is specific to the display of sensor data, showing information for any sensor in a generic way. If you add a custom field to any of the sensor classes, you will want to derive from `SensorPanel` and display the custom data in place of the generic `Float3` data.

```
public class SensorPanel {
    private Bitmap p_bitmap;
    private Canvas p_canvas;
    private int p_width,p_height;
    private Paint p_paint;
    private TextPrinter p_text;
    private BaseSensor p_sensor;
    public Float2 position;

    SensorPanel(int width,int height) {
        p_width = width;
        p_height = height;
        p_sensor = new BaseSensor();
        position = new Float2(0,0);
        p_bitmap = Bitmap.createBitmap(width, height, Bitmap.Config.
                ARGB_8888);
        p_canvas = new Canvas(p_bitmap);
        p_paint = new Paint();
        p_canvas.drawColor(Color.rgb(180,180,180));
        p_paint.setColor(Color.rgb(230,230,230));
        p_canvas.drawRect(3, 3, p_width-4, 28, p_paint);
        p_text = new TextPrinter();
        Clear();
    }

    public BaseSensor getSensor() {
        return p_sensor;
    }
```

```
public void attachSensor(BaseSensor sensor) {
    p_sensor = sensor;
}

public void Clear() {
    //this clears only the content, not the title
    p_paint.setColor(Color.rgb(230,230,230));
    p_canvas.drawRect(3, 32, p_width-4, p_height-4, p_paint);
    p_text.setCanvas(p_canvas);
    p_text.setColor(Color.BLACK);
    p_text.Draw("Model:",10,55);
    p_text.Draw("Vendor:");
    p_text.Draw("Version:");
    p_text.Draw("Resolution:");
    p_text.Draw("Max range:");
    p_text.Draw("DATA:");
}

public Bitmap getBitmap() {
    return p_bitmap;
}

public Canvas getCanvas() {
    return p_canvas;
}
}
```

Printing Text Lines

Printing lines of text hardly calls for a custom class, but that is exactly what this class does—it facilitates the printing of multiple lines of text by keeping track of the line number. The class makes it easy to print a bunch of lines without having to manually keep track of the position of each additional line. Just call the first overload of Draw() with the initial position, and additional calls to overloaded Draw() (with only a single String parameter) will automatically drop to the next line. The font and spacing can be fine-tuned.

```
public class TextPrinter {
    private Canvas p_canvas;
    private Paint p_paint;
    private float p_x, p_y;
    private float p_spacing;
```

This constructor overload calls the second one with a null value for Canvas. This is useful for times when you want to use TextPrinter as a global, versus just declaring it for short-term use in a called method, where it will be created and destroyed repeatedly. For the long-term global use, we'll want to set the `Canvas` for drawing every time through the game loop (because it is not permanent).

```
TextPrinter() {
    this(null);
}

TextPrinter(Canvas canvas) {
    p_canvas = canvas;
    p_paint = new Paint();
    p_x = p_y = 0;
    p_spacing = 22;
    setTextSize(18);
    setColor(Color.WHITE);
}

public void setCanvas(Canvas canvas) {
    p_canvas = canvas;
}

public void setLineSpacing(float spacing) {
    p_spacing = spacing;
}

public void setTextSize(float size) {
    p_paint.setTextSize(size);
}

public void setColor(int color) {
    p_paint.setColor(color);
}

public void Draw(String text, float x, float y) {
    p_x = x;
    p_y = y;
    Draw(text);
}

public void Draw(String text) {
    p_canvas.drawText(text, p_x, p_y, p_paint);
    p_y += p_spacing;
}
}
```

The `Sensors` **Class**

This class encapsulates all the sensors and acts like a manager or container for all the sensors in one place. Some sensors may not be available on every Android device, so we have to remember to handle nulls.

```
public class Sensors implements SensorEventListener {
    SensorManager sensors=null;
    AccelerometerSensor accelerometer=null;
    GravitySensor gravity=null;
    CompassSensor compass=null;
    GyroscopeSensor gyroscope=null;
    LightSensor light=null;
    PressureSensor pressure=null;
    ProximitySensor proximity=null;
    LinearAccelerationSensor linear=null;
```

The constructor creates all the sensor objects at once. Any sensors that are not available on the device will be returned as a null.

```
Sensors() {
    //create sensor manager object
    sensors = (SensorManager)getSystemService(SENSOR_SERVICE);

    //create individual sensor objects
    accelerometer = new AccelerometerSensor(sensors);
    gravity = new GravitySensor(sensors);
    compass = new CompassSensor(sensors);
    gyroscope = new GyroscopeSensor(sensors);
    light = new LightSensor(sensors);
    pressure = new PressureSensor(sensors);
    proximity = new ProximitySensor(sensors);
    linear = new LinearAccelerationSensor(sensors);
}
```

Trapping Sensor Events

The `onSensorChanged()` method is not new in this hour, but we are doing something a bit different this time around. Instead of a single sensor, we have many sensors in this program example. Because each sensor type has an object associated with it, we just figure out which sensor is sending the update and call that particular sensor object with the update data as a parameter.

```
@Override public void onSensorChanged(SensorEvent event) {
    switch (event.sensor.getType()) {

    //process accelerometer update
    case Sensor.TYPE_ACCELEROMETER:
        if (accelerometer.getSensor() != null)
```

```
            accelerometer.Update(event);
        break;

    //process gravity update
    case Sensor.TYPE_GRAVITY:
        if (gravity.getSensor() != null)
            gravity.Update(event);
        break;

    //process compass update
    case Sensor.TYPE_MAGNETIC_FIELD:
        if (compass.getSensor() != null)
            compass.Update(event);
        break;

    //process gyroscope update
    case Sensor.TYPE_GYROSCOPE:
        if (gyroscope.getSensor() != null)
            gyroscope.Update(event);
        break;

    //process light update
    case Sensor.TYPE_LIGHT:
        if (light.getSensor() != null)
            light.Update(event);
        break;

    //process pressure update
    case Sensor.TYPE_PRESSURE:
        if (pressure.getSensor() != null)
            pressure.Update(event);
        break;

    //process proximity update
    case Sensor.TYPE_PROXIMITY:
        if (proximity.getSensor() != null)
            proximity.Update(event);
        break;

    //process linear accel update
    case Sensor.TYPE_LINEAR_ACCELERATION:
        if (linear.getSensor() != null)
            linear.Update(event);
        break;
    }
}
```

The Unused Accuracy Event

We have to remember to include the unused `onAccuracyChanged()` method to compile the program. This is a required method of the `SensorEventListener` interface.

```
@Override public void onAccuracyChanged(Sensor arg0,int arg1){}
```

Pausing and Resuming the App

Pausing and resuming is a bit more involved this time around than it was in the previous hours covering the sensors. The sensors can *all* be unregistered with a single call, but reregistering them is a bit more involved because that has to be done individually. This is also the place where we need to verify whether sensor hardware is present on the Android device. If a sensor is not found, we need to trap the nulls rather than allow an exception error to occur later when the object is used. You need quite a bit of additional code in the `Resume()` method to display the results of any missing sensors.

```
public void Pause() {
    sensors.unregisterListener(this);
}

public void Resume() {
    //register accelerometer sensor
    if (accelerometer.getSensor() != null)
        sensors.registerListener(this, accelerometer.getSensor(),
                SensorManager.SENSOR_DELAY_NORMAL);
    else
        Log.d("Resume", "Accelerometer sensor is null");

    //register gravity sensor
    if (gravity.getSensor() != null)
        sensors.registerListener(this, gravity.getSensor(),
                SensorManager.SENSOR_DELAY_NORMAL);
    else
        Log.d("Resume", "Gravity sensor is null");

    //register compass sensor
    if (compass.getSensor() != null)
        sensors.registerListener(this, compass.getSensor(),
                SensorManager.SENSOR_DELAY_NORMAL);
    else
        Log.d("Resume", "Compass sensor is null");

    //register gyroscope sensor
    if (gyroscope.getSensor() != null)
        sensors.registerListener(this, gyroscope.getSensor(),
                SensorManager.SENSOR_DELAY_NORMAL);
```

```
    else
        Log.d("Resume", "Gyroscope sensor is null");

    //register light sensor
    if (light.getSensor() != null)
        sensors.registerListener(this, light.getSensor(),
                SensorManager.SENSOR_DELAY_NORMAL);
    else
        Log.d("Resume", "Light sensor is null");

    //register pressure sensor
    if (pressure.getSensor() != null)
        sensors.registerListener(this, pressure.getSensor(),
                SensorManager.SENSOR_DELAY_NORMAL);
    else
        Log.d("Resume", "Pressure sensor is null");

    //register proximity sensor
    if (proximity.getSensor() != null)
        sensors.registerListener(this, proximity.getSensor(),
                SensorManager.SENSOR_DELAY_NORMAL);
    else
        Log.d("Resume", "Proximity sensor is null");

    //register linear acceleration sensor
    if (linear.getSensor() != null)
        sensors.registerListener(this, linear.getSensor(),
                SensorManager.SENSOR_DELAY_NORMAL);
    else
        Log.d("Resume", "Linear acceleration sensor is null");
    }
}
```

The `BaseSensor` Class

Now we come again to the `BaseSensor` class, which was covered earlier this hour. Because we're going over the complete source code for the Tricorder program here, we'll list it again for the sake of completeness.

```
public class BaseSensor {
    protected Sensor p_sensor;
    protected Float3 p_data;

    BaseSensor() {
        p_sensor = null;
        p_data = new Float3(0,0,0);
    }
```

```
    public void Update(SensorEvent event) {
        p_data.x = event.values[0];
        p_data.y = event.values[1];
        p_data.z = event.values[2];
    }

    public Sensor getSensor() {
        return p_sensor;
    }

    public String getName() {
        return p_sensor.getName();
    }

    public String getVendor() {
        return p_sensor.getVendor();
    }

    public int getVersion() {
        return p_sensor.getVersion();
    }

    public float getResolution() {
        return p_sensor.getResolution();
    }

    public float getMaximumRange() {
        return p_sensor.getMaximumRange();
    }

    public Float3 getData() {
        return p_data;
    }
}
```

The Various Sensor Classes

We have already gone over the individual sensor classes earlier this hour. Here they are again without any notes, just to be thorough.

```
public class AccelerometerSensor extends BaseSensor {
    AccelerometerSensor(SensorManager sm) {
        p_sensor = sm.getDefaultSensor(Sensor.TYPE_ACCELEROMETER);
    }
    public void Update(SensorEvent event) {
        super.Update(event);
    }
}
```

```java
public class LinearAccelerationSensor extends BaseSensor {
    LinearAccelerationSensor(SensorManager sm) {
        p_sensor = sm.getDefaultSensor(Sensor.TYPE_LINEAR_ACCELERATION);
    }
    public void Update(SensorEvent event) {
        super.Update(event);
    }
}

public class ProximitySensor extends BaseSensor {
    ProximitySensor(SensorManager sm) {
        p_sensor = sm.getDefaultSensor(Sensor.TYPE_PROXIMITY);
    }
    public void Update(SensorEvent event) {
        super.Update(event);
    }
}

public class GravitySensor extends BaseSensor {
    GravitySensor(SensorManager sm) {
        p_sensor = sm.getDefaultSensor(Sensor.TYPE_GRAVITY);
    }
    public void Update(SensorEvent event) {
        super.Update(event);
    }
}

public class PressureSensor extends BaseSensor {
    PressureSensor(SensorManager sm) {
        p_sensor = sm.getDefaultSensor(Sensor.TYPE_PRESSURE);
    }
    public void Update(SensorEvent event) {
        super.Update(event);
    }
}

public class GyroscopeSensor extends BaseSensor {
    GyroscopeSensor(SensorManager sm) {
        p_sensor = sm.getDefaultSensor(Sensor.TYPE_GYROSCOPE);
    }
    public void Update(SensorEvent event) {
        super.Update(event);
    }
}

public class CompassSensor extends BaseSensor {
    CompassSensor(SensorManager sm) {
        p_sensor = sm.getDefaultSensor(Sensor.TYPE_MAGNETIC_FIELD);
```

```
    }
    public void Update(SensorEvent event) {
        super.Update(event);
    }
}

public class LightSensor extends BaseSensor {
    LightSensor(SensorManager sm) {
        p_sensor = sm.getDefaultSensor(Sensor.TYPE_LIGHT);
    }
    public void Update(SensorEvent event) {
        super.Update(event);
    }
}
```

Summary

We are now done with the Android sensors. The code presented in this hour should help you to handle any sensor needs that may arise. Although sensors are not common in most video games, we have this functionality now encapsulated for later use.

Q&A

Q. What type of game can you imagine playing that uses the accelerometer and linear acceleration sensors?

A. Discuss a game in which physical movement while carrying the Android device is a part of the gameplay—such as walking a highwire!

Q. What are some drawbacks to reading all the sensors continually while a game is playing, even if some sensors are not used?

A. That may be a waste of processing power that could go to the gameplay or rendering. It may be helpful to selectively enable or disable reading of specific sensors in a game.

Workshop

Quiz

1. What type of variable was used to read sensor data?

2. What is the name of the base sensor class used to read a single sensor?

3. Which sensor reports the angular motion (rotation) of the device?

Answers

1. Float3

2. BaseSensor

3. Gyroscope

Activities

It would be interesting to see all the sensors displayed graphically, the way they were presented in previous hours covering the sensors. Modify the Tricorder program so that it draws the sensor data graphically rather than displaying it as text. You may want to remove all the sensor panels and graph the data on the screen, using a different color for each sensor.

Playing with the Audio System

In this hour you will learn to tap into the audio system of Android devices for playback of video game music and sound effects. The Android SDK supports the audio system by providing us with a class, SoundPool, that can load and play audio files through the integrated audio mixer. The Android SDK includes classes with methods for loading and playing multimedia content very easily. You will learn how to load audio assets and play them. Both music and sound effects files are treated the same; it's just a matter of length and memory usage, although music is usually handled a bit differently using the MediaPlayer class.

Playing Audio Using MediaPlayer

The class android.media.MediaPlayer gives us access to the multimedia system, exposing methods for loading and playing audio and video files on Android. The Media Player is a useful tool for streaming large audio/video assets without loading them entirely into memory because of the limited memory available to Android apps and games. But the Media Player is not suitable for a game with numerous sound effects. It is not a mixer-based audio system; its purpose is to play from a single source at a time. We can use the Media Player component to play music files for the background music of a game and then use android.media.SoundPool for mixed sound effects (covered later this hour).

Supported Audio Formats

Several common audio file formats are supported by the Android SDK. The following list shows the most common audio formats likely to be used in a game project. For the complete list of asset files supported by the Android SDK, see https://developer.android.com/guide/appendix/media-formats.html.

▶ WAV

▶ OGG

▶ MIDI

▶ MP3

BY THE WAY

An easy way to convert audio files from one format to another is with a free audio editor program called Audacity: http://audacity.sourceforge.net. It can convert to and from WAV, MP3, and OGG.

Initializing `MediaPlayer`

The import library `android.media.MediaPlayer` must be included in the program to gain access to the `MediaPlayer` class. To create a `MediaPlayer` object, use the static method `MediaPlayer.create()` as follows:

```
MediaPlayer mp = MediaPlayer.create(this, resource);
```

Adding Sound Files to the Project

The *resource* parameter should be the identifier for a resource found in the project's .\res\raw folder. By default, .\res is part of a standard Android project, but the \raw subfolder is *not* created automatically. Thus, you have to add this folder to the project yourself manually. Figure 14.1 shows the .\res\raw folder in the Audio Demo project (covered later this hour).

For instance, this resource identifier represents a file called Music in the .\res\raw folder (excluding the extension).

```
MediaPlayer mp = MediaPlayer.create(this, R.raw.music);
```

BY THE WAY

You must add the .\res\raw folder to the project manually by creating this folder and then copying your audio files into the new folder. In doing so, the asset manager will detect the files and add them to the project.

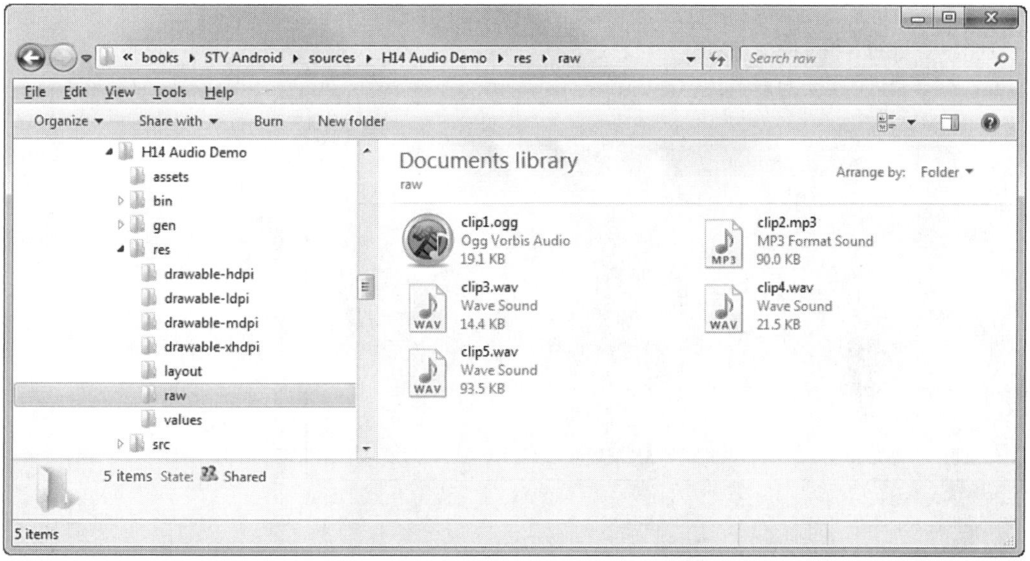

FIGURE 14.1
Audio files are added to the .\res\raw folder of a project. Note that different audio file formats may be used interchangeably.

Resource identifiers begin with the capital letter R. This object, R, represents the .\res folder of the project, with an itemized list of assets detected there by Eclipse. From R, or .\res, we can go into the \raw subfolder via R.raw. Now, when you type this into Eclipse, it will pop up a list of assets found in the folder. This is very helpful.

WATCH OUT

Digital sampled audio is not a good choice for music because of memory use. A compressed MP3 or OGG file might only be about 4MB, but it expands to 40MB when loaded. Streaming *might* work, but there is a performance hit. The small, nonsampled MIDI format is recommended for longer music tracks.

What if you have an audio file in a format or codec not supported by Android? No problem, you can convert it to a supported format using a free audio editing tool called Audacity, shown in Figure 14.2.

Just drag your audio file onto Audacity or load the file using File, Open. After opening an audio clip, use File, Export to export the file to a new format. See Figure 14.3.

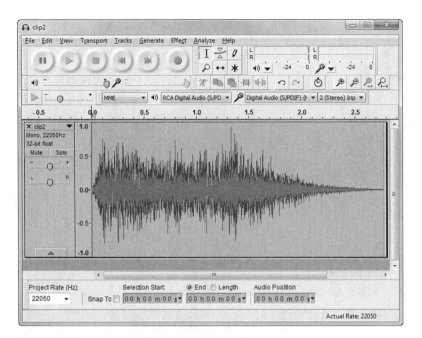

FIGURE 14.2
Using Audacity to convert audio files from one format to another.

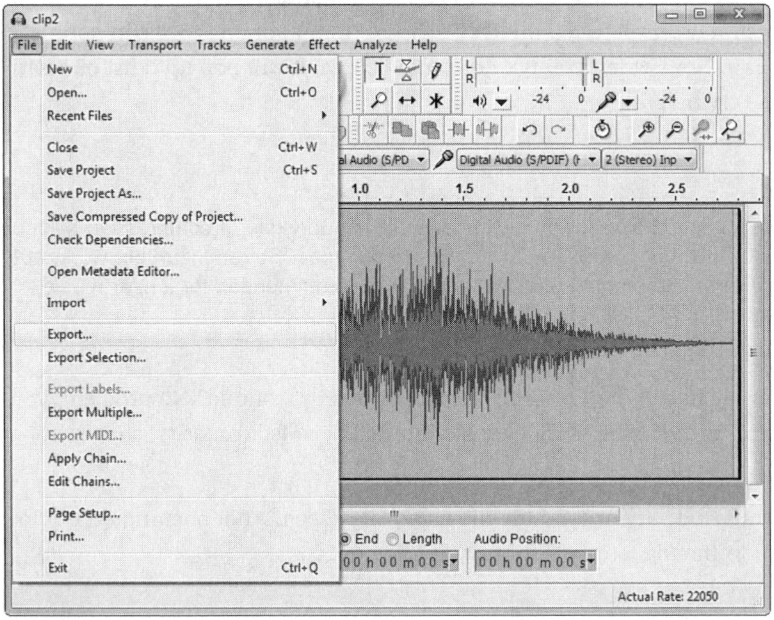

FIGURE 14.3
Preparing to export an audio file to a new format.

This opens the Export File dialog, which allows you to enter a filename and choose the export audio format, as shown in Figure 14.4. Here are the audio formats supported by Audacity:

▶ AIFF (Apple) signed 16-bit PCM

▶ WAV (Microsoft) signed 16-bit PCM

▶ GSM 6.10 WAV (mobile)

▶ MP3

▶ Ogg Vorbis

▶ FLAC

▶ MP2

▶ M4A (AAC) (FFmpeg)

▶ AC3 (FFmpeg)

▶ AMR (narrow band) (FFmpeg)

▶ WMA (version 2) (FFmpeg)

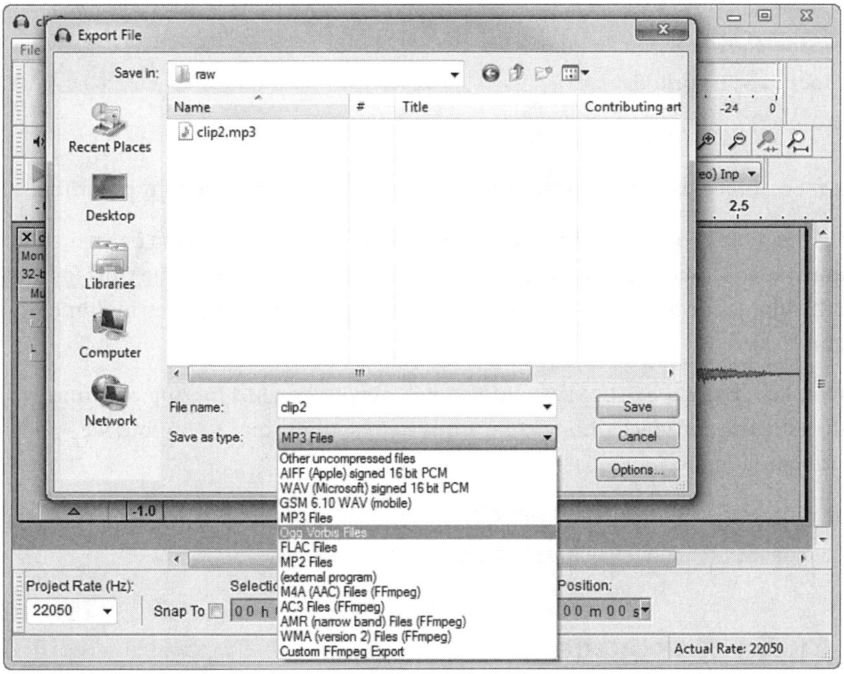

FIGURE 14.4
Selecting the new audio file format.

Playing a Sound Clip

A `MediaPlayer` object contains the audio sample that it will play directly, so a call to `MediaPlayer.start()` causes the loaded audio sample to begin playing.

To pause playback, use `MediaPlayer.pause()`.

Similarly, to stop playback entirely, use `MediaPlayer.stop()`.

Playing Audio Using `SoundPool`

The class `android.media.SoundPool` is used to play more than one audio sample at a time, so it is used for playing sound effects in a game.

BY THE WAY

Asset file extensions are ignored. Because of this, asset filenames must be unique without regard for the extension. That is, **sound1.mp3** and **sound1.ogg** cannot be stored in the same folder because the files are added to the resource manager using the key "sound1" for both files.

Initializing `SoundPool`

First, we'll create a `SoundPool` variable:

```
SoundPool soundPool=null;
```

Normally, the `SoundPool` object is initialized in the `onCreate()` event method of a program.

The first parameter of the `SoundPool` constructor is the number of sound channels to be created for the mixer. This example uses 4, but you may want to use up to 10 or 20, if your game calls for that many. Don't overdo it, though, or the mixer will needlessly waste memory and processing time. A reasonable upper limit is 20.

The second parameter, `AudioManager.STREAM_MUSIC`, will always be used for app or game audio. There are other streams for voice phone calls, for system sounds, and so on, but we wouldn't use them for game audio.

The third parameter is not used and is always set to zero.

```
soundPool = new SoundPool(4, AudioManager.STREAM_MUSIC, 0);
```

Loading an Audio Resource

Audio files copied into the .\res\raw folder of the project are automatically parsed by the resource manager when you refresh, save, or build the project. They are then added to the

`R.raw` list, identified by name (sans the extension). An easy way to index the audio resources at runtime is by using a `java.util.HashMap`. A hash map is like an index with a definable key and value pair for each item stored within it. We can use the `HashMap.put()` method to add audio samples to the hash collection.

This technique works really well because we do not need to keep track of the *sound identifiers* this way, only the index of the hash where they are stored. Normally, we have to keep track of the identifier returned by `SoundPool.load()`, but the hash map translates the index number into the sound identifier on-the-fly.

First, load the audio sample using `SoundPool.load()`, which returns an identifier. Then, store that identifier in the hash map with an index number.

```
int id = soundPool.load(this, R.raw.clip1, 1);
soundPoolMap.put(0, id);
```

Combining both statements into one results in a very clean line of code for loading and storing an audio sample:

```
soundPoolMap.put(0, soundPool.load(this, R.raw.clip1, 1));
```

Just replace `R.raw.clip1` with the name of the audio resource you want to load.

Playing an Audio Resource

After audio is loaded into the hash map—which, again, is nothing more than an indexed lookup of *identifiers*—we can then play a sample using the `SoundPool.play()` method.

The first parameter of this method will be the index of the sample in the hash map. The remaining parameters never need to change (unless you want to play the sample with some special effects).

The second and third parameters are the left and right channel volume levels, respectively, with a range of 0.0 to 1.0 (full volume).

The fourth parameter is the priority, which is usually set to 0.

The fifth parameter is the loop mode, where 0 is no loop, [ms]1 is loop endlessly, and any other value is the number of times to loop (that is, 1 will repeat once, 2 will repeat twice).

```
soundPool.play(sound_id, 1f, 1f, 1, 0, 1f);
```

DID YOU KNOW

Repeatedly playing the *same* sample will cause it to stop and restart each time, but playing different samples will cause them to mix together in the audio stream. To play the same sound mixed, it is necessary to load the sound multiple times or use an additional `SoundPool` object.

The Audio Demo Program

The Audio Demo program has no output other than a black screen. You tap the screen to hear an audio sample play. You can modify the source code to change the sample number and hear a different sound (five total, numbered 0 to 4).

```java
package android.program;

import java.util.HashMap;
import android.app.Activity;
import android.content.Context;
import android.media.AudioManager;
import android.media.SoundPool;
import android.os.Bundle;
import android.view.MotionEvent;
import android.view.View;
import android.view.View.OnTouchListener;

public class Game extends Activity implements OnTouchListener {
    DrawView drawView=null;
    SoundPool soundPool=null;
    HashMap<Integer, Integer> soundPoolMap;

    @Override public void onCreate(Bundle savedInstanceState) {
        super.onCreate(savedInstanceState);
        setTitle("Audio Demo");

        //create the view and touch listener
        drawView = new DrawView(this);
        setContentView(drawView);
        drawView.setOnTouchListener(this);

        //create the sound pool
        soundPool = new SoundPool(4, AudioManager.STREAM_MUSIC, 0);
        soundPoolMap = new HashMap<Integer, Integer>();

        //load the sound files
        soundPoolMap.put(0, soundPool.load(this, R.raw.clip1, 1));
        soundPoolMap.put(1, soundPool.load(this, R.raw.clip2, 1));
        soundPoolMap.put(2, soundPool.load(this, R.raw.clip3, 1));
        soundPoolMap.put(3, soundPool.load(this, R.raw.clip4, 1));
        soundPoolMap.put(4, soundPool.load(this, R.raw.clip5, 1));
    }

    @Override public boolean onTouch(View v, MotionEvent event) {
        playSound( 3 );
        return true;
    }
```

```
public class DrawView extends View {
    public DrawView(Context context) {
        super(context);
    }
}

public void playSound(int soundId) {
    soundPool.play(soundId, 1f, 1f, 1, 0, 1f);
}
}
```

Summary

The audio system of the Android can be programmed using `MediaPlayer` (generally) for music and `SoundPool` for sound effects or any other audio needs. The source code to load and play audio files is not difficult, but it is a bit complex, so this is one component of the Android SDK that would benefit from a wrapper class to consolidate the code and make it easier to use. We will have to do just that when building our Android game engine.

Q&A

Q. What is the main problem with using MP3 or OGG or any other sampled audio format for the background music in a game?

A. The problem is memory consumption because these files are decompressed. An option is to stream them using the `MediaPlayer` class.

Q. Describe what happens when Eclipse detects new files in the .\res\raw folder of a project.

A. Eclipse reloads the `R.raw` collection with the audio files found in that folder.

Workshop

Quiz

1. What is the purpose of the .\res\raw folder in a project?

2. Which Android class is best used for video game music?

3. Which Android class is best used for video game sound effects?

Answers

1. This folder is for storing audio files and other game resources.

2. `MediaPlayer`

3. `SoundPool`

Activities

Modify the Audio Demo program so that it displays several boxes on the screen and plays a different audio sample depending on which box has been tapped on the screen. These boxes may be a precursor for a simple graphical user interface.

PART III

Android Gameplay

HOUR 15
Building an Android Game Engine

What You'll Learn in This Hour:

▶ Designing an Android game engine
▶ Creating an Android library project
▶ Writing the core engine classes
▶ Testing the engine with a demo project

The first step of developing a game for a new hardware platform like the Android OS is to study the hardware and learn how to tap into it for the purposes of utilizing the hardware for a game. We have done that over the previous 14 hours, having learned about the development tools, display system, resource manager, touch input system, hardware sensors (such as the accelerometer), and the audio system. Understanding the hardware is important for a game developer because you want to gain as much control over a system as possible to eke out every bit of performance.

A logical next step is to encapsulate that hardware in code that abstracts it, taking the sting out of working with low-level hardware (which can be very frustrating) and simplifying access to it through encapsulation. In other words, we want to write Java classes that present us with a game engine rather than the Android SDK. At this level, we do *not want* to see very much Android SDK code. What we want to see instead are classes and methods in our game engine that are layered over the Android SDK. This process increases the legibility of the code, making it easier to make improvements and fix bugs (which will hopefully be few!).

The goal this hour is to learn how to create an Android library project that contains the basic Activity code and then use that library as the basis or "engine" for Android games. At this point, it is important that you understand the basics covered so far in the book before continuing. So, if you tend to skip through a book, it would be a good idea to cover the core hardware hours before continuing so you have a good understanding of the graphics system, file formats, and rendering.

Designing an Android Game Engine

The design for a game engine at this level will not be large or complex. The engine will not include level editors and scripting, as you would expect to find in a professional engine like Unity. No, we're going for a *framework* that brings together all the resources in the Android SDK needed to make a variety of games more easily than would be possible with the Android SDK alone. The goal is not to write code for *others*, but to wrap all the code we've studied so far in easier-to-use containers, or classes, so that our *own* games will be easier to make. Most game engines are not released to the public, either for free or for sale, they are developed internally and maintained internally, not for use by the public. Many game studios *license* a third-party engine (such as Unity) to save time and money, and some studios create their own.

BY THE WAY

The Unity game engine also supports Android and iPhone. Check out http://unity3d.com for details.

Design Goals

We do not need a large, complex engine chock full of features for every game genre. This will be more of a lean engine to assist with making games for Android a little easier. Hopefully, it will also make the code more reusable. You might call this library a framework rather than an engine, and that would be just as appropriate. Let's describe some goals for this engine to help with writing the code for it later. The engine should, at minimum, meet these major design goals:

- Make certain assumptions about the minimum hardware

- Launch a game loop in a thread

- Detect multi-touch user input on the touch screen

- Provide easy access to game asset files

- Provide access to image resources

- Provide access to the audio system

- Provide a customizable animation system

- Can automatically report object collisions

- Can manage actors and other objects internally

- Use an event manager to communicate with components

In addition, these less important but interesting goals can also be implemented in the engine:

▶ Automatically clear the screen with a certain color

▶ Allow either portrait or landscape orientation

▶ Calculate the frame rate of the game loop

▶ Handle string output conversion for all data types

▶ Handle most data type conversions automatically

Engine Components

With the aforementioned goals in mind, let's go over the major components of the engine at this early design stage to determine what direction to take with the source code.

Engine Core

The core of the engine will be a class that inherits from `Activity`, as usual, but which also implements the interface classes such as `Runnable` and `OnTouchListener` for threading and input services, among other things. The core class will also encapsulate the `SurfaceView` and `Canvas` objects that previously were made available via the `DrawView` class (which will no longer be needed). The core includes features such as an event manager that facilitates communication among the engine components. For instance, an event can be generated by the code responsible for detecting user input on the touch screen, and a potential *future* GUI system would consume that event to control the GUI for a game. Another common practice is to have a time generate events at regular intervals (such as one per second for frame-rate timing).

Startup

The startup method is called `Activity.onCreate()`. This is quite specific to the Android platform, and unlike any other startup method I've ever encountered on the many platforms I've used over the years (from Windows Phone to Nintendo DS to Windows to Xbox 360). It's not a bad method; it's just unique to Android. What we want to do with the engine is to abstract away the proprietary stuff and make more of a standardized interface to the Android OS. In other words, you want to be able to write similar code—that's similar code, not necessarily the same code—and compile it on different platforms. This is extremely important today with so many different OSs and devices on the market. Gone are the days of releasing a game only for Windows, Mac, or Linux! Today, the video game market is broad, and you will want to take advantage of every platform that will increase sales and *awareness* of both your brand and your games.

We will invoke a custom method in the engine class called `Engine.load()`, which will be called from `Activity.onCreate()`, after the display surface, context, and resource manager have been initialized, to allow the game to load assets.

There is one additional startup step that the engine will need: a preload initialization event. We need to be able to configure the game with basic settings before the screen is initialized into either portrait or landscape mode. `Engine.init()` will take care of this need for us.

Main Thread

The main thread, or cycle update, takes place in the `Runnable.run()` method, which operates in its own thread. This method contains a `while` loop that is the game loop for the engine and any game that uses the engine. Thus, derived game projects need not include their own game loop. The loop is in the engine! By managing the loop and all updates from the engine, the derived game is freed up to focus on gameplay rather than logistics, such as timing, updates, and drawing, at a lower level. The derived game can operate at one level higher, from a coding perspective, and allow the engine to take care of the messy details, so to speak.

The engine will do some updates automatically, such as detecting user input on the touch screen, calculating frame rate, and doing cyclic timing. Some processes need to run at the maximum speed of the processor, and these are called *cycle updates*. But updating and drawing game entities—scenes, actors and props—takes place at timed intervals. Drawing will take place at approximately 60 frames per second (fps) in a method called `Engine.draw(delta)`, and updating will run at the untimed, full-cycle speed in a method called `Engine.update(delta)`. In both cases, the `delta` parameter is a millisecond value representing the time since the previous timed draw or untimed update, respectively. The `delta` value makes it possible to synchronize animations and other gameplay behaviors to a consistent runtime.

The full-cycle-speed update is also where engine-level processes take place, such as automated collision detection, entity management, and so on.

Rendering

Rendering is the most important component of a game, although it depends on other components to work correctly. The Android mechanism for drawing *can* work via `Activity.onDraw()`, but as you learned early on, this is limited to the user interface and not suitable for a real-time game. Rendering takes place via the `SurfaceHolder` and `SurfaceView` classes. But, instead of creating an inner class this time, like we did with the `DrawView` custom class in prior hours, the engine will define these objects and use them internally without a helper class. The `SurfaceView` class ends up being useful only to return its surface via the `getHolder()` method and need not be subclassed.

The rendering portion of the engine takes place in the main `while` loop, explained earlier. The `Engine.draw(delta)` method call allows the game project (which is a subclass of the engine) to draw entities at the gameplay level without regard for the underlying logistics. This significantly frees up the programmer or designer to focus on gameplay code. But even more important, this separation of game *engine* from game *play* code makes it possible to write updates to the engine without rewriting any game code.

Creating an Android Library Project

Our Android game engine will have its own project, separate from any game or app that uses it. The project will be a special type of project configured as a *library*. A library project contains reusable code that does not run on its own. To use the library project, you must create another project that *uses* or *consumes* the library's features in order to make a game.

A simple library project might have only a single class with static methods. For instance, you could store reusable vector math functions in a class using methods, so that the methods are called directly (without instantiating the class). For instance, if you had a *fictional* class called `VectorMath`, and it contained a static method called `DotProduct()`, you would call this method with

```
VectorMath.DotProduct()
```

The class stored in a library project may have to be resolved with a complete namespace, such as `android.engine.VectorMath`, but that can be resolved with an `import` statement.

TRY IT YOURSELF ▼

New Android Project

1. Click the New Project button or use File, New, Android Project. The New dialog appears, as shown in Figure 15.1.

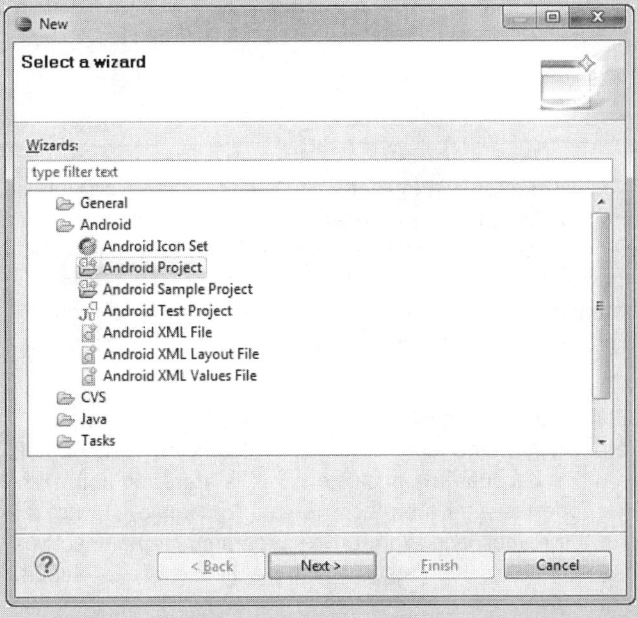

FIGURE 15.1
The New dialog in Eclipse.

▼

2. Choose Android Project from the list of project templates. Next up is the New Android Project dialog, shown in Figure 15.2. The Project Name is not extremely important here from a coding perspective; it is just a label for identifying the project in the Eclipse workspace.

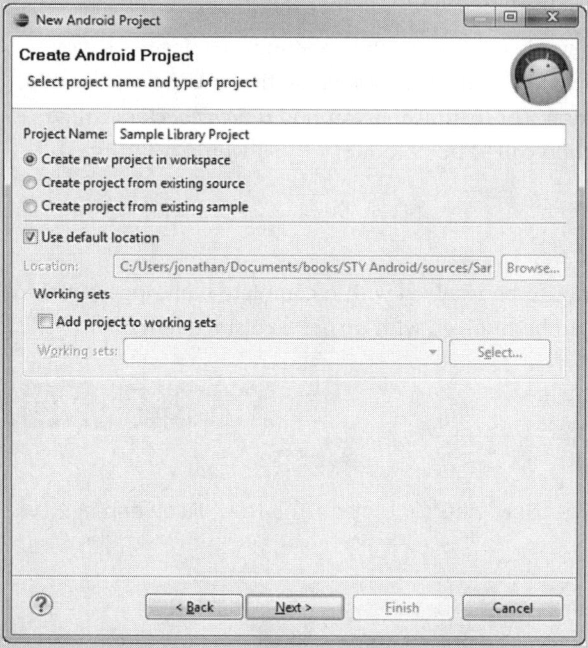

FIGURE 15.2
The New Android Project dialog.

3. The next dialog in the Android project wizard, shown in Figure 15.3, lets you select the build target. Android 4.0.3 is selected in this example. In some cases, you may need to choose an older version. For instance, when targeting an Android 3.2 device, such as the Toshiba Thrive 7" tablet used for testing the code, the Android 3.2 target can be selected. It is a simple matter to change the build target in the project properties later, so don't be concerned at this point if you believe a change may be needed. You do not need to create a separate project for each device.

4. The Application Info dialog comes up, shown in Figure 15.4. The Package Name field is important, but you can change the package name later if necessary. However, I recommend choosing the desired name at this stage because the package name is stored in both the project properties and in the source code file—it's a bit inconvenient to change, but not difficult by any means. The package is the *namespace*, from a C++ programming perspective. It is the wrapper around other classes, binding them together, giving them a shared scope.

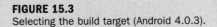

FIGURE 15.3
Selecting the build target (Android 4.0.3).

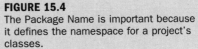

FIGURE 15.4
The Package Name is important because
it defines the namespace for a project's
classes.

5. In Figure 15.5, I have entered a package name of **game.engine** and an activity name of **Engine**. Thus, the complete class name is `game.engine.Engine`. This is how it will be referenced in game projects that use the engine library. You may prefer to use your name or company name for the package, but the choice is ultimately yours.

FIGURE 15.5
Entering the package name and activity name for the new project.

Converting to a Library Project

The new Android project is generated by Eclipse as a standard runnable program. Here is the base source code found in the new `Engine.java` file:

```
package game.engine;

import android.app.Activity;
import android.os.Bundle;
```

```
public class Engine extends Activity {

    @Override
    public void onCreate(Bundle savedInstanceState) {
        super.onCreate(savedInstanceState);
        setContentView(R.layout.main);
    }
}
```

We will be making changes to this code. But first, the project has to be converted so that it will compile as a linkable rather than an executable library (embedded inside an .APK file—an Android Package).

DID YOU KNOW

An APK file is an Android Package, a renamed ZIP file containing the compiled binary and assets ready to run on an Android device. You can verify this by opening the APK file in the \bin folder of an Android project. The first two characters are PK—the initials of Phil Katz, inventor of the ZIP compression algorithm.

To convert a regular project into a library project, open the Project menu in Eclipse and choose Properties. From the list of filters on the left, choose Android. The Android project build targets and libraries will be shown. From this dialog screen, you can add additional libraries that the project depends on, if needed—for instance, a third-party library that you intend to use in a game. This is pretty common for larger, more complex games that need additional features.

BY THE WAY

A good example of a third-party library is Box2D, a physics library. Check out http://box2d.org/links/ for details on the Box2D library for Android (JBox2D).

In Figure 15.6, note the lower panel titled Library. A single check box, Is Library, will convert this project to a library project. That's all you need to do.

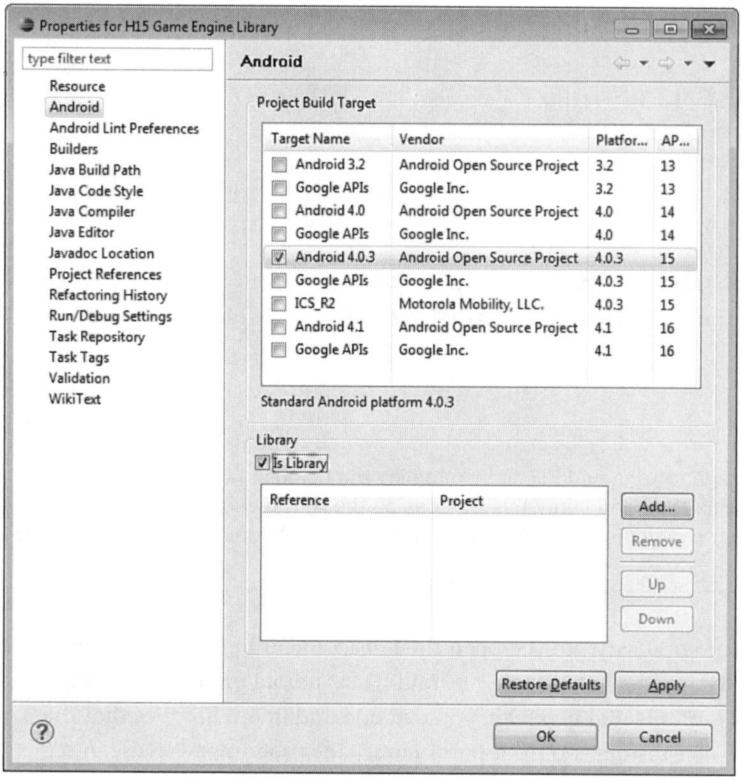

FIGURE 15.6
Changing the project type to a library project.

Writing the Core Engine Classes

A few core engine classes are necessary to get the engine up and running with basic functionality. Over the next several hours we will add additional classes to the engine until it is fully featured and capable of handling just about any genre of game you may want to develop.

WATCH OUT

The "engine" discussed in this section will grow and evolve from one hour to the next and will not be a single, large, complete engine until the final hour. Some code will be revised as well, so you will see the library evolve as needed. I encourage you to develop your own engine in parallel with the concepts described here over the next several hours and add your own flair to the project. Go above and beyond the essentials suggested in the book!

Engine Class

While building the core engine class, one thing we want to ensure is that it will be easy to port any Android demo or game to the engine with a minimum of fuss. This means that, at least until the engine matures, we need to expose the basic Android rendering objects to the game class, including such basic objects as the `SurfaceHolder` and `Canvas` used for drawing. Eventually, you will want to move common features *inside* the engine. But until those features are added and tested, it is helpful to keep the internals publicly visible to subclasses (consumers) of the engine.

Following is the source code for the core of the engine, the `Engine` class, found in the `Engine.java` source file. This is an early version of the core engine that will see improvement during upcoming hours as new features are added. The file should be included in the game engine library project (not the game demo).

Note that additional source code files will be added after this one before it will be a completely usable library for building a game project.

```
/**
 * Android Game Engine Core Class
 */
package game.engine;
import java.math.BigDecimal;
import android.app.Activity;
import android.os.Bundle;
import android.renderscript.Float2;
import android.renderscript.Float3;
import android.content.pm.ActivityInfo;
import android.graphics.*;
import android.util.Log;
import android.view.*;
import android.view.View.OnTouchListener;


/**
 * Engine Core Class
 */
public abstract class Engine extends Activity implements Runnable,
OnTouchListener {
    private SurfaceView p_view;
    private Canvas p_canvas;
    private Thread p_thread;
    private boolean p_running, p_paused;
    private int p_pauseCount;
    private Paint p_paintDraw, p_paintFont;
    private Typeface p_typeface;
    private Point[] p_touchPoints;
```

```java
private int p_numPoints;
private long p_preferredFrameRate, p_sleepTime;

/**
 * Engine constructor
 */
public Engine() {
    Log.d("Engine","Engine constructor");
    p_view = null;
    p_canvas = null;
    p_thread = null;
    p_running = false;
    p_paused = false;
    p_paintDraw = null;
    p_paintFont = null;
    p_numPoints = 0;
    p_typeface = null;
    p_preferredFrameRate = 40;
    p_sleepTime = 1000 / p_preferredFrameRate;
    p_pauseCount = 0;
}

/**
 * Abstract methods that must be implemented in the sub-class!
 */
public abstract void init();
public abstract void load();
public abstract void draw();
public abstract void update();

/**
 * Activity.onCreate event method
 */
@Override
public void onCreate(Bundle savedInstanceState) {
    super.onCreate(savedInstanceState);
    Log.d("Engine","Engine.onCreate start");

    //disable the title bar
    requestWindowFeature(Window.FEATURE_NO_TITLE);

    //set default screen orientation
    setScreenOrientation(ScreenModes.LANDSCAPE);

    /**
     * Call abstract init method in sub-class!
     */
    init();
```

```
    //create the view object
    p_view = new SurfaceView(this);
    setContentView(p_view);

    //turn on touch listening
    p_view.setOnTouchListener(this);

    //create the points array
    p_touchPoints = new Point[5];
    for (int n=0; n<5; n++) {
        p_touchPoints[n] = new Point(0,0);
    }

    //create Paint object for drawing styles
    p_paintDraw = new Paint();
    p_paintDraw.setColor(Color.WHITE);

    //create Paint object for font settings
    p_paintFont = new Paint();
    p_paintFont.setColor(Color.WHITE);
    p_paintFont.setTextSize(24);

    /**
     * Call abstract load method in sub-class!
     */
    load();

    //launch the thread
    p_running = true;
    p_thread = new Thread(this);
    p_thread.start();

    Log.d("Engine","Engine.onCreate end");
}

/**
 * Runnable.run thread method (MAIN LOOP)
 */
@Override
public void run() {
    Log.d("Engine","Engine.run start");

    Timer frameTimer = new Timer();
    int frameCount=0;
    int frameRate=0;
    long startTime=0;
    long timeDiff=0;
```

```
while (p_running) {

    if (p_paused) continue;

    /**
     * Calculate frame rate
     */
    frameCount++;
    startTime = frameTimer.getElapsed();
    if (frameTimer.stopwatch(1000)) {
        frameRate = frameCount;
        frameCount = 0;

        //reset touch input count
        p_numPoints = 0;
    }

    /**
     * Call abstract update method in sub-class!
     */
    update();

    /**
     * Rendering section, lock the canvas.
     * Only proceed if the SurfaceView is valid.
     */
    if (beginDrawing()) {

        p_canvas.drawColor(Color.BLUE);

        /**
         * Call abstract draw method in sub-class!
         */
        draw();

        int x = p_canvas.getWidth()-150;
        p_canvas.drawText("ENGINE", x, 20, p_paintFont);
        p_canvas.drawText(toString(frameRate) + " FPS", x, 40,
            p_paintFont);
        p_canvas.drawText("Pauses: " + toString(p_pauseCount),
            x, 60, p_paintFont);

        /**
         * Complete the rendering process by
         * unlocking the canvas.
         */
        endDrawing();
    }
```

```java
    /**
     * Calculate frame update time and sleep if necessary.
     */
    timeDiff = frameTimer.getElapsed() - startTime;
    long updatePeriod = p_sleepTime - timeDiff;
    if (updatePeriod > 0) {
        try {
            Thread.sleep( updatePeriod );
        }
        catch(InterruptedException e) {}
    }

}
Log.d("Engine","Engine.run end");
System.exit(RESULT_OK);
}

/**
 * BEGIN RENDERING
 * Verify that the surface is valid and then lock the canvas.
 */
private boolean beginDrawing() {
    if (!p_view.getHolder().getSurface().isValid()) {
        return false;
    }
    p_canvas = p_view.getHolder().lockCanvas();
    return true;
}

/**
 * END RENDERING
 * Unlock the canvas to free it for future use.
 */
private void endDrawing() {
    p_view.getHolder().unlockCanvasAndPost(p_canvas);
}

/**
 * Activity.onResume event method
 */
@Override
public void onResume() {
    Log.d("Engine","Engine.onResume");
    super.onResume();
    p_paused = false;
    /*p_running = true;
    p_thread = new Thread(this);
    p_thread.start();*/
}
```

```java
/**
 * Activity.onPause event method
 */
@Override
public void onPause() {
    Log.d("Engine","Engine.onPause");
    super.onPause();
    p_paused = true;
    p_pauseCount++;
    /*p_running = false;
    while (true) {
        try {
            p_thread.join();
        }
        catch (InterruptedException e) { }
    }*/
}

/**
 * OnTouchListener.onTouch event method
 */
@Override
public boolean onTouch(View v, MotionEvent event) {
    //count the touch inputs
    p_numPoints = event.getPointerCount();
    if (p_numPoints > 5) p_numPoints = 5;

    //store the input values
    for (int n=0; n<p_numPoints; n++) {
        p_touchPoints[n].x = (int)event.getX(n);
        p_touchPoints[n].y = (int)event.getY(n);
    }
    return true;
}

/**
 * Shortcut methods to duplicate existing Android methods.
 */
public void fatalError(String msg) {
    Log.e("FATAL ERROR", msg);
    System.exit(0);
}

/**
 * Drawing helpers
 */
public void drawText(String text, int x, int y) {
    p_canvas.drawText(text, x, y, p_paintFont);
}
```

```java
/**
 * Engine helper get/set methods for private properties.
 */
public SurfaceView getView() {
    return p_view;
}

public Canvas getCanvas() {
    return p_canvas;
}

public void setFrameRate(int rate) {
    p_preferredFrameRate = rate;
    p_sleepTime = 1000 / p_preferredFrameRate;
}

public int getTouchInputs() {
    return p_numPoints;
}

public Point getTouchPoint(int index) {
    if (index > p_numPoints)
        index = p_numPoints;
    return p_touchPoints[index];
}

public void setDrawColor(int color) {
    p_paintDraw.setColor(color);
}

public void setTextColor(int color) {
    p_paintFont.setColor(color);
}

public void setTextSize(int size) {
    p_paintFont.setTextSize((float)size);
}

public void setTextSize(float size) {
    p_paintFont.setTextSize(size);
}

/**
 * Font style helper
 */
public enum FontStyles {
    NORMAL (Typeface.NORMAL),
    BOLD (Typeface.BOLD),
```

```
        ITALIC (Typeface.ITALIC),
        BOLD_ITALIC (Typeface.BOLD_ITALIC);
        int value;
        FontStyles(int type) {
            this.value = type;
        }
    }

    public void setTextStyle(FontStyles style) {
        p_typeface = Typeface.create(Typeface.DEFAULT, style.value);
        p_paintFont.setTypeface(p_typeface);
    }

    /**
     * Screen mode helper
     */
    public enum ScreenModes {
        LANDSCAPE (ActivityInfo.SCREEN_ORIENTATION_LANDSCAPE),
        PORTRAIT (ActivityInfo.SCREEN_ORIENTATION_PORTRAIT);
        int value;
        ScreenModes(int mode) {
            this.value = mode;
        }
    }
    public void setScreenOrientation(ScreenModes mode) {
        setRequestedOrientation(mode.value);
    }

    /**
     * Round to a default 2 decimal places
     */
    public double round(double value) {
        return round(value,2);
    }

    /**
     * Round to any number of decimal places
     */
    public double round(double value, int precision) {
        try {
            BigDecimal bd = new BigDecimal(value);
            BigDecimal rounded = bd.setScale(precision, BigDecimal.
                    ROUND_HALF_UP);
            return rounded.doubleValue();
        }
        catch (Exception e) {
            Log.e("Engine","round: error rounding number");
        }
```

```
        return 0;
    }

    /**
     * String conversion helpers
     */
    public String toString(int value) {
        return Integer.toString(value);
    }

    public String toString(float value) {
        return Float.toString(value);
    }

    public String toString(double value) {
        return Double.toString(value);
    }

    public String toString(Float2 value) {
        String s = "X:" + round(value.x) + "," +
            "Y:" + round(value.y);
        return s;
    }

    public String toString(Float3 value) {
        String s = "X:" + round(value.x) + "," +
            "Y:" + round(value.y) + "," +
            "Z:" + round(value.z);
        return s;
    }
}
```

Timer Class

The Timer class is essential to the engine because it keeps track of the frame rate and helps determine when `Thread.sleep()` needs to be called (toward the end of the loop). This Timer class is a good, general-purpose timer that uses `System.currentTimeMillis()` and provides a `stopwatch()` method for quick and easy timing. If you need more than one timer, create another instance of the Timer class, given that it's lightweight. The class should be added to a file called `Timer.java` and included in the game engine library project (not the game demo).

```
/**
 * Timer Class for Android Game Engine
 */
package game.engine;
```

```java
public class Timer {
    private long p_start;
    private long p_stopwatchStart;

    public Timer() {
        p_start = System.currentTimeMillis();
        p_stopwatchStart = 0;
    }

    public long getElapsed() {
        return System.currentTimeMillis() - p_start;
    }

    public void rest(int ms) {
        long start = getElapsed();
        while (start + ms > getElapsed()) {
            try {
                Thread.sleep( 1 );
            } catch (InterruptedException e) {}
        }
    }

    public void resetStopwatch() {
        p_stopwatchStart = getElapsed();
    }

    public boolean stopwatch(long ms) {
        if (getElapsed() > p_stopwatchStart + ms) {
            resetStopwatch();
            return true;
        }
        else
            return false;
    }
}
```

TextPrinter Class

We used TextPrinter in a previous hour, and it was very useful. Every useful feature studied in prior hours will be used to get the engine up and running as quickly as possible, with excellent gameplay features from the start. Following is the source code for the class. The class should be added to a file called TextPrinter.java and included in the game engine library project (not the game demo).

```java
/**
 * TextPrinter Class for Android Game Engine
 * This class helps with printing lines of text with auto line
```

```
 * increment and reusable properties.
 */
package game.engine;

import android.graphics.Canvas;
import android.graphics.Color;
import android.graphics.Paint;

public class TextPrinter {
    private Canvas p_canvas;
    private Paint p_paint;
    private float p_x, p_y;
    private float p_spacing;

    public TextPrinter() {
        this(null);
    }

    public TextPrinter(Canvas canvas) {
        p_canvas = canvas;
        p_paint = new Paint();
        p_x = p_y = 0;
        p_spacing = 22;
        setTextSize(18);
        setColor(Color.WHITE);
    }

    public void setCanvas(Canvas canvas) {
        p_canvas = canvas;
    }

    public void setLineSpacing(float spacing) {
        p_spacing = spacing;
    }

    public void setTextSize(float size) {
        p_paint.setTextSize(size);
    }

    public void setColor(int color) {
        p_paint.setColor(color);
    }

    public void draw(String text, float x, float y) {
        p_x = x;
        p_y = y;
        draw(text);
    }
```

```java
    public void draw(String text) {
        p_canvas.drawText(text, p_x, p_y, p_paint);
        p_y += p_spacing;
    }
}
```

Texture Class

The `Texture` class encapsulates `android.graphics.Bitmap`, making it very easy to create a `Bitmap` object and load an image into memory from a file in the assets folder. This early version of the class is very basic and may see enhancements over time. It exposes a method, `getBitmap()`, to be used for drawing elsewhere in the program. The class should be added to a file called `Texture.java` and included in the game engine library project (not the game demo).

```java
/**
 * Texture Class for Android Game Engine
 */
package game.engine;

import java.io.IOException;
import java.io.InputStream;
import android.content.Context;
import android.graphics.Bitmap;
import android.graphics.BitmapFactory;

public class Texture {

    private Context p_context;
    private Bitmap p_bitmap;

    public Texture(Context context) {
        p_context = context;
        p_bitmap = null;
    }

    public Bitmap getBitmap() {
        return p_bitmap;
    }

    public boolean loadFromAsset(String filename) {
        InputStream istream=null;
        BitmapFactory.Options options = new BitmapFactory.Options();
        options.inPreferredConfig = Bitmap.Config.ARGB_8888;
        try {
            istream = p_context.getAssets().open(filename);
            p_bitmap = BitmapFactory.decodeStream(istream,null,options);
            istream.close();
```

```
        } catch (IOException e) {
            return false;
        }
        return true;
    }
}
```

Engine Test Demo Project

You will need another project to test the engine library. This part of engine development starts to become *very* interesting! After the grueling work trying to understand the hardware systems, all that hard work begins to pay off here! At this point, the lower-level Android code is *stuffed* or hidden away in the engine, and we begin to write code at a higher level. It's still the same Java language, but we're no longer using the Android SDK—it's all engine from this point on. When you come upon new SDK features you need, it's fine to use them in your game code directly, but even *better* to add them to the engine first.

WATCH OUT

If you try to "run" the engine library project, it will crash. You cannot run the engine project directly because it calls abstract methods that must be implemented in a subclass. Be sure to highlight your test project (or its source file), not the engine project. You may optionally choose the correct project from the Run icon drop-down list.

TRY IT YOURSELF ▼

Creating the Engine Demo Project

1. Go ahead and create a new Android project like usual. You do not need to do anything special here, just a normal runnable project. I recommend calling the project "Engine Demo."

2. Open the project properties and choose the Android filter on the left. The lower panel shows the libraries being used by your project (which will be empty). Click the Add button. A list of library projects in the Eclipse workspace will be found in the list. In Figure 15.7, one library project is listed: H15 Game Engine Library, which is the name of the example provided for this hour. Your own library might have a different name than the one shown here.

3. Choose the engine library project you created earlier and click the OK button. The project properties dialog, shown in Figure 15.8, will now cite the engine library as a reference. This means that the public classes in the library are now visible and available to your game project. You can either import the game.engine package and subclass `Engine`, or subclass `game.engine.Engine` without an import line.

FIGURE 15.7
Adding a reference to the engine library.

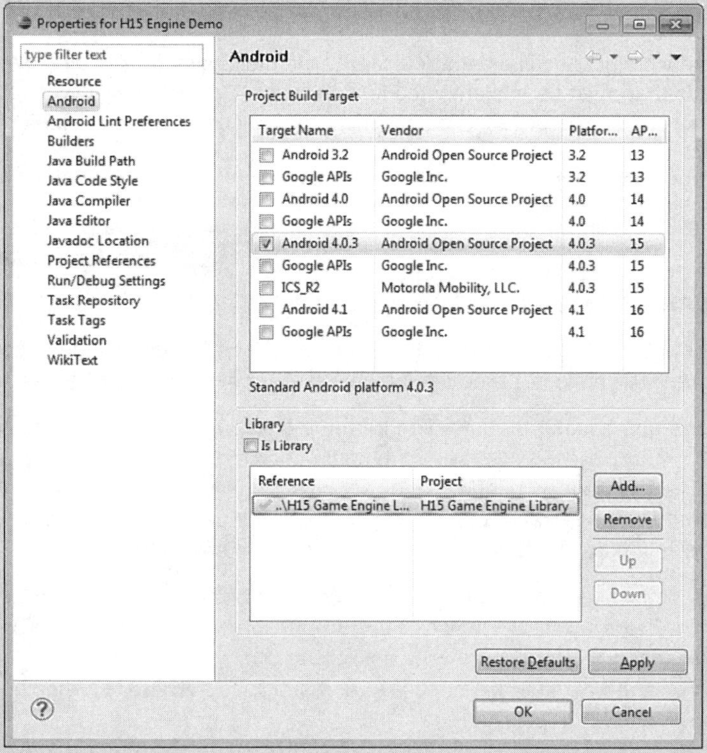

FIGURE 15.8
The engine library has been added to this project as a reference.

Engine Demo Source Code

Following is the source code for the engine demo test project shown in Figure 15.9. The test program demonstrates several important features for this early build of the engine, including multi-touch input, text output, bitmap loading and drawing, and a separation of engine and game code. The source code is a bit light on comments. This is intentional. I wanted you to see the basic code without any clutter to demonstrate how clean the code is with the engine functionality hidden away in the parent class. Note, for instance, the ease with which a bitmap file is loaded and how easy it is to print text and draw shapes.

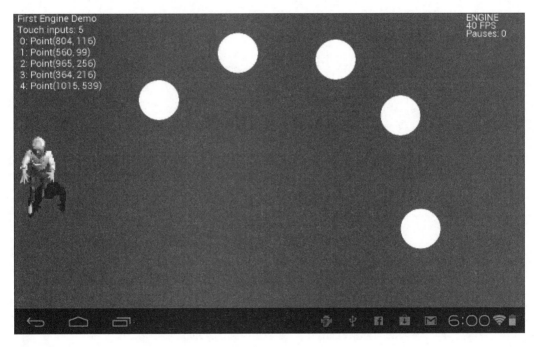

FIGURE 15.9
The first test program—the engine is off to a good start!

```
/**
 * This project consumes the game.engine.Engine class, and so it must
 * reference the library containing this class.
 *
 * Note: The use of 'super.' is only to illustrate which methods are
 * inherited from the Engine class and not needed.
 */

package android.program;
```

```java
//import java.text.DecimalFormat;
import android.graphics.Canvas;
import android.graphics.Color;
import android.graphics.Paint;
import android.graphics.Point;
import android.util.Log;
import game.engine.*;

public class Game extends game.engine.Engine {
    TextPrinter tp;
    Paint paint;
    Canvas canvas;
    Timer timer;
    Texture zombie;

    public Game() {
        Log.d("Game","Game constructor");
        paint = new Paint();
        canvas = null;
        zombie = null;
        tp = new game.engine.TextPrinter();
        tp.setColor(Color.WHITE);
        tp.setTextSize(24);
        tp.setLineSpacing(28);
        timer = new Timer();
    }

    /**
     * Abstract init method called by engine.
     */
    public void init() {
        Log.d("Game","Game.init");
        //(this is the default orientation)
        super.setScreenOrientation(Engine.ScreenModes.LANDSCAPE);
    }

    /**
     * Abstract load method called by engine.
     */
    public void load() {
        Log.d("Game","Game.load");
        zombie = new Texture(this);
        if (!zombie.loadFromAsset("zombie.png")) {
            super.fatalError("Error loading zombie");
        }
    }
```

```java
/**
 * Abstract draw method called by engine.
 */
public void draw() {
    Log.d("Game","Game.draw");
    paint.setColor(Color.WHITE);
    canvas = super.getCanvas();

    //draw zombie bitmap
    canvas.drawBitmap(zombie.getBitmap(), 10, 300, paint);

    tp.setCanvas(canvas);
    tp.draw("First Engine Demo", 10, 20);

    if (super.getTouchInputs() > 0) {
        tp.draw("Touch inputs: " + super.getTouchInputs());
        for (int n=0; n<super.getTouchInputs(); n++) {
            String s = " " + n + ": " + super.getTouchPoint(n).toString();
            tp.draw(s);
            Point p = super.getTouchPoint(n);
            if (p.x != 0 && p.y != 0)
                canvas.drawCircle(p.x, p.y, 50, paint);
        }
    }
    if (timer.stopwatch(500)) {
        super.drawText("**TIMER**", super.getCanvas().getWidth()/2, 20);
    }
}

/**
 * Abstract update method called by engine.
 */
public void update() {
    Log.d("Game","Game.update");
}
}
```

BY THE WAY

It is not necessary to use *super.* in front of public properties and methods inherited from a parent class, but I've used it in these early examples to self-document the engine code to assist with understanding how the engine works. You can also use *this.* in the same manner or not use any prefix pointer at all.

Logging the Engine Demo

You may have noticed a lot of Log statements in the engine and game code. That is pretty normal when developing a new engine because you need to keep an eye on how it is running from both a large-scale perspective (for the benefit of anyone who will use your engine) as well as from a close-up perspective (for your own debugging needs). Perusing the log output of the engine running reveals some very interesting truths about how an Android program works.

For instance, notice how well the engine handles the situation where the surface is being created (asynchronously) while the game loop continues to run. The first four instances of Game.update printed in the log are missing their corresponding Game.draw output lines. This tells me that the surface was not yet ready when the loop began running, but updating was still taking place. This happened for four cycles! Very interesting, indeed!

Note also the ordering of the logged events. First, the Engine constructor runs, followed immediately by the Game constructor. Then we see a block defined by Engine.onCreate start and Engine.onCreate end, and between these two lines, a call to Game.init and Game.load. If you study the source code for the test project, you'll see that init() and load() are indeed called by onCreate(), and so on. But after these processes are understood and seem to be working reasonably well—and without bugs—some of the log output can be removed. After the engine is working well, you will want to pay more attention to critical processes such as loading assets, and the game loop is no longer of real concern.

```
05-25 14:11:53.030: D/Engine(28105): Engine constructor
05-25 14:11:53.030: D/Game(28105): Game constructor
05-25 14:11:53.030: D/Engine(28105): Engine.onCreate start
05-25 14:14:01.740: D/Game(28167): Game.init
05-25 14:11:53.050: D/Game(28105): Game.load
05-25 14:11:53.050: D/Engine(28105): Engine.onCreate end
05-25 14:11:53.050: D/*(28105): Engine.onResume
05-25 14:11:53.050: D/Engine(28105): Engine.run start
05-25 14:11:53.050: D/Game(28105): Game.update
05-25 14:11:53.080: D/Game(28105): Game.update
05-25 14:11:53.100: D/Game(28105): Game.update
05-25 14:11:53.120: D/Game(28105): Game.update
05-25 14:11:53.140: D/Game(28105): Game.update
05-25 14:11:53.190: D/Game(28105): Game.draw
05-25 14:11:53.220: D/Game(28105): Game.update
05-25 14:11:53.240: D/Game(28105): Game.draw
05-25 14:11:53.260: D/Game(28105): Game.update
    .
    .
    .
```

```
05-25 14:11:59.020: D/Game(28105): Game.draw
05-25 14:11:59.040: D/Game(28105): Game.update
05-25 14:11:59.040: D/Game(28105): Game.draw
05-25 14:11:59.060: D/Game(28105): Game.update
05-25 14:11:59.070: D/Game(28105): Game.draw
05-25 14:11:59.090: D/Game(28105): Game.update
05-25 14:11:59.100: D/Game(28105): Game.draw
05-25 14:11:59.120: D/Game(28105): Game.update
05-25 14:11:59.120: D/Game(28105): Game.draw
05-25 14:11:59.130: D/*(28105): Engine.onPause
05-25 14:11:59.150: D/Engine(28105): Engine.run end
```

Summary

The Android game engine has been created! Admittedly, it's in a very simple and crude state at this point, but it has huge potential because the core is working perfectly, and important support classes and methods are already available. We will want to add quite a bit more to the engine in time, including audio (which was notably missing, but not a critical component at this early stage). The very next hour adds sprite functionality to the engine and a complete game example to put the engine to the test in a real-world situation.

Q&A

Q. The game engine project could potentially grow to include virtually unlimited new features without clogging game projects that derive from it. How does this approach to engine building differ from what you might have used or learned about in how other products work (for instance, Unity)?

A. Answers may vary, but a key difference is that some engines are supplied only in binary form without source code.

Q. What are some of the pros and cons of having a separate engine library project versus just putting all the source code files in a single project?

A. Answers will vary.

Workshop

Quiz

1. What method does the `Timer` class use to get the number of milliseconds from the system?

2. What is the name of the engine support class used to load bitmap assets?

3. What are the four abstract classes that must be implemented by any class that derives from `game.engine.Engine`?

Answers

1. `System.currentTimeMillis()`

2. `Texture`

3. `init()`, `load()`, `draw()`, and `update()`.

Activities

See what you can do with the engine already after this initial first version! Try modifying the program so that it draws the zombie image in place of the "finger markers" (white circles).

HOUR 16
Creating a Sprite/Actor Class

What You'll Learn in This Hour:

▶ The difference between a *prop* and an *actor*

▶ Encapsulating sprite functionality in a class

▶ Testing the `Sprite` class in the referenced engine project

A *sprite*, from a video game perspective, is an individual, distinct game object that can be moved or drawn separately from the background. I hesitate to use the word "object" because a sprite can be nothing more than scenery that the player can only see but not touch. For instance, a cloud might be treated as a sprite, without having any interaction with the player. In this hour, you learn how to encapsulate the basic functionality of a *sprite* that will make it possible to begin writing gameplay code on the Android platform.

Static Sprite as a "Prop"

Borrowing terms from theater, a *prop* is something on the stage that can be used by the player in some way. A prop can be a table, bed, shovel, baseball bat, sword, vase, or any other solid object. Note that some props are large and essentially unmovable (within reason), whereas some props are smaller and may be picked up. In general terms, any independent object in the game that the player can touch may be treated as a prop.

For instance, Figure 16.1 contains a small assortment of tree props that can be used in a game (courtesy of Reiner Prokein's free game art website: www.reinerstileset.de). Each tree prop can be added to the game as an individual prop. The logistics of moving and drawing the prop is handled by a `Sprite` class, which we'll go over in a bit.

In a game design that calls for an outdoor scene with trees, each tree would be positioned in the scene according to the design of the game level. However, if the tree is considered a part of the background—in other words, it never gets in the way of the player or other game objects—the tree would not be a sprite or a prop, it would just be an image. Figure 16.2 shows another example of a prop. Although this castle might be described as a building, it is still treated as a prop sprite in source code terms.

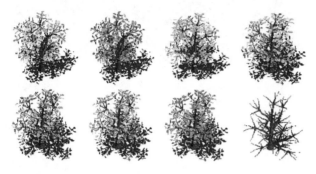

FIGURE 16.1
A small assortment of tree props (courtesy of Reiner Prokein).

FIGURE 16.2
A medieval castle prop (courtesy of Reiner Prokein).

Although a prop contains an image, it is not the *image*, precisely. The image is drawn to represent the prop, but the prop will have additional properties, too, such as position, size, and (possibly) animation frames. That's right. Both a prop and an actor can have either one fixed image, or they can be animated. So the animation factor is not what differentiates a prop from an actor.

Now, let's compare a *prop* with an *actor* by learning what an actor is.

Dynamic Sprite as an "Actor"

Following along with the theater motif, an *actor* is, strictly speaking, an incorrect term to use. An actor is a real person or animal (such as a dog) that *plays a character* in the play. So, although *actor* has become a popularized term in video game theory, it is completely off track when used in conjunction with props; the correct term should be *character*. When perusing the script for a play or film, one does not see actor names (such as Ian McDiarmid), but rather, character names (such as Emperor Palpatine).

We can use either the term *character* or *actor* to describe an interactive game object. In terms of the behavior of a sprite, you can derive the purpose of an object from its sprite type. Whereas a tree and a castle are clearly props, a dragon (shown in Figure 16.3), a knight (see Figure 16.4), and a spaceship (see Figure 16.5) are clearly characters or actors.

FIGURE 16.3
A dragon character sprite (courtesy of Reiner Prokein).

FIGURE 16.4
A knight character sprite (courtesy of Reiner Prokein).

The dragon sprite is clearly a character or actor in the scene of a game, unless it is to be used as a statue. This is a single frame from a very large animation sequence! You will learn how to load and draw animations in an upcoming hour. But, first things first; you will want to learn how to keep track of sprites to use them for gameplay. This is harder than it may sound at first. Just loading and drawing an image is fairly easy, but what about moving the image? What about detecting when it hits another image? These are important considerations for a game to work properly. Unless we use a class to manage prop sprites and actor sprites, the number of global variables will get out of hand very quickly. As it turns out, a `Sprite` class will manage these needs nicely.

FIGURE 16.5
A spaceship character sprite (courtesy of Ron Conley).

To change the theme a bit, let's shift focus from fantasy to science fiction with the spaceship sprite (Figure 16.5). Is it a prop or an actor? This is a difficult question because it seem to be *neither*! Characters go *inside* the ship! They are not affected by the ship in a scene, so it can't be a prop. And yet characters do not interact with the spaceship—at least not from the outside perspective.

As it turns out, the spaceship itself is a character or actor. We ignore human characters and treat the ship as the player, so to speak. Thus, the ship has properties and behaviors like a hero or dragon in a fantasy game.

Encapsulating Basic Sprite Functionality

A sprite can be used for a variety of game genres without any further requirements. Whatever we need for game characters or props, we add to the `Sprite` class directly. That can and does work for many programmers. But consider for a moment the possibility of creating a base `Sprite` class. It would handle the logistical stuff like moving and drawing, while a pair of subclasses handles the unique behaviors of props and actors. This is not a requirement for the Android game engine; it is more of a suggestion.

BY THE WAY

You should add the new `Sprite` class to the game engine project. If you are working on your own engine project in parallel with the instructions here in each hour, each new engine class will be added to the engine project specific to that hour. To avoid confusion, you can find a copy of the current revision of the engine under each hour in the book's resource files (the Eclipse workspace).

Blueprinting Versus Evolving

I find it helpful to *evolve* classes while working on a new game, rather than trying to design them completely in advance of using them. It is more natural to write code in this way. Realistically, this is much faster and more robust, although academicians may disagree and balk at the idea! Granted, a programmer who writes sloppy code may see the *evolving* technique as an excuse to write messy code. But, assuming you think clearly and use creativity to solve problems, you'll find it helpful to start off with a basic, simple, rudimentary `Sprite` class that handles only movement and drawing. Then, as new gameplay requirements are encountered, you modify the class as necessary.

This approach to writing code is most appropriate when you are working alone on a solo game project. When you're working with others who rely on your code, there are obvious problems with it. When others are relying on your code, you can't make huge changes to it without tripping them up and causing delays in their work. So, assuming you are working solo (or have time to develop it before sharing with others), it is perfectly okay to evolve a class (such as `Sprite`) as needs dictate.

Although inheritance is a valid technique in object-oriented programming, too much inheritance reflects a poorly built class structure. Anytime you see numerous classes used in place of one for a single "object" or "purpose," that is most likely a result of dutifully following a static class blueprinting methodology to writing code. That kind of code is a mess to try to use, unless you wrote it. Consider writing good classes from the start, so that inheritance is used only to consume a parent class into a subclass with new and specific goals, rather than to fill in missing functionality.

Introducing the New `Sprite` Class

The simplest game sprite must be able to move and draw (or expose its image so that it can be drawn).

```
/**
 * Sprite Class for Android Game Engine
 */

package game.engine;

import android.graphics.Canvas;
import android.graphics.Color;
import android.graphics.Paint;
import android.graphics.Point;

public class Sprite {
    private Engine p_engine;
    private Canvas p_canvas;
    private Texture p_texture;
```

```
    private Paint p_paint;
    public Point position;

    public Sprite(Engine engine) {
        p_engine = engine;
        p_canvas = null;
        p_texture = new Texture(engine);
        p_paint = new Paint();
        p_paint.setColor(Color.WHITE);
        position = new Point(0,0);
    }

    public void draw() {
        p_canvas = p_engine.getCanvas();
        p_canvas.drawBitmap(p_texture.getBitmap(), position.x,
            position.y, p_paint);
    }

    /**
     * Color manipulation methods
     */
    public void setColor(int color) {
        p_paint.setColor(color);
    }

    public void setPaint(Paint paint) {
        p_paint = paint;
    }

    /**
     * common get/set methods
     */
    public void setTexture(Texture texture) {
        p_texture = texture;
    }

    public Texture getTexture() {
        return p_texture;
    }

    public void setPosition(Point position) {
        this.position = position;
    }

    public Point getPosition() {
        return position;
    }
}
```

Revisiting `Texture`

You may have noticed a reference to `Texture` in the `Sprite` class. `Texture` was introduced in the previous hour. By separating the image in this manner, we can enhance the `Texture` class in order to do animation, which is covered in a future hour. Here is the code for this class again for reference.

```
package game.engine;
import java.io.IOException;
import java.io.InputStream;
import android.content.Context;
import android.graphics.Bitmap;
import android.graphics.BitmapFactory;

public class Texture {
    private Context p_context;
    private Bitmap p_bitmap;

    public Texture(Context context) {
        p_context = context;
        p_bitmap = null;
    }

    public Bitmap getBitmap() {
        return p_bitmap;
    }

    public boolean loadFromAsset(String filename) {
        InputStream istream=null;
        BitmapFactory.Options options = new BitmapFactory.Options();
        options.inPreferredConfig = Bitmap.Config.ARGB_8888;
        try {
            istream = p_context.getAssets().open(filename);
            p_bitmap = BitmapFactory.decodeStream(istream,null,options);
            istream.close();
        } catch (IOException e) {
            return false;
        }
        return true;
    }
}
```

Testing the `Sprite` Class

Creating a sprite object is now fairly easy. The only caveat to using our new `Sprite` class is a requirement imposed by the engine for drawing. As you may recall from Hour 15, "Building an

Android Game Engine," we have two methods that make it possible to draw: `Engine.begin-Drawing()` and `Engine.endDrawing()`. Let's review briefly what happens in these two crucial methods.

In `beginDrawing()`, a `SurfaceView` object, which contains a `SurfaceHolder` object (used for drawing to the Android screen), contains a `Canvas`. In order to draw, we call `lockCanvas()`. At this point, there is an open canvas ready for drawing.

```
p_canvas = p_view.getHolder().lockCanvas();
```

When we are done drawing, the canvas has to be unlocked again for normal use by the Android OS. Thus, in `endDrawing()`, we retrieve the same `SurfaceHolder` object and call `unlockCanvasAndPost()` to complete the drawing cycle.

```
p_view.getHolder().unlockCanvasAndPost(p_canvas);
```

The engine (`game.engine.Engine`) makes a call to the abstract method `draw()` in between the locking and unlocking steps. Now take a look again at the preceding line; `lockCanvas()` returns a `Canvas` object. We set `Engine.p_canvas` (a private property) to that return value. Thus, `p_canvas` is ready to draw.

Before calling `lockCanvas()`, the `p_canvas` variable points to nothing. We don't explicitly set it to `null` (although that might be a good idea after drawing is done), but after the surface is unlocked, the canvas goes out of scope and is no longer relevant.

Realistically, it's *possible* that the canvas will point to the same location in memory in the next cycle through the game loop. But we can't assume that. I've tested it, in fact, and some drawing calls generate a null exception—proving that we can't just initialize the `Canvas` variable once and assume it will remain valid. It has to be renewed *every frame*!

Because of this requirement, the `Sprite` class can draw only when `p_canvas` is valid. That means only from within the abstract `draw()` method. When you create a new `Sprite` object, you must pass the `Engine` object to the new `Sprite` object to give it access to the `Canvas` for drawing. Passing `this` when instantiating a new `Sprite` will suffice to pass the engine object along. After that, `Sprite` is able to draw itself by accessing `Engine.getCanvas()`.

Sprite Demo Source Code

Now for the source code to the sample test program. This project must reference the game engine project to build properly. To add a reference to the engine, first create the new Android Application project. If you need help creating a new project, refer to the previous hour for a tutorial walkthrough of the process. We have gone over creating a new project several times now, so you should be familiar with the process.

I named the sample project that goes with this hour "H16 Sprite Demo."

After creating the new project, open the Project Properties (see Figure 16.6). On the left is a list of property screens. Select Project References. This brings up all the other projects in the whole Eclipse workspace. All the projects up to this point in the book are listed because they were all added to the same workspace.

Highlight the version of the engine you need to reference. In this case, we want to reference H16 Game Engine Library. This is the current version of the engine with the addition of the `Sprite` class, but no more. So, the engine provided for this hour parallels the work we're doing in the book.

When you consider how much work we have had to do to get to this point, it is gratifying to note just how short this program is! This is a lot of functionality, composed of numerous hours of work, now abstracted away into the logistical engine—under the hood and out of view, so to speak. We're finally beginning to write gameplay code that looks similar to the code in many other game engines or libraries. The reason this is important at this higher level of programming with the Android SDK is that we are writing code that is similar to the gameplay code on other platforms.

The following code is much more portable than our earlier Android SDK code, which was proprietary and rather difficult to manage. And consider how many of these lines of code are mere *comments*! Take out the comments and logging and the program becomes surprisingly sparse. In fact, we'll be skipping these comments and log output lines starting in the next hour, now that you're familiar with how the engine works.

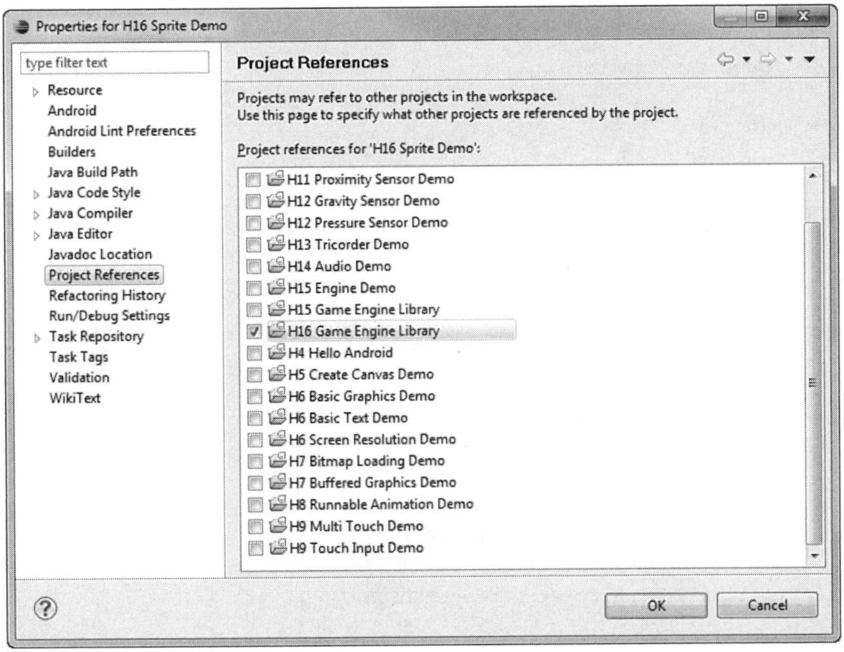

FIGURE 16.6
Adding a reference to the engine project.

BY THE WAY

A bitmap file called `ship1.png` is required for this project to run. Be sure to copy the file into the assets folder. If you need a refresher on those steps, refer to Hour 7, "Loading and Drawing Images."

```
/**
 * H16 Sprite Demo
 * This project consumes the game.engine.Engine class, and so it must
 * reference the library containing this class.
 */

package android.program;

import android.graphics.*;
import android.util.Log;
import game.engine.*;

public class Game extends game.engine.Engine {
    Canvas canvas;
    Paint paint;
    Sprite ship;
    Texture ship_image;
    Point touch;

    public Game() {
        Log.d("Game","Game constructor");
        canvas = null;
        paint = new Paint();
        ship = null;
        ship_image = null;
        touch = new Point(60,60);
    }

    /**
     * Abstract init method called by engine.
     */
    public void init() {
        Log.d("Game","Game.init");

        /**
         * This call is not necessary; engine defaults to landscape.
         * Change this call to use portrait if desired!
         */
        setScreenOrientation(Engine.ScreenModes.LANDSCAPE);
    }

    /**
```

```
    * Abstract load method called by engine.
    */
public void load() {
    Log.d("Game","Game.load");

    //create and load a new sprite
    ship = new Sprite(this);
    ship_image = new Texture(this);
    if (!ship_image.loadFromAsset("ship1.png")) {
        fatalError("Error loading ship");
    }
    ship.setTexture(ship_image);
    ship.position = new Point(60,60);
}

/**
 * Abstract draw method called by engine.
 */
public void draw() {
    canvas = getCanvas();

    drawText("Sprite Demo", 10, 20);
    drawText("Touch: " + toString(touch.x) + "," + toString(touch.y),
    10, 50);

    //draw the ship sprite at touch position
    ship.position = touch;
    ship.draw();
}

/**
 * Abstract update method called by engine.
 */
public void update() {
    //get touch input
    if (getTouchInputs() > 0) {
        touch = getTouchPoint(0);
    }
}
}
```

Testing the `Sprite` Class

Let's run it! The Sprite Demo program is shown in Figure 16.7. Note the engine messages at the upper-right corner and our local project output at the upper-left corner. The spaceship sprite follows your finger (or mouse, if using the emulator), and the touch position is displayed as well.

This is a good test of the most basic functionality of a sprite—movement and drawing. It's a success! But, we have a lot more to do yet.

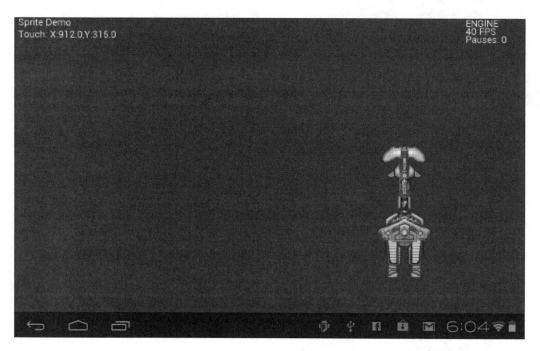

FIGURE 16.7
The Sprite Demo program draws a sprite wherever you touch the screen.

Summary

The game engine now has a rudimentary `Sprite` class! This will be the basis for new techniques we'll learn in upcoming hours—and quite a few awesome new features for the engine.

Q&A

Q. **What is the difference between props and characters (in the context of sprite programming), and how does that differentiation improve game code?**

A. Answers will vary. Refer to the top of the hour for the discussion. Review or discuss your understanding of the concepts.

Q. When your goal is to write robust game code, what technique is better than trying to *blueprint* your classes in advance and rigidly following the class definition?

A. The suggestion in this hour was to *evolve* a class as new features are needed, rather than considering classes static and using inheritance too often.

Workshop

Quiz

1. What helper class does `Sprite` rely on for its source image?

2. Which Android class makes it possible to lock and unlock the screen for drawing?

3. What term describes wrapping a class around a concept, such as a game sprite, and including properties and methods that make it functional?

Answers

1. `Texture`

2. `SurfaceHolder`

3. Encapsulation

Activities

Combine your knowledge of multitouch input with the `Sprite` code in this hour by modifying the example so that the spaceship sprite is drawn up to five times at once as a result of multiple touch points.

Frame Animation Using a Sprite Sheet/Atlas

What You'll Learn in This Hour:

▶ Animating with a single strip

▶ Drawing frames from a strip image

▶ Animating with a sheet (atlas)

▶ Testing sprite animation

Animating with a Single Strip

There are many ways to do frame animation in a video game. Perhaps the simplest method is to load each frame from a series of bitmap files with one frame per file. Using this technique, an array or list stores the frames. Another technique might involve a custom database (random access file) containing frames stored as binary data. For instance, it is possible to store all the bitmap files for an animation in a ZIP archive and then read them using a ZIP library. (The Java Archive utility, called JAR, uses the ZIP format).

These are both valid means to store animation frames. However, experience shows that those two approaches become difficult to manage when a lot of animations are needed in a game. It becomes a logical problem to manage all the files.

DID YOU KNOW

Tired of creating new projects in Eclipse? Try making a copy of your last project instead! Right-click a project name in your workspace (Package Explorer), and select Copy. Then open the Edit menu and choose Paste. A Copy Project dialog appears, allowing you to name the new project. Presto, a complete duplicate of the old project with a new name is ready for your new code!

Arranging Animation Frames

A better approach is to use a technique called *tiling* to store animation frames on a single image. The resulting image is called a *sprite sheet*. Another popular name for it is *texture atlas*, but they both refer to the same thing: an image with two or more frames of animation stored on it. Figure 17.1 shows an example of a simple sprite sheet or texture atlas. (Note: We will use the single term *sprite sheet* from now on).

FIGURE 17.1
A one-row sprite strip with six frames. (Image courtesy of Ari Feldman.)

You'll see some distinct advantages to using a strip such as this to contain frames. One advantage is that only one bitmap file has to be opened (as an asset). Another advantage is that the image itself contains the frames in memory, so no other construct is needed (such as an array or list); the frames can be drawn directly from the strip to the screen.

WATCH OUT
___

This hour does not feature any new improvements to the game engine, but for the sake of consistency, a new project called H17 Game Engine Library can be used with the Animation Demo project this hour.
___

Drawing Frames from a Strip Image

All we need to know to animate a strip is the number of frames and the size of each frame (in pixels). Based on the width, you can calculate the X,Y position of any frame by multiplying the width by the frame number.

```
X = frame * width;
```

The Y position is always 0 because there is only one row in a strip. Figure 17.2 shows the dragon animation strip labeled with frame numbers for reference.

To draw a frame out of the strip, you can use an overload of `Canvas.drawBitmap()` that accepts two `Rect` parameters—one for the source rect (the frame), and one for the destination rect (the output). You can change the destination to scale the sprite smaller or larger this way! See Figure 17.3.

FRAME NUMBERS

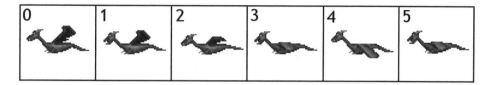

FIGURE 17.2
The frame numbering begins with 0.

FIGURE 17.3
The width and height of each frame is important.

The `drawStripFrame()` method helps with animating a sprite strip. This is a standalone method that you can add to the game engine or to the `Sprite` class if you want.

```
public void drawStripFrame(Sprite sprite, int width, int height, int frame) {
    //define the source rect representing one frame
    Rect src = new Rect(frame*width,0,frame*width+width,height);

    //define the destination location
    int x = sprite.position.x;
    int y = sprite.position.y;
    Rect dst = new Rect(x,y,x+width,y+height);

    //draw the frame
    Paint paint = new Paint();
    canvas.drawBitmap(sprite.getTexture().getBitmap(), src, dst, paint);
}
```

BY THE WAY

To add a bitmap file to an Android project, copy the file (Ctrl+C) as if you are going to copy and paste the file to a new location, such as another folder. Next, in the Package Explorer in Eclipse, locate the \assets folder under your current project and select it. Then paste the file (Ctrl+V) into this location.

Animating with a Sprite Sheet (Texture Atlas)

Figure 17.4 shows a typical sheet with the columns and rows labeled for easy reference.

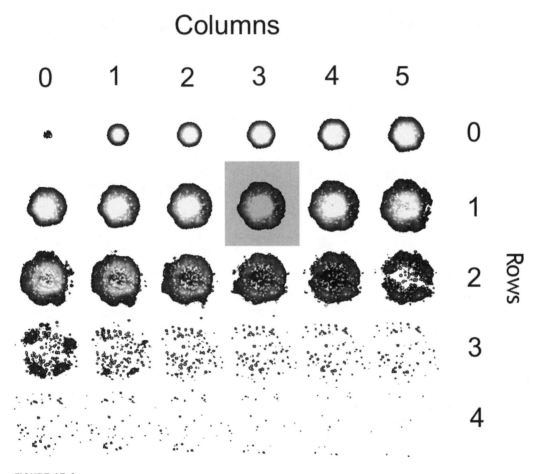

FIGURE 17.4
An animation sheet with 6 columns and 5 rows, for 30 total frames.

The more important of the row and column for animation purposes is the row calculation, so we'll do that one first. To make this calculation, you need to know how many frames there are across from left to right. These are the columns. Here is the formula for calculating the *row* or *Y* position of a frame number on the sprite sheet:

```
Y = ( frame / columns ) * height;
```

To calculate the *column* or *X* position of a frame number on the sprite sheet, a similar-looking calculation is done, but the result is quite different:

```
X = ( frame % columns ) * width;
```

Note that the math operator is not division. The percent symbol (%) is the *modulus operator* in Java. Modulus is similar to division, but instead of returning the quotient (or answer), it returns the remainder!

Why do we care about the remainder? That represents the X position of the frame because X is the extra or leftover amount after the division. Recall that the formula for calculating Y gave us a distinct integer quotient. We want to use the same variables, but modulus gives us the partial column in the row, which represents the X value.

Here is a helper method called `drawSheetFrame()` that has no dependencies, so you can drop it into any game and use it (assuming you're using `game.engine.Engine` due to the `Sprite` and `Texture` classes).

```
public void drawSheetFrame(Sprite sprite, int width, int height,
int columns, int frame) {
    //define the source rect representing one frame
    int u = (frame % columns) * width;
    int v = (frame / columns) * height;
    Rect src = new Rect(u,v,u+width,v+height);

    //define the destination location
    int x = sprite.position.x;
    int y = sprite.position.y;
    Rect dst = new Rect(x,y,x+width,y+height);

    //draw the frame
    Paint paint = new Paint();
    canvas.drawBitmap(sprite.getTexture().getBitmap(), src, dst, paint);
}
```

The Animation Demo

To properly test both animation methods presented in this hour, use the source code that follows for a complete example called Animation Demo. This program animates three sprites on the screen, each with a different size and number of frames for illustration. Figure 17.5 shows the sprite sheet for an asteroid with 64 frames (each 60×60). Figure 17.6 shows the sprite sheet for a walking zombie with 64 frames (each 96×96).

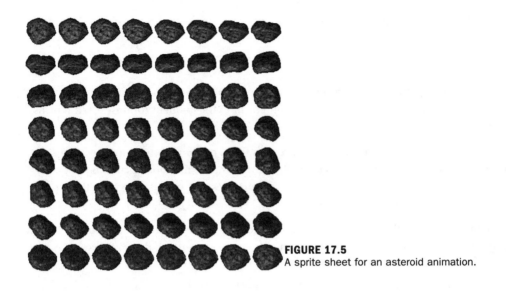

FIGURE 17.5
A sprite sheet for an asteroid animation.

FIGURE 17.6
A sprite sheet for a
zombie animation.

This hour has taken a minimalist approach to animation to show you the techniques without relying heavily on any engine or wrapper class code. This is helpful when learning a new technique, keeping the example simple so you can process it, so to speak.

The Animation Demo program is shown running in Figure 17.7. The frame number is shown below each animating sprite. This program does not *move* the sprites, but you could easily move them by setting the `Sprite.position` property for any of them.

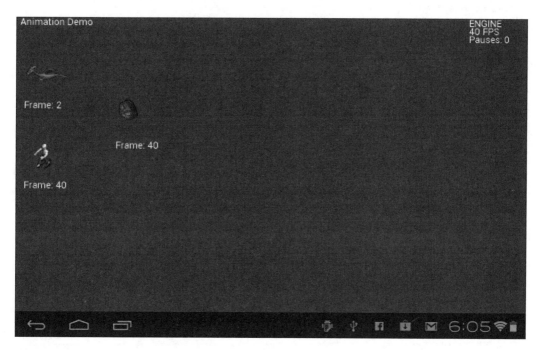

FIGURE 17.7
The Animation Demo program.

The source code for the Animation Demo is shown next. Many of the comments and all the log output code has been removed for the first time. By now you should be familiar with how the engine works, so these helper items should no longer be needed. If you skipped ahead, note that the engine calls several methods in this program, so you may want to refer back to the previous two hours for additional information on how it works.

```
package android.program;
import android.graphics.*;
import game.engine.*;
```

```java
public class Game extends game.engine.Engine {
    Canvas canvas;
    Timer timer;
    Sprite dragon;
    Texture dragon_image;
    int dragon_frame;
    Sprite zombie;
    Texture zombie_image;
    int zombie_frame;
    Sprite asteroid;
    Texture asteroid_image;
    int asteroid_frame;

    public Game() {
        canvas = null;
        timer = new Timer();
        dragon = null;
        dragon_image = null;
        dragon_frame = 0;
        zombie = null;
        zombie_image = null;
        zombie_frame = 0;
        asteroid = null;
        asteroid_image = null;
        asteroid_frame = 0;
    }

    public void init() {
        setScreenOrientation(Engine.ScreenModes.LANDSCAPE);
    }

    public void load() {
        //create and load dragon animation
        dragon = new Sprite(this);
        dragon_image = new Texture(this);
        if (!dragon_image.loadFromAsset("dragon_strip.png")) {
            fatalError("Error loading dragon_strip");
        }
        dragon.setTexture(dragon_image);
        dragon.position = new Point(20,100);

        //create and load zombie animation
        zombie = new Sprite(this);
        zombie_image = new Texture(this);
        if (!zombie_image.loadFromAsset("zombie_walk.png")) {
            fatalError("Error loading zombie_walk");
```

```
    }
    zombie.setTexture(zombie_image);
    zombie.position = new Point(20,300);

    //create and load asteroid animation
    asteroid = new Sprite(this);
    asteroid_image = new Texture(this);
    if (!asteroid_image.loadFromAsset("asteroid_sheet.png")) {
        fatalError("Error loading asteroid_sheet");
    }
    asteroid.setTexture(asteroid_image);
    asteroid.position = new Point(250,200);
}

public void draw() {
    canvas = getCanvas();
    drawText("Animation Demo", 10, 20);

    //draw the dragon
    drawStripFrame(dragon, 128, 128, dragon_frame);
    drawText("Frame: " + toString(dragon_frame), dragon.position.x,
        dragon.position.y + 128);

    //draw the zombie
    drawSheetFrame(zombie, 96, 96, 8, zombie_frame);
    drawText("Frame: " + toString(zombie_frame), zombie.position.x,
        zombie.position.y + 128);

    //draw the asteroid
    drawSheetFrame(asteroid, 60, 60, 8, asteroid_frame);
    drawText("Frame: " + toString(asteroid_frame), asteroid.position.x,
        asteroid.position.y + 128);
}

public void drawStripFrame(Sprite sprite, int width, int height,
int frame) {
    //define the source rect representing one frame
    Rect src = new Rect(frame*width,0,frame*width+width,height);

    //define the destination location
    int x = sprite.position.x;
    int y = sprite.position.y;
    Rect dst = new Rect(x,y,x+width,y+height);

    //draw the frame
    Paint paint = new Paint();
    canvas.drawBitmap(sprite.getTexture().getBitmap(), src, dst, paint);
}
```

```java
public void drawSheetFrame(Sprite sprite, int width, int height,
int columns, int frame) {
    //define the source rect representing one frame
    int u = (frame % columns) * width;
    int v = (frame / columns) * height;
    Rect src = new Rect(u,v,u+width,v+height);

    //define the destination location
    int x = sprite.position.x;
    int y = sprite.position.y;
    Rect dst = new Rect(x,y,x+width,y+height);

    //draw the frame
    Paint paint = new Paint();
    canvas.drawBitmap(sprite.getTexture().getBitmap(), src, dst, paint);
}

public void update() {
    //set animation to 20 fps
    if (timer.stopwatch(50)) {

        //update dragon animation
        dragon_frame++;
        if (dragon_frame > 5)
            dragon_frame = 0;

        //update zombie animation
        zombie_frame++;
        if (zombie_frame > 63)
            zombie_frame = 0;

        //update asteroid animation
        asteroid_frame++;
        if (asteroid_frame > 63)
            asteroid_frame = 0;
    }
}
}
```

Summary

This has been a rather quick jaunt through the basic concepts and techniques used to do sprite animation *the manual way*. No additional Android SDK features were needed to get animation to work, which gives us control over how animation is handled by our own games. In the following hour, however, you will learn some advanced animation techniques and will add them to the engine for future use.

Q&A

Q. Why do you suppose the Android SDK doesn't already handle strip and atlas frame animation, given it's so useful?

A. Most SDKs are designed to give the programmer access to a hardware system, such as an Android device. Features such as frame animation involve gameplay code that is best left up to each programmer.

Q. What are some other techniques you can see as useful alternatives to doing animation without a strip or atlas image?

A. Answers will vary; open discussion.

Workshop

Quiz

1. What method draws one frame of animation onto the screen, assuming the parameters are set up correctly?

2. What helper class stores the image data used by `Sprite` to draw a sequence of animation?

3. What is the name of the helper method in this hour's example that draws a frame from a sprite sheet/atlas to the screen?

Answers

1. `Canvas.drawBitmap()`

2. `Texture`

3. `drawSheetFrame()`

Activities

The strip and sheet images used in the example were already created in advance by the author. Try your hand at creating a strip or sheet yourself from either your own animation frames or from an animation found online (Reiner's Tileset is a good source: www.reinerstileset.de). A useful tool for automatically converting individual bitmaps into a strip or sheet is available; it is called Pro Motion, and a trial version is available from Cosmigo (www.cosmigo.com). It takes a while to figure out how to use it, but when you do, it will greatly speed up your work with animation images.

Advanced Multi-Animation Techniques

What You'll Learn in This Hour:

▶ Creating an animation system
▶ Writing the animation base class
▶ Making major changes to the `Sprite` class

Animation is not limited solely to cartoon-style frame flipping, as described in the previous hour. It is possible to do quite a few different forms of animation, and at a higher level, "animation" might even blend in with the behavior of a game character, helping to bring personality, or at the very least, bring some very interesting gameplay options to the table. The term *multi-animation* refers to a system in which more than one type of animation can be applied to a game object or entity (sprite prop or actor) at the *same time*—for instance, doing frame animation while also doing rotation and fading the color to transparent. The techniques you learn in this hour are very useful for gameplay and not limited merely to the suggestions this hour. You will be able to create your own unique forms of animation to affect the characters in your game in creative ways.

Creating an Animation System

The most interesting thing about the animation system being developed this hour is how it simplifies the amount of work done by the `Sprite` class. Frame animation is offloaded to the animation system, with the addition of new capabilities such as color cycling. You will be able to do special effects like fade out, scaling larger or smaller, and moving automatically.

Writing the Animation Base Class

We'll start with the `Animation` base class, which defines the types of changes we can do to a sprite every frame. This frugal class supplies the animation system with five modification methods:

- ▶ adjustFrame()

- ▶ adjustAlpha()

- ▶ adjustScale()

- ▶ adjustRotation()

- ▶ adjustPosition()

Using these five "tweaking" methods, you can create some very creative, custom effects with classes that derive from `Animation`.

```
/**
 * Animation Class
 */
package game.engine;
import android.renderscript.Float2;
import android.graphics.Point;

public class Animation {
    public boolean animating;

    public Animation() {
        animating = false;
    }

    public int adjustFrame(int original) {
        return original;
    }

    public int adjustAlpha(int original) {
        return original;
    }

    public Float2 adjustScale(Float2 original) {
        return original;
    }

    public float adjustRotation(float original) {
        return original;
    }

    public Point adjustPosition(Point original) {
        return original;
    }
}
```

Sprite Class Enhancements

To support the new animation system, the `Sprite` class (introduced in the previous hour) will have to be significantly upgraded. This will not involve a lot of new code, just a few new properties and methods. The most important new method is `Sprite.animate()`. This method iterates the list of stored animation objects and performs an update on each one. This means you can have more than one animation per sprite—for instance, color cycling with frame animation at the same time! After you see how the animation system works, you will be able to devise your own creative animations.

BY THE WAY

To create a sprite object without any animation, use the simpler `Sprite(this)` constructor, which will cause the width and height to be automatically read from the loaded bitmap's dimensions.

```java
/**
 * Sprite Class (modified)
 * Requires game.engine.Engine to build.
 */
package game.engine;
import java.util.LinkedList;
import java.util.ListIterator;
import android.graphics.*;
import android.renderscript.Float2;

public class Sprite {
    private Engine p_engine;
    private Canvas p_canvas;
    private Texture p_texture;
    private Paint p_paint;
    public Point position;
    private int p_width, p_height;
    private int p_columns;
    private int p_alpha;
    private LinkedList<Animation> p_anims;
    private int p_frame;
    private Float2 p_scale;
    private float p_rotation;

    public Sprite(Engine engine) {
        this(engine, 0, 0, 1);
    }

    public Sprite(Engine engine, int width, int height, int columns) {
        p_engine = engine;
        p_width = width;
```

```
        p_height = height;
        p_columns = columns;
        p_canvas = null;
        p_texture = new Texture(engine);
        p_alpha = 255;
        p_paint = new Paint();
        p_anims = new LinkedList<Animation>();
        position = new Point(0,0);
        p_frame = 0;
        p_scale = new Float2(1.0f,1.0f);
        p_rotation = 0.0f;
    }

    public void draw() {
        p_canvas = p_engine.getCanvas();

        //fill in size if this sprite is not animated
        if (p_width == 0 || p_height == 0) {
            p_width = p_texture.getBitmap().getWidth();
            p_height = p_texture.getBitmap().getHeight();
        }

        //define the source rect representing one frame
        int u = (p_frame % p_columns) * p_width;
        int v = (p_frame / p_columns) * p_height;
        Rect src = new Rect(u, v, u+p_width, v+p_height);

        //define the destination location
        int x = position.x;
        int y = position.y;
        int w = (int)(p_width * p_scale.x);
        int h = (int)(p_height * p_scale.y);
        Rect dst = new Rect(x, y, x+w, y+h);

        //draw the frame
        p_paint.setAlpha(p_alpha);
        p_canvas.drawBitmap(p_texture.getBitmap(), src, dst, p_paint);
    }

    //add an animation technique to this sprite
    public void addAnimation(Animation anim) {
        p_anims.add(anim);
    }

    //run through all of the animations
    public void animate() {
        if (p_anims.size() == 0) return;
```

```java
        ListIterator<Animation> iterator = p_anims.listIterator();
        while (iterator.hasNext()) {
            Animation anim = iterator.next();
            if (anim.animating) {
                p_frame = anim.adjustFrame(p_frame);
                p_alpha = anim.adjustAlpha(p_alpha);
                p_rotation = anim.adjustRotation(p_rotation);
                p_scale = anim.adjustScale(p_scale);
                position = anim.adjustPosition(position);
            }
            else
            {
                p_anims.remove(anim);
                return;
            }
        }
    }

    /**
     * Color manipulation methods
     */
    public void setAlpha(int alpha) {
        p_alpha = alpha;
    }

    public int getAlpha() {
        return p_alpha;
    }

    public void setPaint(Paint paint) {
        p_paint = paint;
    }

    /**
     * common get/set methods
     */
    public void setTexture(Texture texture) {
        p_texture = texture;
    }

    public Texture getTexture() {
        return p_texture;
    }

    public void setPosition(Point position) {
        this.position = position;
    }
```

```java
    public Point getPosition() {
        return position;
    }

    public int getWidth() {
        return p_width;
    }

    public void setWidth(int width) {
        p_width = width;
    }

    public int getHeight() {
        return p_height;
    }

    public void setHeight(int height) {
        p_height = height;
    }

    public Point getSize() {
        return new Point(p_width,p_height);
    }

    public int getFrame() {
        return p_frame;
    }

    public void setFrame(int frame) {
        p_frame = frame;
    }

    public Float2 getScale() {
        return p_scale;
    }

    public void setScale(Float2 scale) {
        p_scale = scale;
    }

    public void setScale(float scale) {
        p_scale = new Float2(scale,scale);
    }
}
```

Alpha Animation

Some animation techniques are intended to run once and then terminate. This might seem like a mistake at first glance, but there is actually a very good reason for it. While a game is playing, if you want to do a special effect (like an alpha fade), that effect should run only once, not repeatedly. By default, some animations run once, and others run repeatedly, depending on the most common usage. For instance, frame animation continually loops. Some, like the throb animation (which cycles the scale value of a sprite) will wrap once and then terminate. That one is especially interesting in a space "shoot-em-up" type game! Following is the `AlphaAnimation` class.

Because this is the first derived animation class, a brief explanation will be helpful. The `Sprite` class has a method called `addAnimation()`, which adds new objects to the internal `LinkedList<Animation>` list. The list makes it possible to have more than one animation applied to a single sprite at a time.

Each derived animation may have its own constructor with any needed parameters to initialize the animation effect. `AlphaAnimation`, for instance, makes use of three:

- `int minAlpha`
- `int maxAlpha`
- `int change`

The first two define the range for the alpha channel value, from 0 to 255. The third parameter, `change`, describes the speed—forward or backward—that the alpha value should change. This will normally be 1 or −1, but could be any larger (or smaller) value to cause the alpha value to change more quickly.

This example illustrates how to add this animation technique to a sprite:

```
sprite.addAnimation(new AlphaAnimation(0, 255, 1));
```

It adds a new instance of the alpha animation technique to a sprite, with a range of 0 to 255 and an increment of 1. This is a very straightforward, simple use of the technique, which will cause the sprite's image to slowly fade into view.

```
/**
 * AlphaAnimation Class
 */
package game.engine;

public class AlphaAnimation extends Animation {
    private int p_minAlpha;
    private int p_maxAlpha;
    private int p_change;
```

```java
    public AlphaAnimation(int minAlpha, int maxAlpha, int change) {
        this.p_minAlpha = minAlpha;
        this.p_maxAlpha = maxAlpha;
        this.p_change = change;
        animating = true;
    }

    @Override
    public int adjustAlpha(int original) {
        int modified = original;
        modified += p_change;
        if (modified < p_minAlpha) {
            modified = p_minAlpha;
            animating = false;
        }
        if (modified > p_maxAlpha) {
            modified = p_maxAlpha;
            animating = false;
        }
        return modified;
    }
}
```

Frame Animation

Frame animation is the usual sort of animation that we normally think of when using the term *animation*. Now, however, frame animation can be embedded inside the functionality of Sprite via the animation system. As you may recall, in the previous hour we explored frame animation and wrote a pair of helper methods to animate frames on a strip of a sheet (atlas). That functionality is built into the Sprite class directly, and the way in which frames are cycled is handled by a custom animation class called FrameAnimation. It's a good partnership between the two classes and gives us more versatility.

At this point, you should create quite a few new classes for the engine project—one new class for each subclass of Animation. It would be helpful to see a quick example of how to add a class that automatically has the code specifying its base class. Use the File menu to choose New, Class to bring up the New Java Class dialog shown in Figure 18.1. Be sure to have the Game Engine Library project highlighted because the currently selected project is where the new class will be added.

In this case, I have entered the name of this new class as FrameAnimation in the Name field. Below it is another field called Superclass. This is where you will want to enter **game.engine. Animation**. This helper dialog will make it a bit easier to create new derived classes, so I recommend using it!

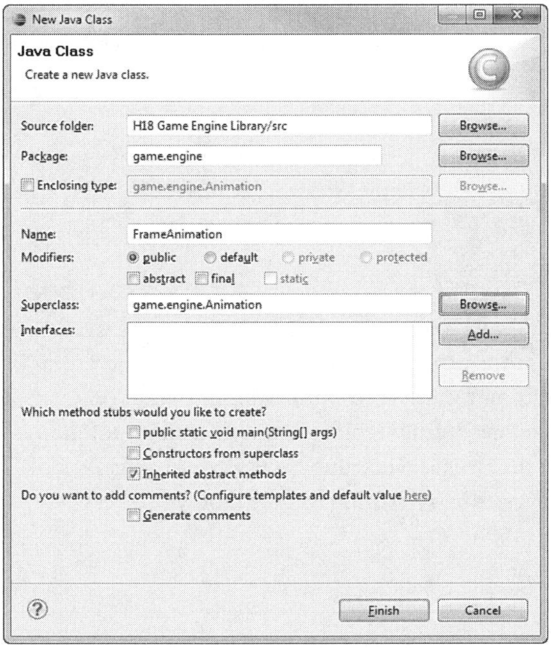

FIGURE 18.1
Adding a new Java class to the project.

Here is the source code for the `FrameAnimation` class.

```java
/**
 * FrameAnimation Class
 */
package game.engine;

public class FrameAnimation extends Animation {
    private int p_firstFrame;
    private int p_lastFrame;
    private int p_direction;

    public FrameAnimation(int firstFrame, int lastFrame, int direction) {
        animating = true;
        p_firstFrame = firstFrame;
        p_lastFrame = lastFrame;
        p_direction = direction;
    }

    @Override
    public int adjustFrame(int original) {
        int modified = original + p_direction;
```

```
        if (modified < p_firstFrame)
            modified = p_lastFrame;
        else if (modified > p_lastFrame)
            modified = p_firstFrame;
        return modified;
    }
}
```

Spin Animation

Although the SpinAnimation class works, we'll have to come back to it later because the Sprite class does not have support for matrix transforms yet, and that is required to do rotation. We *can* do scaling by tweaking the destination rectangle (a parameter in the drawBitmap() method), but true transforms will eventually replace manual scaling, rotation, and translation (movement). Until then, know that this is what the SpinAnimation class looks like, and it is plugged into the engine, but Sprite.draw() cannot do rotation yet.

```
/**
 * SpinAnimation Class
 */
package game.engine;

public class SpinAnimation extends Animation {
    private float p_angleDist, p_velocity;

    public SpinAnimation(float velocity) {
        animating = true;
        this.p_velocity = velocity;
        this.p_angleDist = 0.0f;
    }

    @Override
    public float adjustRotation(float original) {
        float modified = original;
        float fullCircle = (float)(2.0 * Math.PI);
        p_angleDist += p_velocity;
        if (p_angleDist > fullCircle)
            animating = false;
        modified += p_velocity;
        return modified;
    }
}
```

WATCH OUT

The SpinAnimation class works, but the Sprite class can't use it until we add matrix transform support to it. Until then, rotation is not so much broken as it is a future enhancement.

Throb Animation

The term *throb* refers to a sprite growing quite large and then shrinking back to normal rather quickly. When repeated, it will appear to throb. The amount of scaling that occurs is entirely up to you via constructor parameters. Specify the minimum scale, maximum scale, and change value. Perhaps the throb animation will be very slight, from 0.9 to 1.1 or so, and a scale change speed of 0.01—which would be quite slow. Or you could use a larger range from a tiny 0.1 (10 percent normal size) to 3.0 (300 percent enlargement). This animation is designed to run once and then terminate. If you prefer to have it repeat, you could modify this or create a similar class with slightly different behavior.

```java
/**
 * ThrobAnimation Class
 */
package game.engine;
import android.renderscript.Float2;

public class ThrobAnimation extends Animation {
    private float p_startScale, p_endScale, p_speed;
    private boolean p_started;

    public ThrobAnimation(float startScale, float endScale, float speed) {
        p_started = false;
        animating = true;
        this.p_startScale = startScale;
        this.p_endScale = endScale;
        this.p_speed = speed;
    }

    @Override
    public Float2 adjustScale(Float2 original) {
        Float2 modified = original;
        if (!p_started) {
            modified.x = p_startScale;
            modified.y = p_startScale;
            p_started = true;
        }
        modified.x += p_speed;
        modified.y += p_speed;
        if (modified.x >= p_endScale)
            p_speed *= -1;
```

```
        else if (modified.x <= p_startScale)
            animating = false;

        return modified;
    }
}
```

Circular Movement Animation

The circular movement animation technique is very interesting because it demonstrates how the animation system can be used to add behaviors to game objects that go beyond the norm for animation. This one, for example, causes a sprite to revolve around a point at a certain radius. This can be quite useful in gameplay because it can be combined with other animations. For instance, if you're doing a space shooter game, you could use this technique to give your ship orbiting helper drones!

```
/**
 * CircularMovementAnimation Class
 */
package game.engine;
import android.graphics.Point;

public class CircularMovementAnimation extends Animation {
    private int p_radius;
    private Point p_center;
    private double p_angle;
    private float p_velocity;

    public CircularMovementAnimation(int centerx, int centery, int radius,
    double angle, float velocity) {
        animating = true;
        this.p_center = new Point(centerx,centery);
        this.p_radius = radius;
        this.p_angle = angle;
        this.p_velocity = velocity;
    }

    @Override
    public Point adjustPosition(Point original) {
        Point modified = original;
        p_angle += p_velocity;
        modified.x = (int)(p_center.x+(float)(Math.cos(p_angle)*p_radius));
        modified.y = (int)(p_center.y+(float)(Math.sin(p_angle)*p_radius));
        return modified;
    }
}
```

Animation System Demo

The animation system is quite a significant update to the engine and requires a solid example to illustrate how it works. Figure 18.2 shows the program running; the complete source code follows. It is remarkable how much gameplay functionality we have for such a short Android program!

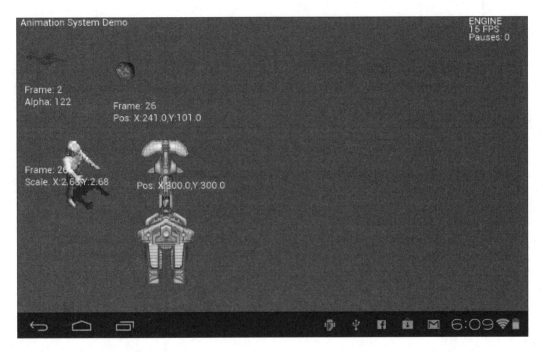

FIGURE 18.2
The Animation System Demo.

```
/**
 * H18 Animation System Demo
 * Requires game.engine.Engine to build.
 */
package android.program;
import android.graphics.*;
import game.engine.*;

public class Game extends game.engine.Engine {
    Canvas canvas;
    Timer timer;
    Sprite dragon;
    Texture dragon_image;
```

```
Sprite zombie;
Texture zombie_image;
Sprite asteroid;
Texture asteroid_image;
Sprite ship;
Texture ship_image;

public Game() {
    canvas = null;
    timer = new Timer();
    dragon = null;
    dragon_image = null;
    zombie = null;
    zombie_image = null;
    asteroid = null;
    asteroid_image = null;
    ship = null;
    ship_image = null;
}

public void init() {
    setScreenOrientation(Engine.ScreenModes.LANDSCAPE);
}

public void load() {
    /**
     * create dragon sprite
     */
    dragon = new Sprite(this, 128, 128, 6);
    dragon_image = new Texture(this);

    if (!dragon_image.loadFromAsset("dragon_strip.png")) {
        fatalError("Error loading dragon_strip");
    }
    dragon.setTexture(dragon_image);
    dragon.position = new Point(20,60);
    dragon.setAlpha(0);

    /**
     * create zombie sprite
     */
    zombie = new Sprite(this, 96, 96, 8);
    zombie_image = new Texture(this);
    if (!zombie_image.loadFromAsset("zombie_walk.png")) {
        fatalError("Error loading zombie_walk");
    }
    zombie.setTexture(zombie_image);
    zombie.position = new Point(20,260);
```

```
    /**
     * create asteroid sprite
     */
    asteroid = new Sprite(this, 60, 60, 8);
    asteroid_image = new Texture(this);
    if (!asteroid_image.loadFromAsset("asteroid_sheet.png")) {
        fatalError("Error loading asteroid_sheet");
    }
    asteroid.setTexture(asteroid_image);
    asteroid.position = new Point(300,90);

    /**
     * create ship sprite (NO FRAMES)
     */
    ship = new Sprite(this);
    ship_image = new Texture(this);
    if (!ship_image.loadFromAsset("ship1.png")) {
        fatalError("Error loading ship1");
    }
    ship.setTexture(ship_image);
    ship.position = new Point(300,300);
    ship.setScale(0.5f);

    /**
     * Add animation techniques to the sprites
     */

    dragon.addAnimation(new FrameAnimation(0, 5, 1));
    dragon.addAnimation(new AlphaAnimation(0, 255, 5));

    zombie.addAnimation(new FrameAnimation(0, 63, 1));
    zombie.addAnimation(new ThrobAnimation(0.5f, 3.0f, 0.01f));

    asteroid.addAnimation(new FrameAnimation(0, 63, 1));
    asteroid.addAnimation(new CircularMovementAnimation(
            asteroid.position.x, asteroid.position.y,
            60, 0.0, 0.1f) );

    ship.addAnimation(new ThrobAnimation(0.2f, 1.5f, 0.1f));
}

public void draw() {
    canvas = getCanvas();
    drawText("Animation System Demo", 10, 20);

    //draw the dragon
    dragon.draw();
    int x = dragon.position.x;
```

```
    int y = dragon.position.y + 128;
    drawText("Frame: " + toString(dragon.getFrame()), x, y);
    drawText("Alpha: " + dragon.getAlpha(), x, y+30);

    //draw the zombie
    zombie.draw();
    x = zombie.position.x;
    y = zombie.position.y + 128;
    drawText("Frame: " + zombie.getFrame(), x, y);
    drawText("Scale: " + toString(zombie.getScale()), x, y+30);

    //draw the asteroid
    asteroid.draw();
    x = asteroid.position.x;
    y = asteroid.position.y + 128;
    drawText("Frame: " + asteroid.getFrame(), x, y);
    drawText("Pos: " + toString(asteroid.position.x) + ", " +
toString(asteroid.position.y), x, y+30);

    //draw the ship
    ship.draw();
    x = ship.position.x;
    y = ship.position.y+128;
    drawText("Pos: " + toString(ship.position.x) + ", " +
    toString(ship.position.y), x, y+30);

}

public void update() {
    //set animation to 50 fps
    if (timer.stopwatch(20)) {

        //update dragon animation
        dragon.animate();

        //reset alpha animation
        if (dragon.getAlpha() >= 255) {
            dragon.setAlpha(0);
            dragon.addAnimation(new AlphaAnimation(0, 255, 1));
        }

        //update zombie animation
        zombie.animate();

        //reset throb animation
        if (zombie.getScale().x <= 0.5f) {
            zombie.addAnimation(new ThrobAnimation(0.5f, 3.0f, 0.01f));
        }
```

```
//update asteroid animation
asteroid.animate();

//update ship animation
ship.animate();

//reset throb animation
if (ship.getScale().x <= 0.2f) {
    ship.addAnimation(new ThrobAnimation(0.2f, 1.5f, 0.1f));
}

        }
    }
}
```

Summary

The advanced animation system is now finished and ready for new animation techniques. Anytime you are working on gameplay code and find yourself writing code for a repeatable process with game sprites, consider writing an animation technique to add some versatility to your game. Over time, you should develop quite a library of such animations. This thought is a bit beyond the scope of this hour, but it's not too far of a stretch to imagine moving this animation code into a *scripting system*, based on a script language such as LUA or Python. We aren't going to cover scripting in this book, but libraries for scripting are available for Java. Imaging storing animation scripts inside text files that are loaded at runtime rather than compiled! It just keeps getting better and better after you have a rudimentary engine up and running.

Q&A

Q. The ability to expand the animation system with new features makes this a truly useful resource for a game designer because it can be challenging to try to produce special effects entirely in the art. What are some advantages and disadvantages to a programmable animation system?

A. Answers will vary.

Q. Describe how the programmable animation system works.

A. Subclasses of `Animation` will implement one or more of the modifier methods to effect a change to one or more animation properties (such as `adjustScale()`).

Workshop

Quiz

1. What is the name of the base sprite animation class used to make programmable animation?

2. What new functionality does the `Sprite` class need in order to make programmable animation fully functional?

3. Which `Animation` method makes it possible for a subclass to modify the animation frame?

Answers

1. `Animation`

2. The `Sprite` class needs matrix transformation support.

3. `adjustFrame()`

Activities

The animation system is meant to be used in such a way that a sprite can be given *more than one* animation at a time. We aren't quite there yet in terms of engine support, though. But see if you can come up with your own new animation subclass to produces an interesting effect.

HOUR 19

Manipulating Sprites with Matrix Transforms

What You'll Learn in This Hour:

▶ Using matrix translation
▶ Using matrix rotation
▶ Using matrix scaling
▶ Combining all three transforms into one matrix
▶ Drawing animation frames with matrix transforms

This hour delves into the awesome subject of matrix transforms, giving us the capability to rotate, scale, and translate a sprite. Although we can already translate (move) and scale a sprite using the known drawBitmap() methods, an additional overload of the method takes a Matrix parameter instead. Because matrix math is much faster than trigonometry (that is, using sine and cosine), and because a matrix can handle all three transforms at once, this is clearly where we want to go with our 2D rendering system.

Matrix Translation

To draw with matrix transforms, we use an overloaded version of the drawBitmap() method, which looks like this:

```
void drawBitmap(Bitmap bitmap, Matrix matrix, Paint paint)
```

Conceptually, the matrix parameter passed to drawBitmap() is *three matrices*, one each for rotation, scaling, and translation. It is possible to use three separate matrices and combine them into one by multiplying them together before rendering (and that is often preferred). The Matrix class *can* do some limited work with the transforms internally with one matrix (see Figure 19.1), but it's easier (and more importantly, standardized) to separate them, one matrix per transform. We'll examine the internal structure of a matrix shortly. It is a better practice to use three separate matrices and combine them before rendering.

COLUMNS

$$\begin{bmatrix} 11 & 12 & 13 & 14 \\ 21 & 22 & 23 & 24 \\ 31 & 32 & 33 & 34 \\ 41 & 42 & 43 & 44 \end{bmatrix}$$

ROWS

FIGURE 19.1
A typical matrix is composed of 4 columns and 4 rows.

The Matrix class contains a 3×3 matrix for transforming coordinates, but the illustrations featuring a 4×4 grid apply just as well because the concepts are the same. Matrices store values used to transform an object. Beginning with an identity matrix, addition and multiplication of matrices results in extremely fast transforms!

Addition and subtraction of matrices is done with the help of a zero matrix. Just like adding zero to any real number results in the unchanged number, so adding or subtracting a matrix from a zero matrix results in the original *unchanged* matrix. Think of this as a starting point when performing addition or subtraction operations on a matrix. Remember, a matrix represents a system, or sequence, of equations. Figure 19.2 shows an illustration of a zero matrix.

$$\begin{bmatrix} 0 & 0 & 0 & 0 \\ 0 & 0 & 0 & 0 \\ 0 & 0 & 0 & 0 \\ 0 & 0 & 0 & 0 \end{bmatrix}$$

FIGURE 19.2
An example of a zero matrix.

An identity matrix, illustrated in Figure 19.3, is used for multiplication and division operations. An identity matrix is filled with zeroes, except for the diagonal from upper left to lower right, represented by matrix elements 11, 22, 33, 44. We use an identity matrix to reset any existing transformations back to the origin (0,0,0). Every transform must start with the identity matrix; otherwise, transforms become additive.

$$\begin{bmatrix} 1 & 0 & 0 & 0 \\ 0 & 1 & 0 & 0 \\ 0 & 0 & 1 & 0 \\ 0 & 0 & 0 & 1 \end{bmatrix}$$

FIGURE 19.3
An example of an identity matrix.

We'll begin our study of transforms with the simplest one: *translation*, or simply, *movement*. Translation is a mathematical term that involves movement on a Cartesian coordinate system and may be calculated with simple addition.

Coordinate Systems

To help visualize how translation works in a coordinate system, take a look at Figure 19.4. The directions in which values increase (+) and decrease (–) are important to keep in mind as you are translating your game objects on the screen. The Z axis is often hard to visualize. Whereas the X and Y axes appear flat, the Z axis goes *in* and *out* of the diagram, giving it depth.

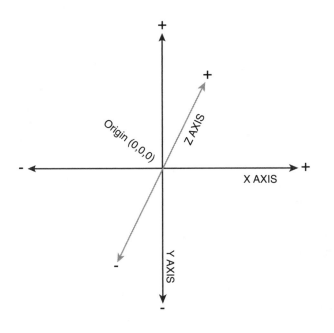

FIGURE 19.4
A 3-axis coordinate system.

Note the position of the *origin* label, which refers to the intersection point of the two axes at (0,0). The origin can be redefined in your game by adding a *center point* value to any translation calculations you need to perform on any game object. For instance, in the previous hour you used an animation subclass called `CircularMovementAnimation` to move an object around a center point on a circular path. This class uses a fixed center point. That point becomes the origin of a local coordinate system for each object.

Now take a look at Figure 19.5, which shows the four quadrants of the Cartesian system. On an Android screen, the origin refers to the upper-left corner of the screen. On an Android screen, the origin is at the upper left; X increases to the right, and Y increases downward toward the bottom of the screen. Thus, you may be tempted to view an Android screen with 4th quadrant coordinates. But that would be wrong because Y *decreases* downward in the 4th quadrant. So, which quadrant represents the screen of an Android (or any other computer display)? Unfortunately for us, *none of them* map to a screen!

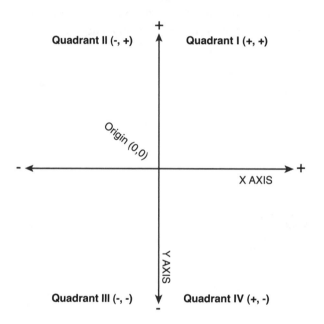

FIGURE 19.5
The four quadrants of a Cartesian coordinate system.

The way we can solve this dilemma is by using the 1st quadrant and inverting the Y values. This is inconvenient, but we can solve the problem by inverting any results for Y by multiplying it by –1. Thus, we have to work with an *inverted 1st quadrant*. It's not really as complex as that might sound because we aren't using any complex trigonometry calculations—-most of that is done by support class methods.

A cleaner view of the coordinate system we use for a 2D, sprite-based game is shown in Figure 19.6 The two axes are easier to read in this simpler view without the third dimension. You can translate each object in your game based on an individual coordinate system, or you can use a global coordinate system.

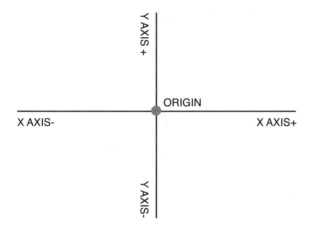

FIGURE 19.6
A simpler view of a 2D coordinate system with two axes.

Based on this simpler view of the coordinate system, we can illustrate how translation works by showing two frames of *before* and *after* translation occurring on a specific point. In Figure 19.7, a point is located at (100,–50). This phrase is really an incorrect way to put it because a point is a coordinate pair; a point is not an object located somewhere—it *is* the coordinate. A point has one dimension, which means it does not exist except as a location. (And, no, this isn't quantum mechanics, so we can know the position of a point—although a probability point might be fun to try to simulate).

The point at (100,–50) is translated by the values (*X:–200*, *Y:+150*) to arrive at a destination point of (–100,100). In gameplay code, we can cause a game object to move by a certain amount without regard for the destination, or we can explicitly move it to a specific location. The former technique involves *velocity*, whereas the latter involves *relocation*. If you want to give an object the ability to move but want it to stay put for a while, you would set its velocity to (0,0).

Matrix Translation Options

Because it is understood now that the `Matrix` class uses a single shared matrix for all thee types of transforms, how exactly does it store them? Take a look at Figure 19.8, which shows where in the matrix the translation values are stored.

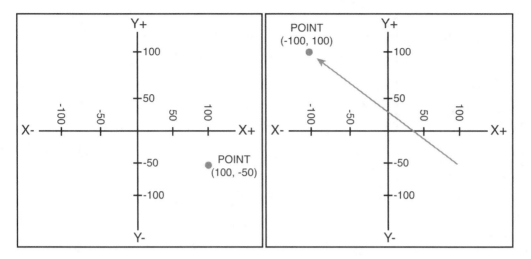

FIGURE 19.7
Translating a point to a new location creates a line.

$$\begin{bmatrix} 0 & 0 & 0 & 0 \\ 0 & 0 & 0 & 0 \\ 0 & 0 & 0 & 0 \\ x & y & z & 0 \end{bmatrix}$$

FIGURE 19.8
Illustration showing where the translation values are stored in the matrix.

The Matrix class has several methods for doing translation. We're not going to obsessively cover every single one in detail, just the useful ones (you're free to explore the rest by opening the JavaDoc page on the Matrix class). First, we'll take a look at the explicit setting with a method called setTranslate():

```
void Matrix.setTranslate(float dx, float dy)
```

Next, we have two additional methods for tweaking the translation values of a matrix. The first, postTranslate(), applies a translation to the matrix *after* the other transforms (rotation and scaling).

```
boolean  postTranslate(float dx, float dy)
```

And preTranslate() applies the translation *before* the other transforms.

```
boolean  preTranslate(float dx, float dy)
```

In case you were wondering why it is important to *pre-* or *post-*translate, it has to do with the identity or reset state of a matrix and whether transforms have already been applied. Generally, you will need to do rotation and scaling before translation, or the object's position will be translated with rotation and scaling applied as well, with bizarre results!

Matrix Rotation

As you learned in the previous section on translation, an overloaded version of the `drawBitmap()` method is used to draw with transforms stored in a matrix. The very same method is used for rotation and scaling as well because all three transforms are stored in the same matrix passed in this call:

```
void drawBitmap(Bitmap bitmap, Matrix matrix, Paint paint)
```

We can set the rotation value explicitly using the `setRotate()` method:

```
void  setRotate(float degrees)
```

There is also a `postRotate()` and `preRotate()` method pair for rotation, and each takes a degree parameter:

```
boolean  postRotate(float degrees)
boolean  preRotate(float degrees)
```

Figure 19.9 shows the position of the rotation values in the matrix. I think you'll agree that this is difficult to discern. Although translation was obvious, rotation is a bit confusing in how it is stored.

$$\begin{bmatrix} y & 0 & y & 0 \\ 0 & xz & xz & 0 \\ y & xz & xyz & 0 \\ 0 & 0 & 0 & 0 \end{bmatrix}$$

FIGURE 19.9
Illustration showing where the rotation values are stored in the matrix.

WATCH OUT

It is generally better to use *radians* rather than *degrees* for rotation because trig functions like sine and cosine always work with radians. To convert from one to the other, use `Math.toDegrees()` or `Math.toRadians()`.

To help you see where this matrix result comes from, here are three tables, numbered 19.1, 19.2, and 19.3, showing how each value of the rotation vector is calculated and stored in the matrix—one each for the X, Y, and Z values, respectively. It is indeed quite complex only when all three vector properties are stored together. Individually, the X, Y, and Z components are straightforward sine and cosine calculations.

TABLE 19.1   X Rotation Matrix

	C1	C2	C3	C4
R1	1	0	0	0
R2	0	$\cos(\theta)$	$-\sin(\theta)$	0
R3	0	$\sin(\theta)$	$\cos(\theta)$	0
R4	0	0	0	1

TABLE 19.2   Y Rotation Matrix

	C1	C2	C3	C4
R1	$\cos(\theta)$	0	$-\sin(\theta)$	0
R2	0	1	0	0
R3	$\sin(\theta)$	0	$\cos(\theta)$	0
R4	0	0	0	1

TABLE 19.3   Z Rotation Matrix

	C1	C2	C3	C4
R1	$\cos(\theta)$	$-\sin(\theta)$	0	0
R2	$\sin(\theta)$	$\cos(\theta)$	0	0
R3	0	0	1	0
R4	0	0	0	1

Matrix Scaling

The scaling transform also shares the matrix with rotation and translation. We can set the scale value explicitly using the setScale() method:

```
void  setScale(float sx, float sy)
```

Likewise, we have two familiar support methods available for scaling:

```
boolean  postScale(float sx, float sy)
boolean  preScale(float sx, float sy)
```

Figure 19.10 shows the position of the scale values in the matrix along the diagonal.

$$\begin{bmatrix} x & 0 & 0 & 0 \\ 0 & y & 0 & 0 \\ 0 & 0 & z & 0 \\ 0 & 0 & 0 & 0 \end{bmatrix}$$

FIGURE 19.10
Illustration showing where the scale values are stored in the matrix.

Matrix Transforms Demo

Now that you have basic matrix transforms under your belt, so to speak, you can use this powerful new technique to revolutionize the Sprite class. It's going to require a bit of extra work to upgrade the class. To support transforms, the existing Sprite class, which supports frame animation, will need an additional scratch bitmap used to hold a single frame that is then transformed and drawn to the screen.

Combining Three Matrices

The Sprite class will use four matrices in total to support transforms:

▶ Translate matrix

▶ Rotate matrix

▶ Scale matrix

▶ Combined matrix

We'll need to add these new matrices to the Sprite class and initialize them properly:

```
private Matrix p_mat_translate;
private Matrix p_mat_scale;
private Matrix p_mat_rotate;
private Matrix p_matrix;
```

Just prior to drawing, each of the three transform matrices is set to its associated value from local Sprite properties. Then a fourth matrix will combine them all into one that can be passed along for rendering.

The scale matrix is set with the following line (note that parameters are local to the `Sprite` class):

```
p_mat_scale.setScale(p_scale.x, p_scale.y);
```

The rotate matrix is set with

```
p_mat_rotate.setRotate( (float)Math.toDegrees(p_rotation));
```

The translate matrix is set with

```
p_mat_translate.setTranslate(position.x, position.y);
```

Finally, the three are combined into one using `Matrix.postConcat()`, which combines them.

```
p_matrix = new Matrix(); //set to identity
p_matrix.postConcat(p_mat_scale);
p_matrix.postConcat(p_mat_rotate);
p_matrix.postConcat(p_mat_translate);
```

Rendering Frames to a Scratch Bitmap

The `drawBitmap()` method is quite useful, but one thing it cannot do is draw animation frames *and* use transforms at the same time. To accomplish this feat, we must render a sprite frame in two steps. First, one frame is copied to a scratch bitmap. Second, the scratch bitmap is drawn to the screen with transforms.

These are the new properties to add to the `Sprite` class:

```
private Bitmap p_frameBitmap;
private Canvas p_frameCanvas;
```

At the appropriate place in the code, they are created like so:

```
p_frameBitmap = Bitmap.createBitmap(p_width, p_height, Config.ARGB_8888);
p_frameCanvas = new Canvas(p_frameBitmap);
```

All of the code previously written to draw a frame out of a sprite sheet still applies, but we have made a minor change to the `drawBitmap()` line. Rather than drawing directly to the screen, the frame is drawn to the scratch bitmap via `p_frameCanvas`:

```
p_frameCanvas.drawBitmap(p_texture.getBitmap(), src, dst, p_paint);
```

After this line, the scratch bitmap (`p_frameBitmap`) contains a single frame of animation. It is this bitmap that can now be drawn to the screen with transforms.

Getting the Screen Resolution (Precanvas)

An issue will come up frequently during the `load()` event if we don't add a new feature to the engine. That issue is the capability to get the screen resolution *before* the canvas has been created. This comes up when you want to initialize game objects on the screen without knowing exactly what type of Android device the game is running on—for instance, placing certain sprites randomly on the screen. Remember, the canvas is null until the drawing stage, so during `load()`, there is no canvas. After the canvas is valid, it's easy to get the screen resolution (via `Canvas`). Prior to that, though, we have to use another technique.

```
private Point p_screenSize;
```

This initialization code is added to the `onCreate()` event in Engine.java *prior* to calling the abstract `load()` method. In order to use `DisplayMetrics` in the following code, be sure to add `import android.util.DisplayMetrics` in your program.

```
//get the screen dimensions
DisplayMetrics dm = new DisplayMetrics();
getWindowManager().getDefaultDisplay().getMetrics(dm);
p_screenSize = new Point(dm.widthPixels,dm.heightPixels);
```

Next, these helper methods are added to Engine.java to provide access to the screen size.

```
public Point getSize() {
    return p_screenSize;
}

public int getScreenWidth() {
    return p_screenSize.x;
}

public int getScreenHeight() {
    return p_screenSize.y;
}
```

"Warping" Behavior

It's time for a new type of animation, a subclass like those demonstrated in the previous hour. This is where we blur the line between *animation* and *behavior* because this new technique is very clearly a behavior—in other words, it involves the movement or activity of a sprite and not just what it looks like. Take a look at Figure 19.11 for an illustration of the technique. In this illustration, game objects are moving toward the left in one direction. When they hit the left edge, they are automatically sent to the right edge again. The new animation class is called `WarpRect`. Let's peruse the code first and then explain how it works.

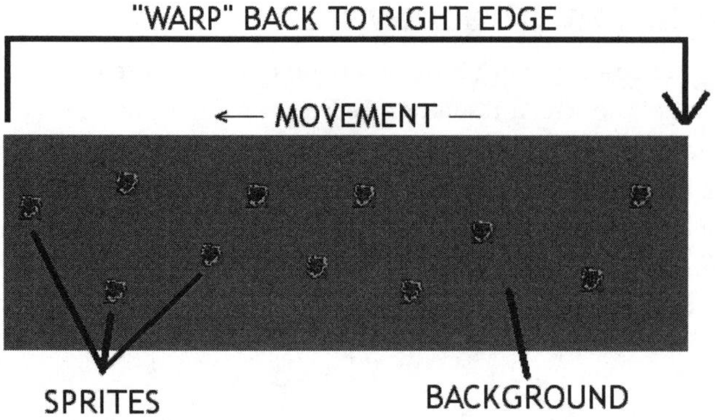

FIGURE 19.11
Illustration showing how warping from one edge to another works.

```
/**
 * WarpRect class - derived from Animation
 * Requires game.engine.Engine to build.
 */
package game.engine;
import android.graphics.Point;
import android.graphics.Rect;
import android.renderscript.Float2;

public class WarpRect extends Animation {
    private Rect p_bounds;
    private Float2 p_velocity;
    private Point p_size;

    public WarpRect(Rect bounds, Point size, Float2 velocity) {
        animating = true;
        p_bounds = bounds;
        p_velocity = velocity;
        p_size = size;
    }

    @Override
    public Point adjustPosition(Point original) {
        Point modified = original;
        modified.x += p_velocity.x;
        modified.y += p_velocity.y;

        if (modified.x < p_bounds.left)
            modified.x = p_bounds.right-p_size.x;
        else if (modified.x > p_bounds.right-p_size.x)
            modified.x = p_bounds.left;
```

```
        if (modified.y < p_bounds.top)
            modified.y = p_bounds.bottom-p_size.y;
        else if (modified.y > p_bounds.bottom-p_size.y)
            modified.y = p_bounds.top;

        return modified;
    }
}
```

As you can tell from the code, `WarpRect` affects only the position and no other sprite property. The purpose of this animation is to set a boundary and velocity for an object, cause it to move, and keep the object inside the boundary by warping around at the edges. As an object hits the top edge, it is moved to the bottom edge, and so on. This behavior contrasts with a reboundlike behavior, in which a sprite will bounce off of a boundary wall rather than warping to the other side. Both behaviors are useful in a variety of gameplay scenarios. For instance, you can use movement of objects (such as clouds) moving from right to left, warping back to the right edge, to simulate the appearance of movement.

Updated `Sprite` Class

Because the `Sprite` class has undergone significant changes again this hour, we'll show the source code for the class with the new code highlighted in bold. It has become quite a complex, versatile class for the game engine, extremely capable at this point of handling most gameplay needs.

```
/**
 * Sprite Class
 * Requires game.engine.Engine to build.
 */
package game.engine;
import java.util.LinkedList;
import java.util.ListIterator;
import android.graphics.*;
import android.graphics.Bitmap.Config;
import android.renderscript.Float2;

public class Sprite {
    private Engine p_engine;
    private Canvas p_canvas;
    private Texture p_texture;
    private Paint p_paint;
    public Point position;
    private int p_width, p_height;
    private int p_columns;
    private int p_alpha;
    private LinkedList<Animation> p_anims;
```

```
private int p_frame;
private Float2 p_scale;
private float p_rotation;
private Matrix p_mat_translate;
private Matrix p_mat_scale;
private Matrix p_mat_rotate;
private Matrix p_matrix;
private Bitmap p_frameBitmap;
private Canvas p_frameCanvas;

public Sprite(Engine engine) {
    this(engine, 0, 0, 1);
}

public Sprite(Engine engine, int width, int height, int columns) {
    p_engine = engine;
    p_width = width;
    p_height = height;
    p_columns = columns;
    p_canvas = null;
    p_texture = new Texture(engine);
    p_alpha = 255;
    p_paint = new Paint();
    p_anims = new LinkedList<Animation>();
    position = new Point(0,0);
    p_frame = 0;
    p_scale = new Float2(1.0f,1.0f);
    p_rotation = 0.0f;
    p_mat_translate = new Matrix();
    p_mat_scale = new Matrix();
    p_mat_rotate = new Matrix();
    p_matrix = new Matrix();
    p_frameBitmap = null;
    p_frameCanvas = null;
}

public void draw() {
    p_canvas = p_engine.getCanvas();

    //fill in size if this sprite is not animated
    if (p_width == 0 || p_height == 0) {
        p_width = p_texture.getBitmap().getWidth();
        p_height = p_texture.getBitmap().getHeight();
    }

    //create the frame scratch bitmap
    if (p_frameBitmap == null) {
        p_frameBitmap = Bitmap.createBitmap(p_width, p_height, Config.
```

```
ARGB_8888);
            p_frameCanvas = new Canvas(p_frameBitmap);
        }

        /**
         * First, copy the animation frame onto a scratch bitmap.
         */

        //define the source rect representing one frame
        int u = (p_frame % p_columns) * p_width;
        int v = (p_frame / p_columns) * p_height;
        Rect src = new Rect(u, v, u+p_width, v+p_height);

        //define the destination location
        int x = 0;// position.x;
        int y = 0;// position.y;
        int w = p_width; //(int)(p_width * p_scale.x);
        int h = p_height; // (int)(p_height * p_scale.y);
        Rect dst = new Rect(x, y, x+w, y+h);

        //copy frame onto temp bitmap
        p_paint.setAlpha(p_alpha);
        p_frameCanvas.drawBitmap(p_texture.getBitmap(), src, dst, p_paint);


        /**
         * Second, draw the scratch bitmap using matrix transforms.
         */

        //update transform matrices
        p_mat_scale = new Matrix();
        p_mat_scale.setScale(p_scale.x, p_scale.y);
        p_mat_rotate = new Matrix();
        p_mat_rotate.setRotate( (float)Math.toDegrees(p_rotation));
        p_mat_translate = new Matrix();
        p_mat_translate.setTranslate(position.x, position.y);
        p_matrix = new Matrix(); //set to identity
        p_matrix.postConcat(p_mat_scale);
        p_matrix.postConcat(p_mat_rotate);
        p_matrix.postConcat(p_mat_translate);

        //draw frame bitmap onto screen
        p_canvas.drawBitmap(p_frameBitmap, p_matrix, p_paint);
    }

    //add an animation technique to this sprite
    public void addAnimation(Animation anim) {
        p_anims.add(anim);
    }
```

```java
//run through all of the animations
public void animate() {
    if (p_anims.size() == 0) return;

    ListIterator<Animation> iterator = p_anims.listIterator();
    while (iterator.hasNext()) {
        Animation anim = iterator.next();
        if (anim.animating) {
            p_frame = anim.adjustFrame(p_frame);
            p_alpha = anim.adjustAlpha(p_alpha);
            p_rotation = anim.adjustRotation(p_rotation);
            p_scale = anim.adjustScale(p_scale);
            position = anim.adjustPosition(position);
        }
        else
        {
            p_anims.remove(anim);
            return;
        }
    }
}

/**
 * Color manipulation methods
 */
public void setAlpha(int alpha) {
    p_alpha = alpha;
}

public int getAlpha() {
    return p_alpha;
}

public void setPaint(Paint paint) {
    p_paint = paint;
}

/**
 * common get/set methods
 */
public void setTexture(Texture texture) {
    p_texture = texture;
}

public Texture getTexture() {
    return p_texture;
}
```

```java
public void setPosition(Point position) {
    this.position = position;
}

public Point getPosition() {
    return position;
}

public int getWidth() {
    return p_width;
}

public void setWidth(int width) {
    p_width = width;
}

public int getHeight() {
    return p_height;
}

public void setHeight(int height) {
    p_height = height;
}

public Point getSize() {
    return new Point(p_width,p_height);
}

public int getFrame() {
    return p_frame;
}

public void setFrame(int frame) {
    p_frame = frame;
}

public Float2 getScale() {
    return p_scale;
}

public void setScale(Float2 scale) {
    p_scale = scale;
}

public void setScale(float scale) {
    p_scale = new Float2(scale,scale);
}
```

```
    public float getRotation() {
        return p_rotation;
    }

    public void setRotation(float radians) {
        p_rotation = radians;
    }
}
```

The Sprite Transforms Demo

Following is the complete source code for the Sprite Transforms Demo program shown in
Figure 19.12. The asteroid sprites are moving in random locations and warping within the
box shown on the screen. The spaceship is independent of the asteroids and does not interact
with them in any way. The purpose of the spaceship is to show dramatically how rotation and
scaling work in conjunction with translation. Because all the sprites in this scene are drawing
with transforms, it's an effective demonstration of the new capabilities. You will need to use
bitmap files for this project: asteroid_sheet.png and ship1.png. Both are included in the book
resource files.

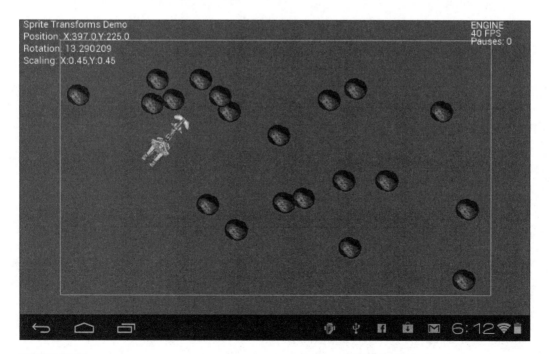

FIGURE 19.12
The Sprite Transforms Demo draws a bunch of sprites with matrix transforms.

```
package android.program;
import java.util.LinkedList;
import java.util.ListIterator;
import java.util.Random;
import android.graphics.*;
import android.graphics.Paint.Style;
import android.renderscript.Float2;
import game.engine.*;

public class Game extends game.engine.Engine {
    Canvas canvas;
    Timer timer;
    Point touch,oldTouch;
    LinkedList<Sprite> asteroids;
    Texture asteroid_image;
    Sprite ship;
    Texture ship_image;
    Random rand;
    Paint paint;
    Rect boundary;

    public Game() {
        canvas = null;
        paint = new Paint();
        timer = new Timer();
        asteroids = null;
        asteroid_image = null;
        ship = null;
        ship_image = null;
    }

    public void init() {
        setScreenOrientation(Engine.ScreenModes.LANDSCAPE);
        rand = new Random();
        touch = oldTouch = new Point(0,0);
    }

    public void load() {
        int x,y,w,h;
        w = getScreenWidth();
        h = getScreenHeight();
        boundary = new Rect(100,50,w-100,h-50);

        asteroid_image = new Texture(this);
        if (!asteroid_image.loadFromAsset("asteroid_sheet.png")) {
            fatalError("Error loading asteroid_sheet");
        }
```

```
    asteroids = new LinkedList<Sprite>();
    for (int n=0; n<20; n++) {
        Sprite asteroid = new Sprite(this, 60, 60, 8);
        asteroid.setTexture(asteroid_image);
        x = boundary.left;
        y = boundary.top;
        w = boundary.width();
        h = boundary.height();
        asteroid.position = new Point(x+rand.nextInt(w),
                y+rand.nextInt(h));
        asteroid.addAnimation(new FrameAnimation(0, 63, 1));
        Float2 vel = new Float2(rand.nextFloat()*10-5.0f,
                rand.nextFloat()*10-5.0f);
        asteroid.addAnimation(new WarpRect(boundary,
                new Point(60,60), vel));
        asteroids.add(asteroid);
    }

    ship = new Sprite(this);
    ship_image = new Texture(this);
    if (!ship_image.loadFromAsset("ship1.png")) {
        fatalError("Error loading ship1");
    }
    ship.setTexture(ship_image);
    ship.position = new Point(200,200);
    ship.addAnimation(new ThrobAnimation(0.2f, 0.8f, 0.001f));
    int cx = getScreenWidth()/2-60;
    int cy = getScreenHeight()/2-60;
    ship.addAnimation(new CircularMovementAnimation(
            cx,cy,200,0,0.05f));

}

public void draw() {
    canvas = getCanvas();
    drawText("Sprite Transforms Demo", 10, 20);
    drawText("Position: " + toString(ship.position), 10, 50);
    drawText("Rotation: " + toString(ship.getRotation()), 10, 80);
    drawText("Scaling: " + toString(ship.getScale()), 10, 110);

    //draw the asteroids with transforms
    ListIterator<Sprite> iter = asteroids.listIterator();
    while (iter.hasNext()) {
        Sprite asteroid = (Sprite)iter.next();
        asteroid.draw();
    }
```

```
        //draw the ship sprite with transforms!
        ship.draw();

        //draw border to show WrapRect boundary
        paint.setColor(Color.WHITE);
        paint.setStyle(Style.STROKE);
        this.getCanvas().drawRect(boundary, paint);

    }

    public void update() {
        if (timer.stopwatch(20)) {

            //animate the asteroid sprite group
            ListIterator<Sprite> iter = asteroids.listIterator();
            while (iter.hasNext()) {
                Sprite asteroid = (Sprite)iter.next();
                asteroid.animate();
            }

            //animate the ship sprite
            ship.animate();
            //manually update rotation
            float r = ship.getRotation();
            ship.setRotation(r + 0.01f);
            //manually reset scaling
            if (ship.getScale().x <= 0.2f)
                ship.addAnimation(new ThrobAnimation(0.2f, 0.8f, 0.001f));
        }
    }
}
```

Summary

This hour concludes our work on sprite animation and matrix transforms. It has been quite a hard job over the past three hours to get to this point, as I'm sure you will agree! But now we're beginning to see a major payoff after all our hard work. The Sprite class is completely decked out with awesome capabilities and ready to be put to the test in a serious game project! We're essentially done with this aspect of the engine and need to move into some new gameplay techniques in the very next hour, which will cover collision detection.

Q&A

Q. The `Sprite` class can now do real-time transforms. How does this improve the capabilities of the class over the earlier version?

A. Answers will vary, but try to focus on how transforms use matrixes, which simplify (and speed up) transform calculations.

Q. The addition of support for multiple animations in a single sprite opens the door for doing unique special effects, such as rotating one sprite around another. What are some interesting effects you can recall from some classic video games that might be duplicated now in your own games?

A. Answers will vary, but discussion should resolve around some classic arcade games.

Workshop

Quiz

1. What `Sprite` methods allow you to manipulate the scale of a sprite?

2. What data type makes it possible for `Sprite` to use transforms?

3. What `Sprite` method updates the animation(s) currently in use?

Answers

1. `getScale()` and `setScale()`

2. `Matrix`

3. `animate()`

Activities

The `Sprite` class has matured significantly in the past few hours, so if you have not spent much time with it beyond the example in this hour, a good exercise will be for you to write your own new code using `Sprite` to put it through its paces. See what it can do and get creative with the transforms it can now do!

Entity Grouping

What You'll Learn in This Hour:

- ▶ Adding an entity grouping system to the engine
- ▶ Making the necessary engine enhancements
- ▶ Adding behavior to the game entities
- ▶ Demonstrating entity grouping

This hour covers a very big subject that is high in concept but fairly low in complexity, leading up to collision detection in the next hour. Entity grouping is the use of a list for game entities that is automatically updated by the engine. The way this works is that animations or behaviors are used to specify the activity of an entity (that is, sprite), which means "fire and forget" sprites. Give a sprite entity a simple behavior and "cut it loose" to wreak havoc—entirely on its own, so to speak. We'll follow this up in the next hour by covering collision detection, which works well with entity grouping—because, as it turns out, it's fairly easy to check for collisions after you have a grouping system in place.

Entity Grouping

The concept behind entity grouping is extremely simple. We don't need to borrow any algorithms or develop any techniques; all that is required is a LinkedList and some creativity. You were introduced to entity grouping in the previous hour when the asteroid sprites were managed using a list. The basic code will be used again here, but it will be moved inside Engine.java with some required properties and helper methods. The approach this hour is to build the example as we go along, while learning about grouping. So, let's begin with some work on the core engine again (which hasn't been touched for a while now).

Engine Enhancements

Open up the core engine class in Engine.java. You may follow along while perusing the finished project under H20 in the sources, or make the changes yourself to the base H19 engine library project if you prefer to build things as a good learning experience. Because the engine source code is rather lengthy, we'll just note the changes rather than repeating the entire code listing. For reference, go back to Hour 15, "Building an Android Game Engine."

Add this new private property to the list of privates at the top of the class:

```
private LinkedList<Sprite> p_group;
```

To use this class, an import is needed. While we're at it, the iterator class will be imported as well.

```
import java.util.LinkedList;
import java.util.ListIterator;
```

Next, initialize the `LinkedList` object in the class constructor under `public  Engine()`:

```
p_group = new LinkedList<Sprite>();
```

Now for the new group update and draw code. The `run()` method in Engine.java is the thread update method, as you'll recall from back in Hour 8, "Bringing Your Game to Life with Looping." There are only a few minor additions to the method that will bring to life our entity group. Note the changes in bold.

```
@Override
    public void run() {
        Log.d("Engine","Engine.run start");

        Timer frameTimer = new Timer();
        int frameCount=0;
        int frameRate=0;
        long startTime=0;
        long timeDiff=0;

        while (p_running) {
            // Process frame only if not paused
            if (p_paused) continue;

            // Calculate frame rate
            frameCount++;
            startTime = frameTimer.getElapsed();
            if (frameTimer.stopwatch(1000)) {
                frameRate = frameCount;
                frameCount = 0;

                //reset touch input count
                p_numPoints = 0;
            }
```

```
        // Call abstract update method in sub-class
        update();

        // Rendering section, lock the canvas
        // Only proceed if the SurfaceView is valid
        if (beginDrawing()) {

            p_canvas.drawColor(Color.BLACK);

            /**
             * NEW CODE
             * Draw the group entities with transforms
             */
            ListIterator<Sprite> iter = p_group.listIterator();
            while (iter.hasNext()) {
                Sprite spr = (Sprite)iter.next();
                spr.animate();
                spr.draw();
            }

            // Call abstract draw method in sub-class
            draw();

            int x = p_canvas.getWidth()-150;
            p_canvas.drawText("ENGINE", x, 20, p_paintFont);
            p_canvas.drawText(toString(frameRate) + " FPS", x, 40,
                p_paintFont);
            p_canvas.drawText("Pauses: " + toString(p_pauseCount),
                x, 60, p_paintFont);

            // Complete the rendering process by unlocking the canvas
            endDrawing();
        }

        // Calculate frame update time and sleep if necessary
        timeDiff = frameTimer.getElapsed() - startTime;
        long updatePeriod = p_sleepTime - timeDiff;
        if (updatePeriod > 0) {
            try {
                Thread.sleep( updatePeriod );
            }
            catch(InterruptedException e) {}
        }
    }
    Log.d("Engine","Engine.run end");
    System.exit(RESULT_OK);
}
```

Further down in the code of Engine.java, add the following new methods to the `Engine` class:

```
/**
 * Entity grouping methods
 */

public void addToGroup(Sprite sprite) {
    p_group.add(sprite);
}

public void removeFromGroup(Sprite sprite) {
    p_group.remove(sprite);
}

public void removeFromGroup(int index) {
    p_group.remove(index);
}
```

That's all we need at this point to do rudimentary entity grouping inside the engine. Now, let's take a look at some new animation classes we'll need for the example this hour, and then we'll take a look at the working demo.

Throb Animation Update

The `ThrobAnimation` class introduced in the previous hour needs some tweaking. It is still useful as a one-time animation sequence, but I want to give it a new feature that will cause the throb scale effect to loop if desired. This can be done with an additional constructor parameter to flag a repeat. The changes are noted in bold. While making the minor modifications, I've taken the opportunity to add another constructor and improve the logic code a bit as well. This way, the class can be used as originally intended, or the repeat flag can be used. In C++, this would be a simple matter of using an optional parameter, but in Java we have to use an overload.

```
package game.engine;
import android.renderscript.Float2;

public class ThrobAnimation extends Animation {
    private float p_startScale, p_endScale, p_speed;
    private boolean p_started, p_repeat;

    public ThrobAnimation(float startScale, float endScale, float speed) {
        this(startScale, endScale, speed, false);
    }

    public ThrobAnimation(float startScale, float endScale, float speed,
            boolean repeat) {
        p_started = false;
        animating = true;
```

```
        this.p_startScale = startScale;
        this.p_endScale = endScale;
        this.p_speed = speed;
        this.p_repeat = repeat;
    }

    @Override
    public Float2 adjustScale(Float2 original) {
        Float2 modified = original;
        if (!p_started) {
            modified.x = p_startScale;
            modified.y = p_startScale;
            p_started = true;
        }
        modified.x += p_speed;
        modified.y += p_speed;
        if (modified.x > p_endScale) {
            p_speed *= -1;
        }
        else if (modified.x < p_startScale) {
            if (!p_repeat)
                animating = false;
            else
                p_speed *= -1;
        }
        return modified;
    }
}
```

Warp Behavior Update

In the previous hour, I introduced an animation subclass called WarpRect. We're going to rename and enhance this class to make it more useful. The new name will be WarpBehavior. Going along with this theme, any animation that is more about logic than appearance will use the term *Behavior* instead of *Animation* in the class name. This is important because you will most likely create a lot of such classes over time and there is clearly a difference between the two types. In addition to the name change, this class also features a new constructor overload (for convenience, not new functionality).

An interesting use of this class involves warping objects around the perimeter of the entire screen. Because the origin or pivot point of a sprite is at the upper-left corner, there is a difference in logic between warping from the left or top and the right or bottom. To balance out the discrepancy, it is helpful to specify a negative value for the left and top edges. This will have the effect of showing an object sliding off the edge of the screen rather than popping off.

```
package game.engine;
import android.graphics.Point;
import android.graphics.Rect;
import android.renderscript.Float2;

public class WarpBehavior extends Animation {
    private Rect p_bounds;
    private Float2 p_velocity;
    private Point p_size;

    public WarpBehavior(Rect bounds, int w, int h, Float2 velocity) {
        this(bounds, new Point(w,h), velocity);
    }

    public WarpBehavior(Rect bounds, Point size, Float2 velocity) {
        animating = true;
        p_bounds = bounds;
        p_velocity = velocity;
        p_size = size;
    }

    @Override
    public Point adjustPosition(Point original) {
        Point modified = original;
        modified.x += p_velocity.x;
        modified.y += p_velocity.y;

        if (modified.x < p_bounds.left)
            modified.x = p_bounds.right-p_size.x;
        else if (modified.x > p_bounds.right-p_size.x)
            modified.x = p_bounds.left;

        if (modified.y < p_bounds.top)
            modified.y = p_bounds.bottom-p_size.y;
        else if (modified.y > p_bounds.bottom-p_size.y)
            modified.y = p_bounds.top;

        return modified;
    }
}
```

Fence Behavior

We will introduce a new behavior class this hour! Remember, anytime you are tempted to write reusable gameplay logic, consider putting that code into a subclass of *Animation* and add it to the engine rather than writing custom code in the game loop! For this behavior, I want to limit the player's ship to the boundary of the screen. It is simple logic to prevent a sprite from going off the screen; it's sort of the opposite of the warp behavior. As such, we might call this *fencing*, or *corralling*.

Here is the `FenceBehavior` class. It is extremely simple in nature—just stop an object if it reaches the fence border, and move it back behind the fence if necessary.

```
package game.engine;
import android.graphics.Point;
import android.graphics.Rect;

public class FenceBehavior extends Animation {
    private Rect p_fence;

    public FenceBehavior(Rect fence) {
        p_fence = fence;
        animating = true; //just means it is active
    }

    @Override
    public Point adjustPosition(Point original) {
        Point modified = original;

        if (modified.x < p_fence.left)
            modified.x = p_fence.left;
        else if (modified.x > p_fence.right)
            modified.x = p_fence.right;
        if (modified.y < p_fence.top)
            modified.y = p_fence.top;
        else if (modified.y > p_fence.bottom)
            modified.y = p_fence.bottom;

        return modified;
    }
}
```

Entity Grouping Demo

Now we want the main project to test the new entity grouping functionality of the engine. Obviously, there is much work yet to be done to make the grouping system versatile for a large game project, but it's a good start. For quick reference, Figure 20.1 shows the output of the project. Note that the figure shows what appear to be stationary sprites; in fact, the asteroids are moving quite fast and are being warped by the `WarpBehavior` class, and the ship is moving because of user input. Note also that the background should now be black instead of blue. That is due to a quick change while we were working in the Engine class. In the future, it will be helpful to add a support method to the engine that will make it possible to change the background color or possibly use a background image.

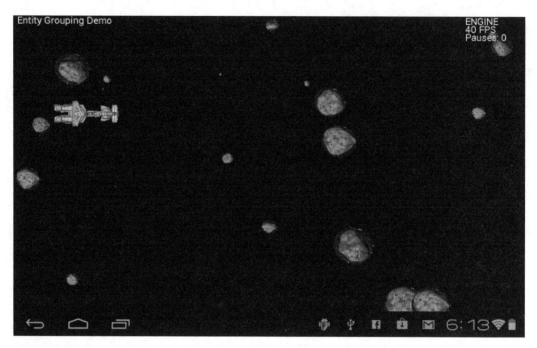

FIGURE 20.1
The Entity Grouping Demo program.

BY THE WAY

When you make changes to the code in Engine.java or any other class file in the engine library project, you have to Save All and then use Project, Clean to rebuild the engine for the changes to show up in the code editor.

Here is the source code for the example. It is astonishing how short this code listing is, given how much activity is happening on the screen. We have asteroids zooming across the screen while animating. The player's ship is moving in response to user touch input while also cycling the scale in a subtle way to help with the sensation of movement. This isn't a complex example, but it's a lot of behavior in a small package thanks to the new animation and behavior features in the engine. We are truly working with some advanced gameplay code now at a fairly high level. In fact, this type of code is only one level away from *script code*.

```
/**
 * H20 Entity Grouping Demo
 * Requires game.engine.Engine to build.
 */
package android.program;
import java.util.Random;
import android.graphics.*;
import android.renderscript.*;
import game.engine.*;

public class Game extends game.engine.Engine {
    Canvas canvas;
    Paint paint;
    game.engine.Timer timer; //avoid conflict with java.util.Timer
    Random rand;
    Texture asteroid_image;
    Sprite ship;
    Texture ship_image;

    public Game() {
        canvas = null;
        paint = new Paint();
        timer = new Timer();
        rand = new Random();
        asteroid_image = null;
        ship = null;
        ship_image = null;
    }

    public void init() {
        setScreenOrientation(Engine.ScreenModes.LANDSCAPE);
    }

    public void load() {

        asteroid_image = new Texture(this);
        if (!asteroid_image.loadFromAsset("asteroid_sheet.png")) {
            fatalError("Error loading asteroid_sheet");
        }

        int w = getScreenWidth();
        int h = getScreenHeight();
        Rect boundary = new Rect(-60,-60,w,h);

        for (int n=0; n<20; n++) {
            Sprite asteroid = new Sprite(this, 60, 60, 8);
            asteroid.setTexture(asteroid_image);
```

```
            asteroid.position = new Point(w+rand.nextInt(w), rand.nextInt(h-60));
            asteroid.addAnimation(new FrameAnimation(0, 63, 1));
            Float2 vel = new Float2(rand.nextFloat()*-50.0f, 0);
            asteroid.addAnimation(new WarpBehavior(boundary, 60, 60, vel));
            asteroid.setFrame(rand.nextInt(63));
            asteroid.setScale(rand.nextFloat()*2.0f);
            addToGroup(asteroid);
        }

        ship = new Sprite(this);
        ship_image = new Texture(this);
        if (!ship_image.loadFromAsset("ship3.png")) {
            fatalError("Error loading ship3");
        }
        ship.setTexture(ship_image);
        ship.position = new Point(100, h/2);
        ship.addAnimation(new ThrobAnimation(0.8f, 1.2f, 0.001f, true));
        ship.addAnimation(new FenceBehavior(new Rect(0,0,200,h-64)));
    }

    public void draw() {
        canvas = getCanvas();
        drawText("Entity Grouping Demo", 10, 20);
        ship.draw();
    }

    public void update() {
        Point touch=null;
        int inputs = getTouchInputs();

        if (timer.stopwatch(20)) {
            if (inputs > 0) {
                touch = getTouchPoint(0);
                if (touch.x < 200) {
                    if (touch.y < getScreenHeight()/2-20) {
                        ship.position.y -= 5.0f;
                    }
                    else if (touch.y > getScreenHeight()/2+20) {
                        ship.position.y += 5.0f;
                    }
                }
            }

            ship.animate();
        }
    }
}
```

Figure 20.2 shows the player's spaceship featured in the demo. It has been prerotated by 90 degrees to face the right. Because that is the orientation the sprite will always be in for this sort of game, it makes sense to make changes to the art in advance to cut down on code manipulation that would otherwise be required. Consider doing this anytime you are working on a game. Try to avoid messy code to get art where you want it, and pre-edit images in advance to keep your code cleaner. This also benefits by being easier to modify later.

FIGURE 20.2
The player's spaceship sprite.

Figure 20.3 shows the asteroid animation sheet/atlas for reference. We have used this sprite before. It's not especially interesting, just useful for testing new game code when you want a sci-fi setting. In this hour's example, the asteroid sprites are being used as a background without interaction to make the ship appear to be flying through space.

FIGURE 20.3
The asteroid sheet/atlas.

Summary

This hour introduced a new entity grouping system to the engine that makes it fairly easy to add automated behaviors to a game with a minimum of source code. The engine is truly beginning to feel like a functional engine rather than just a graphics wrapper for Android.

Q&A

Q. The animation system in this rudimentary Android game engine seems to support a lot more than just frame animation, it can be used for game logic, too, such as moving things around. Should this functionality be moved into a more appropriate class, such as a class called Behavior? Discuss the pros and cons.

A. Answers will vary.

Q. The new entity system that automatically moves sprites does not seem to let the programmer do anything with the objects manually. This seems to be a problem, or is that intentional? Discuss the issue.

A. Answers should reflect a need to "get" objects out of the entity system as needed, and this functionality is not yet included.

Workshop

Quiz

1. Which class handles the list of automated entities in the engine?

2. Which class makes it easier to loop through a list and is preferred when using a list?

3. When iterating through a list, which method returns the next object in the list?

Answers

1. `java.util.LinkedList`

2. `java.util.ListIterator`

3. `next()`

Activities

The `WarpBehavior` class makes some assumptions that could be customized with additional parameters or constructor overloads. See what interesting things you can do with the class to give it even more useful functionality.

HOUR 21

Collision Detection

What You'll Learn in This Hour:

▶ Collision detection techniques

▶ Bounding rectangles (box collision)

▶ Bounding circles (radial collision)

▶ Testing collision detection

Collision detection makes a game look and feel realistic by allowing objects to hit each other and react to those collision events. This hour explores the two most common and efficient techniques for detecting collisions between game objects, with a theoretical discussion of the algorithms and an applied example.

Collision Detection Techniques

The two collision techniques we will study get their names from the techniques they employ: *bounding rectangles* and *bounding circles*. We'll study each in detail and then create an example to test collisions.

Bounding Rectangles (Box Collision)

The most common technique used in video games to test for collisions is the *bounding rectangle* technique, also known as *box collision*. The name comes from the use of a rectangle that surrounds the entire shape of the object and is often derived from the frame size (with animation) or actual dimensions of the image loaded from a bitmap file (in cases where no animation is involved).

To determine whether two game objects have collided, we can create a bounding box around each one and then compare the boxes to see if they overlap. The box may be a Rect stored in the game object, or it may be generated on-the-fly. The latter approach is the norm because it recalculates the boundary as the object is moving, taking into account the X,Y position and width/height properties. Figure 21.1 shows an illustration of five objects with their bounding boxes.

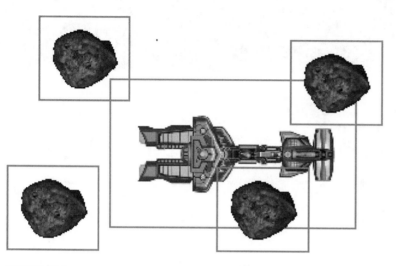

FIGURE 21.1
Five game objects with bounding boxes.

This illustration shows some of the flaws in the bounding box collision detection technique. As you can see, none of the objects are actually colliding, but their bounding boxes are! This is a legitimate problem. How do we solve it?

The short answer is: *We don't*. The bounding boxes in this illustration have been slightly exaggerated, but they are often large, as shown, to take into account the differences in animation frames (where some frames take up more room than others). Because animation frames must all be the same size, the bounding box is defined by the largest frame. If an object is actively rotating, the bounding box around the object while it is in a diagonal orientation will be quite large. This poses a problem for us.

One solution is to adjust the bounding rectangle so that it represents the *bulk* of the shape rather than just the outer perimeter of the image. A good average reduction that produces consistent results is 25%, with up to 50% if the shape is dense (with few or no convex parts).

Figure 21.2 is another illustration, this time showing actual physical contact between the two game objects. If you note how far in the second object intersects the first, you may notice that it's about halfway into the spaceship bounding box. This trend is fairly common, which is why the 25 to 50% figure comes up quite often.

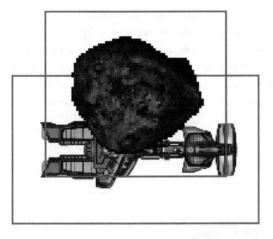

FIGURE 21.2
A collision is more apparent between larger game objects.

Bounding Circles (Radial Collision)

The second common technique for collision detection uses bounding circles around two objects. This technique is quite a bit different from bounding rectangles. For a comparison, see Figure 21.3. The bounding circle seems *huge* in comparison. There is a simplicity to the algorithm, based on distance, and this technique works extremely well in some situations.

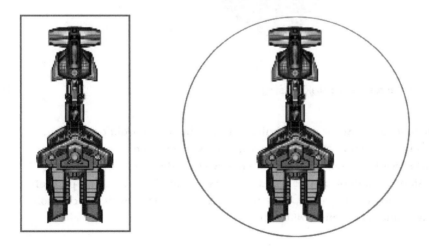

FIGURE 21.3
Comparison of two bounding shapes: rectangle and circle.

Very simply, take the center point of each shape and use a radius value to simulate a circle around the shape. To test for collision, compare the distance between two objects in relation to the radius of each: If the distance is less than the sum of the radii, a collision has occurred. See Figure 21.4, which shows four asteroids again, close to a spaceship. The most surprising example is the asteroid in the lower-right corner: Although it is fully within the bounding circle of the space ship, this clearly shows that no physical collision has occurred! Figure 21.5 demonstrates a problem when objects actually collide.

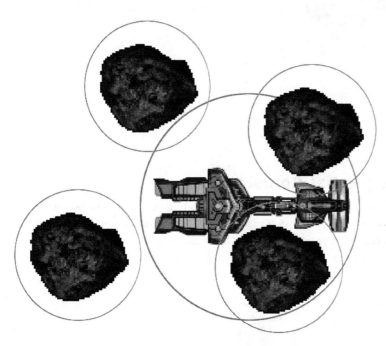

FIGURE 21.4
Bounding circles produce similar results in collision testing.

There really is no rule that you must use one technique or the other when dealing with certain game genres; it's normal to use a mix of the two. In some cases, where a game object has an odd shape (such as the spaceship here), it is helpful to use two bounding shapes to accommodate the object. For instance, a pair of smaller boxes or circles around the fore and aft parts of the ship would work well and produce very good results. For a simpler game with one collision test per object, a single bounding rectangle will suffice.

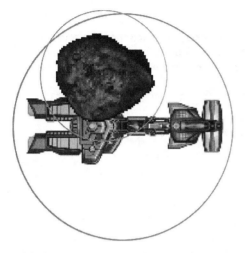

FIGURE 21.5
Physical collision between the two shapes shows the problem with this technique.

Demonstrating Collisions

To demonstrate collision detection, we will build a project called Collision Demo. It is somewhat similar to the project in the previous hour but is considerably enhanced to effectively illustrate this subject with flair. First, we'll make some required enhancements to the engine, including work on the `Engine` class, the `Sprite` class, and then we'll write the code for the program.

Engine Enhancements

The `Engine` class must be modified to handle collision detection internally to properly demonstrate engine-level functionality. We could implement a collision method in the main game and be done with it, but this approach is far more useful long term. These enhancements will presume to use new features not yet added to the `Sprite` class; rest assured, we will modify `Sprite` soon enough.

Remember the abstract methods? We have taken them for granted for several hours now, but now it's time to add a new one! The new `collision()` method notifies the game when a collision occurs. Only a single `Sprite` parameter is needed, thanks to new properties in the `Sprite` class that support collision processing (noted in bold). All these changes will be made to the Engine.java file.

WATCH OUT

There may be minor differences between the code shown on these pages and the code found in the project files. These changes are known, not mistakes. Occasionally a line has to be wrapped or a variable declared slightly differently to save space. The code listed on these pages is always copied from the final version of a source code file.

```java
/**
 * Abstract methods that must be implemented in the subclass!
 */
public abstract void init();
public abstract void load();
public abstract void draw();
public abstract void update();
public abstract void collision(Sprite sprite);
```

Further along in the Engine.java source code file, we need to make additional changes so that the engine automatically tests for collisions when a Sprite object in the entity manager is flagged for it. So, look for the `run()` method. The required changes are also noted next in the `run()` method. Note also that `import android.graphics.Paint.*` is required (and Eclipse will notify you if it isn't already in your engine source listing).

```java
@Override
public void run() {
    Log.d("Engine","Engine.run start");

    ListIterator<Sprite> iter=null, iterA=null, iterB=null;

    Timer frameTimer = new Timer();
    int frameCount=0;
    int frameRate=0;
    long startTime=0;
    long timeDiff=0;

    while (p_running) {
        // Process frame only if not paused
        if (p_paused) continue;

        // Calculate frame rate
        frameCount++;
        startTime = frameTimer.getElapsed();
        if (frameTimer.stopwatch(1000)) {
            frameRate = frameCount;
            frameCount = 0;

            //reset touch input count
            p_numPoints = 0;
```

```
}

// Call abstract update method in sub-class
update();

/**
 * Test for collisions in the sprite group
 * Note that this takes place outside of rendering
 */
iterA = p_group.listIterator();
while (iterA.hasNext()) {
    Sprite sprA = (Sprite)iterA.next();
    if (!sprA.getCollidable()) continue;

    /*
     * Improvement to prevent double collision testing
     */
    if (sprA.getCollided())
        continue; //skip to next iterator

    //iterate the list again
    //ListIterator<Sprite>
    iterB = p_group.listIterator();
    while (iterB.hasNext()) {
        Sprite sprB = (Sprite)iterB.next();
        if (!sprB.getCollidable()) continue;

        /*
         * Improvement to prevent double collision testing
         */
        if (sprB.getCollided())
            continue; //skip to next iterator

        //do not collide with itself
        if (sprA == sprB) continue;

        /*
         * Ignore sprites with the same ID? This is an important
         * consideration. Decide if your game requires it or not.
         */
        if (sprA.getIdentifier() == sprB.getIdentifier())
            continue;

        if (collisionCheck(sprA, sprB)) {
            sprA.setCollided(true);
            sprA.setOffender(sprB);
            sprB.setCollided(true);
            sprB.setOffender(sprA);
```

```
            break; //exit while
        }
    }
}//while

// Rendering section, lock the canvas
// Only proceed if the SurfaceView is valid
    if (beginDrawing()) {

        /**
         * Note: In a future hour this will be moved to
         * the draw() method call so the user can define
         * the color of the background.
         */
        p_canvas.drawColor(Color.BLACK);

     /**
      * Draw the group entities with transforms
      */
    iter = p_group.listIterator();
    while (iter.hasNext()) {
        Sprite spr = (Sprite)iter.next();
        spr.animate();
        spr.draw();

        /**
         * For collision testing purposes, draw boundary
         * around each sprite (temporary).
         */
        if (spr.getCollidable()) {
            if (spr.getCollided()) {
                p_paintDraw.setStyle(Style.STROKE);
                p_paintDraw.setColor(Color.RED);
                p_canvas.drawRect(spr.getBoundsScaled(),
                p_paintDraw);
            }
        }
    }

    // Call abstract draw method in sub-class
    draw();

     /**
      * Print engine debug information (temporary).
      */
```

```
            int x = p_canvas.getWidth()-150;
            p_canvas.drawText("ENGINE", x, 20, p_paintFont);
            p_canvas.drawText(toString(frameRate) + " FPS", x, 40,
                p_paintFont);
            p_canvas.drawText("Pauses: " + toString(p_pauseCount),
                x, 60, p_paintFont);

            /**
             *  Complete the rendering process by unlocking the canvas
             */
            endDrawing();
        }

        /**
         * Notify game of any sprites that have collided
         */
        iter = p_group.listIterator();
        while (iter.hasNext()) {
            Sprite spr = (Sprite)iter.next();
            collision(spr); //notify game
            spr.setCollided(false);
        }

        // Calculate frame update time and sleep if necessary
        timeDiff = frameTimer.getElapsed() - startTime;
        long updatePeriod = p_sleepTime - timeDiff;
        if (updatePeriod > 0) {
            try {
                Thread.sleep( updatePeriod );
            }
            catch(InterruptedException e) {}
        }

    }//while
    Log.d("Engine","Engine.run end");
    System.exit(RESULT_OK);
}
```

The enhancements to run() called on one support method: the collisionCheck() method, which has not been written yet. Add this new collision method to the Engine.java file as well.

```
/**
 * Collision detection
 */
public boolean collisionCheck(Sprite A, Sprite B) {
```

```
    boolean test = Rect.intersects(A.getBoundsScaled(),
        B.getBoundsScaled());
    return test;
}
```

Sprite Enhancements

Quite a few modifications must be made to the `Sprite` class to support collision handling! First, add the following new private properties to the class:

```
private boolean p_collidable, p_collided;
private Sprite p_offender;
private String p_name;
private int p_identifier;
```

Next, initialize these new properties in the constructor method:

```
p_collidable = p_collided = false;
p_offender = null;
p_name = "";
p_identifier = 0;
```

No changes are made to existing methods, but we do need all these new helper and get/set methods to make collision handling possible!

```
public boolean getCollidable() {
    return p_collidable;
}

public void setCollidable(boolean value) {
    p_collidable = value;
}

public boolean getCollided() {
    return p_collided;
}

public void setCollided(boolean value) {
    p_collided = value;
}

public Sprite getOffender() {
    return p_offender;
}

public void setOffender(Sprite value) {
    p_offender = value;
}
```

```
public String getName() {
    return p_name;
}

public void setName(String value) {
    p_name = value;
}

public int getIdentifier() {
    return p_identifier;
}

public void setIdentifier(int value) {
    p_identifier = value;
}

public Rect getBounds() {
    Rect r = new Rect(position.x, position.y,
            position.x + p_width, position.y + p_height);
    return r;
}

public Rect getBoundsScaled() {
    Rect r = getBounds();
    r.right = (int) (r.left + r.width() * p_scale.x);
    r.bottom = (int) (r.top + r.height() * p_scale.y);
    return r;
}
```

Collision Demo Source

The Collision Demo program is a project that uses the engine library again, as usual. The goal of this program is to demonstrate sprite collisions in real-time by highlighting collisions as they occur. This is done by drawing a red box around sprites that are in a collision state. Figure 21.6 shows the program in action.

WATCH OUT

The engine's collision code has some debugging/testing features that will not be found in the Engine.java file in the next hour. Some of the code in this hour is temporary, and the way collisions are handled will also be updated in the following hour to take into account null values.

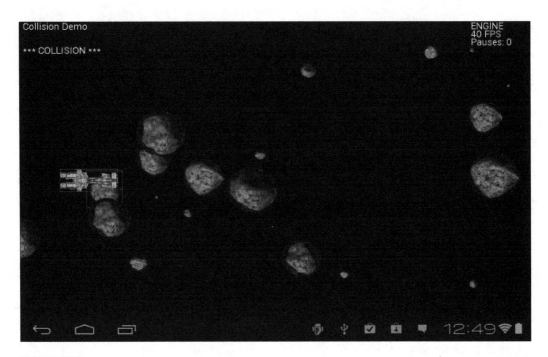

FIGURE 21.6
The Collision Demo highlights sprite collisions in real-time.

Here is the source code for the Collision Demo program. As expected, it is again on the short side, thanks to the engine.

```
/**
 * H21 Collision Demo
 * Requires game.engine.Engine to build.
 */
package android.program;
import java.util.Random;
import android.graphics.*;
import android.renderscript.*;
import game.engine.*;

public class Game extends game.engine.Engine {
    Canvas canvas;
    Paint paint;
    game.engine.Timer timer;
    Random rand;
    Texture asteroid_image;
    Sprite ship;
```

```
Texture ship_image;
boolean collision;

public Game() {
    canvas = null;
    paint = new Paint();
    timer = new Timer();
    rand = new Random();
    asteroid_image = null;
    ship = null;
    ship_image = null;
    collision = false;
}

public void init() {
    setScreenOrientation(Engine.ScreenModes.LANDSCAPE);
}

public void load() {
    asteroid_image = new Texture(this);
    if (!asteroid_image.loadFromAsset("asteroid_sheet.png")) {
        fatalError("Error loading asteroid_sheet");
    }

    int w = getScreenWidth();
    int h = getScreenHeight();
    Rect boundary = new Rect(-60,-60,w,h);

    /**
     * Add very fast warping background sprites
     */
    for (int n=0; n<10; n++) {
        Sprite ast = new Sprite(this, 60, 60, 8);
        ast.setTexture(asteroid_image);
        ast.position = new Point(100+w+rand.nextInt(w), rand.nextInt(h-60));
        ast.addAnimation(new FrameAnimation(0, 63, 1));
        Float2 vel = new Float2(rand.nextFloat()*-100.0f, 0); //fast
        ast.addAnimation(new WarpBehavior(boundary, 60, 60, vel));
        ast.setFrame(rand.nextInt(63));
        ast.setScale(0.1f + rand.nextFloat()); //small

        ast.setCollidable(false);
        ast.setName("scenery");
        ast.setIdentifier(10); //arbitrary # (your choice)

        addToGroup(ast);
    }
```

```
/**
 * Add slower collidable warping sprites
 */
for (int n=0; n<10; n++) {
    Sprite ast = new Sprite(this, 60, 60, 8);
    ast.setTexture(asteroid_image);
    ast.position = new Point(100+w+rand.nextInt(w), rand.nextInt(h-60));
    ast.addAnimation(new FrameAnimation(0, 63, 1));
    Float2 vel = new Float2(rand.nextFloat()*-10.0f, 0); //slow
    ast.addAnimation(new WarpBehavior(boundary, 60, 60, vel));
    ast.setFrame(rand.nextInt(63));
    ast.setScale(1.5f + rand.nextFloat()); //large

    ast.setCollidable(true);
    ast.setName("asteroid");
    ast.setIdentifier(100); //arbitrary # (your choice)

    addToGroup(ast);
}

ship = new Sprite(this);
ship_image = new Texture(this);
if (!ship_image.loadFromAsset("ship3.png")) {
    fatalError("Error loading ship3");
}
ship.setTexture(ship_image);
ship.position = new Point(100, h/2);
ship.addAnimation(new ThrobAnimation(0.8f, 1.2f, 0.001f, true));
ship.addAnimation(new FenceBehavior(new Rect(0,0,200,h-64)));

ship.setName("ship");
ship.setIdentifier(200); //arbitrary #
ship.setCollidable(true);
addToGroup(ship);
}

public void draw() {
    canvas = getCanvas();
    drawText("Collision Demo", 10, 20);
    //ship.draw();

    if (collision) {
        drawText("*** COLLISION ***", 10, 80);
        collision = false;
    }
}
```

```
public void update() {
    Point touch=null;
    int inputs = getTouchInputs();

    if (timer.stopwatch(20)) {
        if (inputs > 0) {
            touch = getTouchPoint(0);
            if (touch.x < 200) {
                if (touch.y < ship.position.y) {
                    ship.position.y -= 5.0f;
                }
                else {
                    ship.position.y += 5.0f;
                }
            }
        }

        ship.animate();

    }
}

/**
 * New abstract collision() method called by engine
 */
public void collision(Sprite sprite) {
    Sprite other = sprite.getOffender();
    if (other == null) return;
    if (sprite.getName() == "ship") {
        if (other.getName() == "asteroid") {
            collision = true;
        }
    }
}
}
```

Summary

This hour introduced the important subject of collision detection. While studying the concepts behind bounding rectangle and bounding circle detection, we made some impressive new enhancements to the engine that enable, via Sprite properties, automatic collision detection with in-game notifications!

Q&A

Q. Discuss the pros and cons of automatically detecting collisions in a game. In some cases, will it ever be used at all? In other cases, will it be used extensively?

A. Answers will vary.

Q. This hour's example is a good test of the performance of the code on various Android devices. If you have an Android device, try the game on your device and note the difference in frame rate compared with the emulator. What do you think the result will be?

A. Results will vary. Discuss before and after running the tests.

Workshop

Quiz

1. What type of collision detection uses a rectangle around each object?

2. What type of collision detection uses the radius of a circle around each object?

3. Which Java method is called to test for collisions in the engine code?

Answers

1. Box collision (or bounding rectangle)

2. Radial collision (or bounding circles)

3. `Rect.intersects()`

Activities

The Collision Demo does a pretty good job of automatically detecting collisions, but it is also a bit slow. Be sure to selectively turn collision on and off for sprites that don't require it. See what kinds of results you can get by changing the collision method to radial for the asteroids in this project.

HOUR 22
Using Linear Velocity for Realistic Movement

What You'll Learn in This Hour:

▶ How to calculate velocity from any direction

▶ How to move based on rotation angle

▶ How to calculate the angle to a target

▶ How to make final changes to the Android game engine

This hour expands on the concepts learned in the last two hours—dealing with transforms and collision detection—to move objects in any direction based on velocity of an angle. We will derive the math calculations needed to move a sprite in any desired direction based on its rotation angle (from a top-down perspective). Moving a sprite at a desired angle is a very important need in most games, so you will no doubt use this technique extensively in your own projects. The next related calculations involve "looking" at a desired target point from a source point and moving toward that target location. Perhaps this might be considered the opposite of calculating velocity from a direction angle. In this case, we know *where* we want the sprite to go, but we don't yet know how to point the sprite in the direction of the target. What we're studying in this hour is basic rocket science, with help from some basic trigonometry to solve these problems. This hour also sees the final changes to the Android game engine!

Calculating Velocity from a Direction

We have done a lot of work already with sprite transforms, so now it's time to put some of these new features to the test in a real-world situation that often comes up in game projects. We'll have a sprite move on the screen based on user input and move in the direction it is facing. This requires some familiar trigonometry functions used in a creative way.

To begin, we need to understand the starting point for trigonometric calculations. The artwork in a game is often oriented with the "front" or "nose" pointing upward. But in our math calculations, that starting point will always be to the right, or 90 degrees clockwise from the up direction, as shown in Figure 22.1.

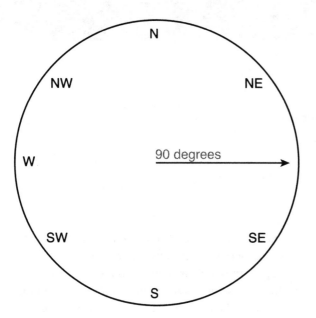

FIGURE 22.1
Trigonometry functions assume angle 0 is right, not up.

WATCH OUT

Math functions dealing with rotation angles and velocities *always* work with radians, not degrees. Using degrees in code is fine, but angles must be converted to radians during calculations. This can be done with `Math.toDegrees()` and `Math.toRadians()`.

We use cosine to calculate the X component and sine to calculate the Y component for the velocity of an object. You can use the `Math.cos()` and `Math.sin()` methods to perform these calculations. The sole parameter passed to both of these methods is the `angle` that an object is facing or moving toward. The angle will be any value from 0 to 360 degrees, including decimal values for partial degrees. When making the calculations, the angle must be converted to radians. Suppose the angle is 10 degrees. We convert this to radians with

```
float radians = Math.toRadians( 10 );
// radians = 0.174532925
```

The angular velocity is calculated using this radian value, rounded to 0.1745 for our purposes (although the complete floating-point value is used with all decimal places in memory).

VelocityX = Math.cos(0.1745)

VelocityY = Math.sin(0.1745)

Figure 22.2 shows a circle with the angle and calculated values. Figure 22.3 shows the relationship between sine and cosine on a right triangle to determine velocity.

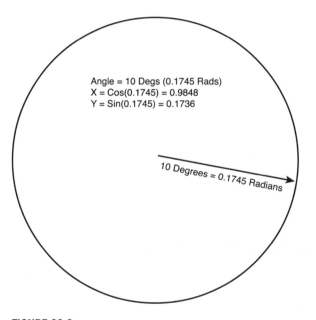

FIGURE 22.2
Calculating angular velocity.

The results are X = 0.9848 and Y = 0.1736, as shown in the illustration. Consider the direction the arrow is facing in the illustration (10 degrees). The X and Y velocity values make sense, given that angle. Considering pixel movement on the screen, at this angle a sprite will move in the X axis much more than in the Y axis, a ratio of about five and a half to one (5.5:1). So when a sprite is moving across the screen at an angle of 10 degrees, it will move 5.5 pixels to the right (+X) for every 1 pixel down (+Y). If the angle were 180, for instance, the arrow would be pointing to the left, which would result in a negative X velocity.

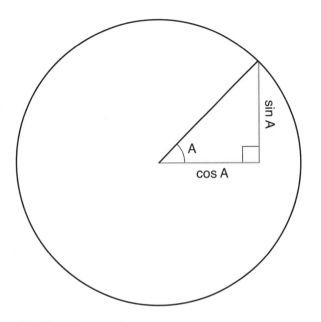

FIGURE 22.3
The relationship between sine and cosine on a right triangle; the hypotenuse gives us our velocity values.

"Pointing" a Sprite in the Direction of Movement

You might be thinking, "Didn't we just do this?" That's an astute question! In fact, in the previous section, you saw how an angle can be used to calculate an X and Y velocity. Now we're going to do the reverse: given the direction a sprite is already moving, we want it to "point" in that direction so that it looks right. For instance, one use for it would be making a spaceship sprite to rotate around a planet and continue to point in the direction it is facing. To more accurately describe this situation, we want a sprite to move and point toward a target.

BY THE WAY

The trigonometry ("circular") functions we've been using may be considered elementary physics. In a sense, then, we're working on our own simple physics engine here, which is a bit of a stretch but still compelling!

Have you ever played a real-time strategy (RTS) game where you can select units, right-click somewhere on the map, and they would move toward that location? That is the basic way most RTS games work. Along the path, if your units encounter enemy units, they will usually fight or shoot at the enemy, unless you tell them to target a specific enemy unit with a similar right-click on it.

We can do something like that with the concept covered here. Sure, a lot more is involved in an RTS game than just moving toward a destination, but at the core of the game is code similar to what we're going to learn about here.

Calculating Angle to Target

In the previous section, we used `Math.cos()` and `Math.sin()` to calculate the respective X and Y components of velocity. These values could then be used to move a sprite in any desired direction. There's a related calculation we can perform to do the opposite: given a sprite's current location and a target location, calculate the angle needed to get there.

We won't be using sine and cosine to calculate the angle. Those trig functions are useful only if you know the angle already. The reverse is knowing where we are already headed—what is that angle?

This concept is powerful in terms of gameplay! Suppose you do know the angle and use it to calculate velocity, then send a bullet on its way, like we did in the previous example. Okay, that's great. But what if you wanted to slow that sprite down, make it stop, and even begin moving in reverse? Not in terms of a bullet, but any sprite, like a spaceship or a car? We can do these things.

BY THE WAY

This code could be used to cause one sprite to continually point at another sprite. Instead of using a target screen coordinate, use the location of a moving target sprite instead!

The secret behind this targeting concept is a trig function called *arctangent*. Arctangent is an inverse trigonometric function; specifically, the inverse of tangent, which itself is opposite over adjacent (side a divided by side b), shown in Figure 22.4. I don't want to get into deriving these trig functions, so let's jump to the `Math` method name. There are two versions: `Math.atan()`, which takes one parameter, and `Math.atan2()`, which takes two parameters (double y, double x; note that y comes before x). This math function returns the angle whose tangent is the quotient of two specified numbers.

We can't just pass the position (X and Y) of a target screen coordinate to this function because the two parameters are actually *delta* values (the difference between the X and Y values of two points). That's not as bad as it sounds, as any math major will tell you. Delta is just the difference between the two points: X2 – X1 and Y2 – Y1.

```
double deltaX = x2 - x1;
double deltaY = y2 - y1;
```

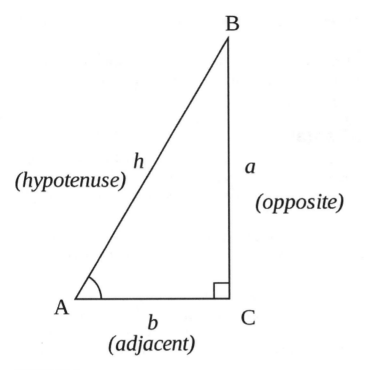

FIGURE 22.4
A right triangle is the basis for trigonometry. Illustration courtesy of Wikipedia.

Having these variables ready, we can calculate the angle toward a target with arctangent (with two deltas), like so:

```
double angle = Math.atan2(deltaY, deltaX);
```

Figure 22.5 is an illustration of velocity-based movement. By using floating-point values for X and Y, a sprite can be made to move very slowly—less than one pixel per cycle.

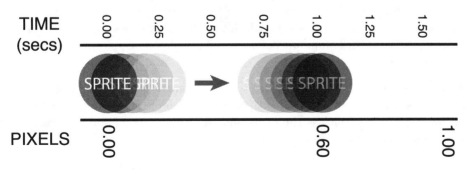

FIGURE 22.5
Using velocity allows for subpixel movement with a float rather than an int.

Enhancing the Engine

There are quite a few enhancements to the engine in addition to the use of velocity. Shifting from manual to automatic velocity is not the sole purpose of these changes; with these enhancements, a game will have the potential to become free of gameplay code and fully based on *behavior* classes. It should be possible to write a simple game entirely using behaviors, while the main game source just does initialization. That functionality would be a very successful test of the engine.

BY THE WAY

The improvements you make to the engine here will result in the final version of the engine. The last three hours will share the engine library produced this hour.

Changes to the Sprite Class

The `Sprite` class needs to be tweaked to support subpixel translation. Presently, a `Point` is used to represent the position of a sprite. That has to be changed to a `Float2` to maintain subpixel positioning between frames (necessary for finer translation control). In the variables section listed next, note the change to `position` and the addition of a new property called `p_alive`.

```
public class Sprite {
    private Engine p_engine;
    private Canvas p_canvas;
    private Texture p_texture;
    private Paint p_paint;
    //public Point position; //CUT
    public Float2 position; //ADDED
    private int p_width, p_height;
    private int p_columns;
    private int p_alpha;
    private LinkedList<Animation> p_anims;
    private int p_frame;
    private Float2 p_scale;
    private float p_rotation;
    private Matrix p_mat_translate;
    private Matrix p_mat_scale;
    private Matrix p_mat_rotate;
    private Matrix p_matrix;
    private Bitmap p_frameBitmap;
    private Canvas p_frameCanvas;
    private boolean p_collidable, p_collided;
    private Sprite p_offender;
    private String p_name;
    private int p_identifier;
    private Float2 p_velocity; //ADDED
    private boolean p_alive; //ADDED
```

Down in the listing a ways, you'll find the `Sprite` constructor. Make the changes noted.

```
public Sprite(Engine engine, int width, int height, int columns) {
    p_engine = engine;
    p_width = width;
    p_height = height;
    p_columns = columns;
    p_canvas = null;
    p_texture = new Texture(engine);
    p_alpha = 255;
    p_paint = new Paint();
    p_anims = new LinkedList<Animation>();
    //position = new Point(0,0); //DELETE
    position = new Float2(0,0); //ADD
    p_frame = 0;
    p_scale = new Float2(1.0f,1.0f);
    p_rotation = 0.0f;
    p_mat_translate = new Matrix();
    p_mat_scale = new Matrix();
    p_mat_rotate = new Matrix();
    p_matrix = new Matrix();
    p_frameBitmap = null;
    p_frameCanvas = null;
    p_collidable = p_collided = false;
    p_offender = null;
    p_name = "";
    p_identifier = 0;
    p_velocity = new Float2(0,0); //ADD
    p_alive = true; //ADD
}
```

Next, look for the `animate()` method and add the new adjustment method call.

```
public void animate() {
    if (p_anims.size() == 0) return;

    ListIterator<Animation> iterator = p_anims.listIterator();
    while (iterator.hasNext()) {
        Animation anim = iterator.next();
        if (anim.animating) {
            p_frame = anim.adjustFrame(p_frame);
            p_alpha = anim.adjustAlpha(p_alpha);
            p_rotation = anim.adjustRotation(p_rotation);
            p_scale = anim.adjustScale(p_scale);
            position = anim.adjustPosition(position);
            p_velocity = anim.adjustVelocity(p_velocity);//NEW
            p_alive = anim.adjustAlive(p_alive);//NEW
        }
        else
```

```
        {
            p_anims.remove(anim);
            return;
        }
    }
}
```

Later in the code listing, look for the get/set methods and make the changes noted for position:

```
//public void setPosition(Point position) { //EDIT
public void setPosition(Float2 position) {
    this.position = position;
}


//public Point getPosition() { //EDIT
public Float2 getPosition() {
    return position;
}
```

A little ways down, look for getBounds() and getBoundsScaled(), and change Rect to RectF (taking into account that position was changed from Point to Float2).

```
public RectF getBounds() { //change to RectF
    RectF r = new RectF(position.x, position.y,
            position.x + p_width, position.y + p_height);
    return r;
}


public RectF getBoundsScaled() { //change to RectF
    RectF r = getBounds();
    r.right = (int) (r.left + r.width() * p_scale.x);
    r.bottom = (int) (r.top + r.height() * p_scale.y);
    return r;
}
```

The last major change involves adding get/set method pairs for the *velocity* and *alive* properties.

```
public Float2 getVelocity() {
    return p_velocity;
}


public void setVelocity(Float2 value) {
    p_velocity = value;
}


public boolean getAlive() {
    return p_alive;
}
```

```java
public void setAlive(boolean value) {
    p_alive = value;
}
```

Enhancing the Animation Class

An important new behavior needs to be added to the animation system: the capability to *destroy* a sprite and remove it from the group. A new property will be added, *animating*, so that the animation can be selectively turned on or off. The adjustPosition() method is changed, and two new methods are added to manipulate the velocity and animation state.

```java
/**
 * Animation Class
 * Requires game.engine.Engine to build.
 */
package game.engine;
//import android.graphics.Point;
import android.renderscript.Float2;

public class Animation {
    public boolean animating;

    public Animation() {
        animating = false;
    }

    public int adjustFrame(int original) {
        return original;
    }

    public int adjustAlpha(int original) {
        return original;
    }

    public Float2 adjustScale(Float2 original) {
        return original;
    }

    public float adjustRotation(float original) {
        return original;
    }

    //NOTE CHANGES!
    //public Point adjustPosition(Point original) {
    public Float2 adjustPosition(Float2 original) {
        return original;
    }
```

```
    //NEW METHOD!
    public Float2 adjustVelocity(Float2 original) {
        return original;
    }

    //NEW METHOD!
    public boolean adjustAlive(boolean original) {
        return original;
    }
}
```

Classing the Velocity Behavior

The VelocityBehavior class is a new Animation derivative with a simple purpose: to cause an object to move in a certain direction based on an angle of direction (in degrees, for convenience). We will use this new behavior for firing rockets from the spaceship to blow up the asteroids (and other types of objects in the next hour). This behavior will modify the *position* and *alive* properties of the sprite it is applied to via adjustPosition() and adjustAlive(), respectively. The really interesting thing about this behavior class is how it uses a timer to autodestroy the sprite after its time has come up.

We could optionally use a new behavior that causes a sprite to self-destruct when it reaches a certain boundary. Instead of warping or fencing, for instance, we could have a sprite die when it hits a boundary. That could be very useful for firing bullets or rockets! But we'll take the timed approach this time—a rocket fired from the ship has a two-second lifetime. Because it moves very fast, it will clear the screen before running out of time. Another option you may enjoy using is giving the bullets a short term of about one-half second, which effectively limits the range of shots being fired from the ship (and looks really great, too). These are all great features for an arcade-style shoot-em-up game like the one we're building, step by step.

This class manipulates an internal velocity value, rather than the new velocity property added to the Sprite class. If you come up with a new behavior that deals with velocity on your own, you may use the built-in velocity property or an independent property—it's up to you.

```
/**
 * VelocityBehavior class - derived from Animation
 * Requires game.engine.Engine to build.
 */
package game.engine;
//import android.graphics.Point;
import android.renderscript.Float2;

public class VelocityBehavior extends Animation {
    private double p_angle;
    private double p_multiplier;
```

```
private double p_velX, p_velY;
private int p_lifetime;
private Timer p_timer;

public VelocityBehavior(double angleDegrees, float speedMultiplier,
        int lifetime) {
    animating = true;
    p_lifetime = lifetime;
    p_timer = new Timer();
    p_angle = angleDegrees;
    p_multiplier = speedMultiplier;
    double angleRadians = Math.toRadians(p_angle);
    //calculate X velocity
    p_velX = Math.cos(angleRadians) * p_multiplier;
    //calculate Y velocity
    p_velY = Math.sin(angleRadians) * p_multiplier;
}

@Override
//public Point adjustPosition(Point original) {
public Float2 adjustPosition(Float2 original) {
    //Point modified = new Point(original.x,original.y);
    Float2 modified = new Float2(original.x,original.y);
    modified.x +=  p_velX;
    modified.y += p_velY;
    return modified;
}

@Override
public boolean adjustAlive(boolean original) {
    boolean modified = original;
    if (p_lifetime > 0) {
        if (p_timer.stopwatch(p_lifetime)) {
            modified = false;
        }
    }
    return modified;
}
}
```

Updating the Circular Movement Class

Now that we're into doing both animations and behaviors, it will make sense to rename this one from CircularMovementAnimation to a name more in tune with behavior rather than appearance: Let's use CirclingBehavior. After all, a sprite with this behavior just circles around a center point at a certain radius, so it's an apt name. You can do this by right-clicking the class file in Package Explorer and choosing Refactor, Rename. This is a useful tool in Eclipse that will rename any references to the class in your other code files as well.

In addition to the name, some changes are required to bring this class in line with the newly enhanced base Animation class. Note the changes in italic and bold.

```
/**
 * CirclingBehavior Class
 */
package game.engine;
//import android.graphics.Point;
import android.renderscript.Float2;

public class CirclingBehavior extends Animation {
    private int p_radius;
    //private Point p_center;
    private Float2 p_center;
    private double p_angle;
    private float p_velocity;

    public CirclingBehavior(int centerx, int centery, int radius,
            double angle, float velocity) {
        animating = true;
        //this.p_center = new Point(centerx,centery);
        this.p_center = new Float2(centerx,centery);
        this.p_radius = radius;
        this.p_angle = angle;
        this.p_velocity = velocity;
    }

    @Override
    //public Point adjustPosition(Point original) {
    public Float2 adjustPosition(Float2 original) {
        //Point modified = original;
        Float2 modified = original;
        p_angle += p_velocity;
        modified.x = (int)(p_center.x + (float)(Math.cos(p_angle) *
                p_radius));
        modified.y = (int)(p_center.y + (float)(Math.sin(p_angle) *
                p_radius));
        return modified;
    }
}
```

Updating the Fence Behavior

This is another class that requires changes to bring it in line with the new changes to `Animation`. The changes involve replacing `Point` with `Float2`, and `Rect` to `RectF`. The changes are shown in italic and bold for easy reference.

```
/**
 * FenceBehavior Class
 */
package game.engine;
//import android.graphics.Point;
//import android.graphics.Rect;
import android.graphics.RectF;
import android.renderscript.Float2;

public class FenceBehavior extends Animation {
    //private Rect p_fence;
    private RectF p_fence;

    //public FenceBehavior(Rect fence) {
    public FenceBehavior(RectF fence) {
        p_fence = fence;
        animating = true; //just means it is active
    }

    @Override
    //public Point adjustPosition(Point original) {
    public Float2 adjustPosition(Float2 original) {
        //Point modified = original;
        Float2 modified = original;

        if (modified.x < p_fence.left)
            modified.x = p_fence.left;
        else if (modified.x > p_fence.right)
            modified.x = p_fence.right;
        if (modified.y < p_fence.top)
            modified.y = p_fence.top;
        else if (modified.y > p_fence.bottom)
            modified.y = p_fence.bottom;
        return modified;
    }
}
```

BY THE WAY

You may be wondering why we didn't do this in advance in the previous hours when the classes were originally written. Does this give you a jaded perspective on the reliability of the code in this book? It shouldn't! This reflects the real-world evolution of an engine to accommodate changes as they arise while working on a game. After a certain point, all the changes will have been made, and the feature set of the engine will be sufficient so that no new changes are needed. This is the last time any changes will be made to the engine. In the remaining two hours you will see how easy it is to make a game now that the hard part is done!

Updating the Warp Behavior

The `WarpBehavior` class also requires changes to conform with the new `Animation` base class. Remember, this isn't a fail situation, because the engine is a work in progress and you're seeing it take shape in real-time, so to speak.

```
/**
 * WarpBehavior class - derived from Animation
 * Requires game.engine.Engine to build.
 */
package game.engine;
import android.graphics.*;
import android.renderscript.Float2;

public class WarpBehavior extends Animation {
    //private Rect p_bounds;
    private RectF p_bounds;
    private Float2 p_velocity;
    private Point p_size;

    //public WarpBehavior(Rect bounds, int w, int h, Float2 velocity) {
    public WarpBehavior(RectF bounds, int w, int h, Float2 velocity) {
        this(bounds, new Point(w,h), velocity);
    }

    //public WarpBehavior(Rect bounds, Point size, Float2 velocity) {
    public WarpBehavior(RectF bounds, Point size, Float2 velocity) {
        animating = true;
        p_bounds = bounds;
        p_velocity = velocity;
        p_size = size;
    }

    @Override
    //public Point adjustPosition(Point original) {
    public Float2 adjustPosition(Float2 original) {
        //Point modified = original;
        Float2 modified = original;
        modified.x += p_velocity.x;
        modified.y += p_velocity.y;
```

```
        if (modified.x < p_bounds.left)
            modified.x = p_bounds.right-p_size.x;
        else if (modified.x > p_bounds.right-p_size.x)
            modified.x = p_bounds.left;

        if (modified.y < p_bounds.top)
            modified.y = p_bounds.bottom-p_size.y;
        else if (modified.y > p_bounds.bottom-p_size.y)
            modified.y = p_bounds.top;

        return modified;
    }
}
```

Engine Enhancements

Quite a few changes are required in the `Engine` class to bring it up to spec with the animation
and sprite changes. The first change involves a modification of the collision iterators to support
the new *alive* property. Both iterator loops are tight through the use of `continue` as a conditional break, so the code is already quite efficient. This additional conditional test using the
`alive` property makes it possible to remove `Sprite` entities from the managed list.

```
/**
 * Test for collisions in the sprite group.
 * Note that this takes place outside of rendering.
 */
iterA = p_group.listIterator();
while (iterA.hasNext()) {
    Sprite sprA = (Sprite)iterA.next();
    if (!sprA.getAlive()) continue;
    if (!sprA.getCollidable()) continue;

    /*
     * Improvement to prevent double collision testing
     */
    if (sprA.getCollided())
        continue; //skip to next iterator

    //iterate the list again
    iterB = p_group.listIterator();
    while (iterB.hasNext()) {
        Sprite sprB = (Sprite)iterB.next();
        if (!sprB.getAlive()) continue;
        if (!sprB.getCollidable()) continue;

        /*
         * Improvement to prevent double collision testing
```

```
        */
        if (sprB.getCollided())
            continue; //skip to next iterator

        //do not collide with itself
        if (sprA == sprB) continue;

        /**
         * Ignore sprites with the same ID.
         */
        if (sprA.getIdentifier() == sprB.getIdentifier())
            continue;

        if (collisionCheck(sprA, sprB)) {
            sprA.setCollided(true);
            sprA.setOffender(sprB);
            sprB.setCollided(true);
            sprB.setOffender(sprA);
            break; //exit while
        }
    }
}
}
```

The next change is also made to run(). The rendering code takes place between calls to begin-Drawing() and endDrawing(). This change is simply part of the evolving engine. Previously, there was quite a bit of debugging going on here (such as outlining colliding objects with a red box). Note also that the *alive* property is also taken into account before animating or drawing a sprite.

There is still some unnecessary code here—the part where "ENGINE" and "FPS" and "Pauses" are displayed in the upper-right corner of the screen. I'll leave these in for now. Perhaps there should be a flag property that will selectively print this info while in a debug mode or something.

The most important change here is that draw() was moved to the top, and the call to p_canvs. drawColor() is commented out. We don't want to just clear the screen anymore—from now on, the background is handled by the game code, not the engine. Thus, draw() is up top in the render section, so we can clear the screen. Previously, draw() was below the entity group code, so that it was impossible to clear the screen or draw a background without hiding the managed game objects.

```
if (beginDrawing()) {

    //p_canvas.drawColor(Color.BLACK);

    //MOVED ABOVE THE p_group SECTION!
    // Call abstract draw method in sub-class
    draw();
```

```
/**
 * Draw the group entities with transforms
 */
iter = p_group.listIterator();
while (iter.hasNext()) {
    Sprite spr = (Sprite)iter.next();
    if (spr.getAlive()) {
        spr.animate();
        spr.draw();
    }
}

/**
 * Print some engine debug info.
 */
int x = p_canvas.getWidth()-150;
p_canvas.drawText("ENGINE", x, 20, p_paintFont);
p_canvas.drawText(toString(frameRate) + " FPS", x, 40,
    p_paintFont);
p_canvas.drawText("Pauses: " + toString(p_pauseCount),
    x, 60, p_paintFont);

// Complete the rendering process by unlocking the canvas
endDrawing();
}
```

Down a little ways in the `run()` method, we need to add some new cleanup code. When you're making a fast-paced action game like a scrolling shoot-em-up, a lot of objects are created and destroyed every cycle (such as bullets and explosions). Now that sprites have an *alive* property, we can clean them out of the group when they're no longer needed. Add this new code near the end of `run()` as shown in bold.

Look for the section of code that calls the `collision()` function in the game sub-class file. It should look like this:

```
/**
 * Notify game of any sprites that have collided.
 * Note that this is a very simplistic implementation,
 * and this code will be improved in the next hour.
 */
iter = p_group.listIterator();
while (iter.hasNext()) {
    Sprite spr = (Sprite)iter.next();
    collision(spr); //notify game
    spr.setCollided(false);
}
```

Completely replace that entire section of code with this new code. This is a more advanced version of the cleanup code in `run()` that removes dead sprites and checks for nulls before calling the `collision()` method in the game sub-class file.

WATCH OUT

This is a *significant* change to the collision logic in the entity manager. You may find it helpful to open the *H23 Game Engine Library* project, go into the Engine.java file, and note the complete code for `run()` just to ensure you understand how it flows together. By the way, H23 is not a typo: Both Hour 22 and Hour 23 share the engine project. These are the final changes you will have to make to the engine!

```
/*
 * Do some cleanup: collision notification, removing
 * 'dead' sprites from the list.
 */
iter = p_group.listIterator();
Sprite spr = null;
while (iter.hasNext()) {
    spr = (Sprite)iter.next();

    //remove from list if flagged
    if (!spr.getAlive()) {
        iter.remove();
        continue;
    }

    //is collision enabled for this sprite?
    if (spr.getCollidable()) {

        //has this sprite collided with anything?
        if (spr.getCollided()) {

            //is the target a valid object?
            if (spr.getOffender() != null) {

                /*
                 * External func call: notify game of collision
                 * (with validated offender)
                 */
                collision(spr);

                //reset offender
                spr.setOffender(null);
            }
```

```
            //reset collided state
            spr.setCollided(false);


        }
    }
}
```

Next, further down in the `Engine` code, add the following new `toString()` methods to print out a `Rect` and a `RectF` variable. These are helper methods.

```
public String toString(Rect value) {
    RectF r = new RectF(value.left, value.top, value.right,
            value.bottom);
    return toString((RectF)r);
}


public String toString(RectF value) {
    String s = "{" + round(value.left) + "," +
        round(value.top) + "," +
        round(value.right) + "," +
        round(value.bottom) + "}";
    return s;
}
```

The next change is a new helper *get* method that returns the size of the sprite group. The game can use this to find out how many sprites are in the group. It may even be necessary at some point to return the whole group; but when possible, it's better to hide such things in the engine and add helper methods to work with the group of entities stored in the list.

```
public int getGroupSize() {
    return p_group.size();
}
```

Further down is the `collisionCheck()` method added in the previous hour. This needs to be modified to work with a `RectF`, as shown. This is necessary because `Sprite.getBounds()` now returns a `RectF`.

```
public boolean collisionCheck(Sprite A, Sprite B) { //change to RectF
    boolean test = RectF.intersects(A.getBounds(), B.getBounds());
    return test;
}
```

Summary

That concludes our hour on rocket science, so to speak. Given that an Android device is much more powerful than the computers NASA used for the Apollo spacecraft that landed on the moon, I think there's some validity to it! The Collision Demo in the previous hour, combined with the engine changes this hour, have solidly rounded out the engine for 2D games. With this foundation in place, you can take it to the next level by expanding into the OpenGL ES realm as a next step.

Q&A

Q. The code experienced massive changes this hour! What is your impression of making such huge changes to so much of the engine code? Do you feel it's better to blueprint the final state of a project up front so that no changes are ever needed?

A. Answers will vary. However, it must be pointed out that this is an educational book, so it's helpful and realistic to show the reader how code evolves. The key here is this fact: No one writes perfect code on their first attempt—not Bill Gates, Linus Torvalds, or anyone.

Q. The linear velocity code seems to have affected most of the classes in the engine. Why did it have such a big impact like that?

A. Discuss how a rudimentary variable or class change requires updates everywhere that it is used.

Workshop

Quiz

1. What are the names of the trig functions used to calculate angular velocity?
2. Which trig function calculates the angle to a target?
3. Which Java method converts a radian angle to degrees?

Answers

1. Sine and cosine
2. Arctangent (or `Math.atan2()`)
3. `Math.ToDegrees()`

Activities

Write your own graphics demo that draws sprites moving in creative ways on the screen, following patterns or math functions as if they are on a graph.

Scrolling the Background

What You'll Learn in This Hour:

▶ Understanding the theory of background scrolling

▶ Creating a shoot-'em-up game

In the previous hour we covered linear velocity, a technique used to simulate firing projectiles (bullets, laser beams missiles, and the like). It is also used to move things in a certain direction. The example started in that hour showed a spaceship (controlled by the player), which could fire laser beams at obstacles on the screen—the start of a shoot-'em-up game. This hour covers background scrolling and ties the two together into a cohesive whole game example—a demo that could be the start of a larger, more fully developed game with enemy ships and the like.

Background Scrolling Overview

Background scrolling adds a layer of depth to a game that simply cannot be done with a fixed background filled with color or a non-moving bitmap. The short explanation is this: A large bitmap is created in memory, and a seamless texture is copied onto that texture—twice, side by side. The key is having a seamless texture that lines up on the left and right edges. That double-wide texture is used as the source image for scrolling.

A rectangle the size of the screen is what actually scrolls, not the background. The background is what you see on the screen, so technically the rectangle defines the background. To scroll the display, that rectangle is moved within the source image, and the portion of the double-wide texture where the rectangle is positioned is copied out to the screen. Because a seamless bitmap is duplicated side by side, the scrolling portion of the game can wrap the scroll position back to the front when an edge is reached, and it will appear to continually scroll without end.

At a certain point, the player might notice that the background looks familiar, especially after playing for several minutes. The key to pulling off a seamless scroll without distracting the player with *déjà vu* is to use a rather boring background—one that does not have sharply distinguishing features that will catch the eye as they go by repeatedly.

Flipping the Scroll Rectangle

Figure 23.1 shows what the texture looks like in memory (with a small gap added to illustrate the separation between the two copies of the source image). In this figure, the left and right sides are a duplicate of the same texture with seamless sides. This means that the pixels on the very edge of each side will line up when put side by side.

FIGURE 23.1
The space background is seamless on the sides and duplicated for scrolling.

To scroll the background, then, we need to load one bitmap containing an image with seamless edges (at least in the direction you want to scroll). Then, with the creative use of features in the `Bitmap` class, paste that image side by side into a double-wide texture. A rectangle will move "inside" the texture, representing what is drawn to the screen (see Figure 23.2).

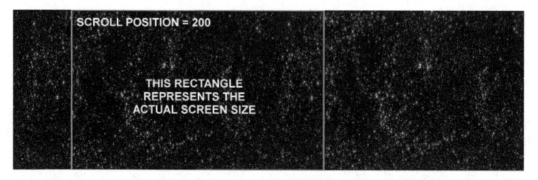

FIGURE 23.2
The scroll rectangle represents the view on the screen.

When the scrolling rectangle reaches one edge of the source texture, it is quickly "jumped" to the opposite side. That's the key; because the pixels on both sides are the same, the player won't notice that the position has moved. The same background pixels will be shown, and the player won't even know that a jump was made in the background scroll position. This process can continue indefinitely or for as long as the background needs to continue scrolling.

To scroll a display in all four directions, rather than just left or right, the code will be similar, but the top and bottom of the source bitmap must also be seamless. And, when you're constructing the double-wide texture, it must be created four times as large as the base image with four copies of the seamless texture copied to it (in four quadrants rather than just two).

Creating the Scroller Texture

Let's look at the code to create the texture used as the source for scrolling a background. Here are some global variables that we will use:

```
Bitmap bg_image2x;
Rect bg_rect;
Point bg_scroll;
```

First, we need to load the base bitmap file into memory. The easiest way to do that is with our own game.engine.Texture class. The bitmap dimensions should be the same as the screen resolution (this is up to the programmer to prepare in advance).

```
Texture tex = new Texture(this);
tex.loadFromAsset("background.png");
```

Next, create a new texture in memory that is twice the width of the screen. This is done using Bitmap.createBitmap() with the dimensions and color depth. Then, to assist with copying the source texture onto this new image, we can create a new Canvas based on the bitmap in order to draw onto it.

```
int w = getScreenWidth();
int h = getScreenHeight();
int w2 = w*2;
bg_image2x = Bitmap.createBitmap(w2, getScreenHeight(),
    Config.ARGB_8888);
Canvas can = new Canvas(bg_image2x);
```

The next step is to copy the source bitmap twice onto this new memory texture so that the image is side by side (and, presumably, the edges are seamless so it will appear to be one large texture).

```
Rect dst = new Rect(0, 0, w-1, h);
can.drawBitmap(tex.getBitmap(), null, dst, null);
dst = new Rect(w, 0, w2, h);
can.drawBitmap(tex.getBitmap(), null, dst, null);
```

Combined into one helper function, we can create the background texture with the result going into the global variable, bg_image2x. This is the result of the function. But rather than return it as a value, it is treated as a global variable in the example. Here is the complete function.

```
public void createBackground() {
    Texture tex = new Texture(this);
    if (!tex.loadFromAsset("space.png")) {
        fatalError("Error loading space");
    }

    //make a bitmap 2x screen width
    int w = getScreenWidth();
    int h = getScreenHeight();
    int w2 = w*2;
    bg_image2x = Bitmap.createBitmap(w2, getScreenHeight(),
        Config.ARGB_8888);
    Canvas can = new Canvas(bg_image2x);

    //stretch bitmap over background
    Rect dst = new Rect(0, 0, w-1, h);
    can.drawBitmap(tex.getBitmap(), null, dst, null);
    dst = new Rect(w, 0, w2, h);
    can.drawBitmap(tex.getBitmap(), null, dst, null);

    //draw red line between two halves of background
    paint.setStyle(Style.STROKE);
    paint.setColor(Color.RED);
    can.drawLine(w, 0, w, h, paint);

    //set initial scroll values
    bg_rect = new Rect(0,0,getScreenWidth(),getScreenHeight());
    bg_scroll = new Point(0,0);
}
```

The *Shoot-'Em-Up* Game

The source code for the *shoot-'em-up* game is shown next with a lot of new functionality compared with the example in the previous hour! As you may recall from Hour 22, "Using Linear Velocity for Realistic Movement," you learned how to calculate velocity. Rather than having two separate examples, they are combined this hour into one simple but interesting game demo. This is not intended to be a fully polished game with a title screen, high score, enemy A.I., and so on. The intent here is to give you a good, working demo of a scrolling shoot-'em-up game and the tools to do complex behaviors. You can take it to the next level and finish it from a game-play perspective (if you have a desire to see it completed). Think of this as the framework, and you can apply your own design to make a really great game!

WATCH OUT

If an asteroid has already collided with another asteroid, bullets will not collide properly! Therefore, the collision system has to take into account the identifier of each sprite. This approach seems to work well but might give you unexpected results if you forget! If you *need* to have two like sprites collide (such as two asteroids), give them each a different identifier.

Figure 23.3 shows the output from the game running on a hardware device (not the emulator). The frame rate is just barely keeping up with 30fps, and the target rate of the engine is 40fps. That's okay because this is not optimized code. Objects are being created and destroyed over and over fairly quickly in some of the methods, so there is quite a bit of wiggle room for improvement. Another performance hit comes from the text displayed on the screen (the so-called debug messages), which can be removed.

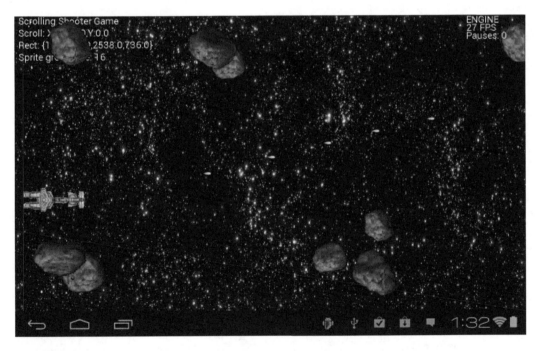

FIGURE 23.3
The shoot-'em-up game includes a scrolling background, moving obstacles, and a ship that moves and fires by touch.

Following is the complete, uninterrupted source code listing for the project called H23 Velocity Scrolling Demo, which combines the concepts of both this and the previous hour into one project. The H23 Game Engine Library project is a dependency.

BY THE WAY

The vertical red line in the background is not a mistake. It is added to show where the division lies between the two halves of the scrolling background buffer and was included to demonstrate that scrolling is working correctly.

```java
/**
 * H23 Scrolling Shooter Game
 * Requires game.engine.Engine to build.
 */

package android.program;
import java.util.Random;
import android.graphics.*;
import android.graphics.Bitmap.Config;
import android.graphics.Paint.Style;
import android.renderscript.*;
import game.engine.*;

public class Game extends game.engine.Engine {
    Canvas canvas;
    Paint paint;
    game.engine.Timer timer, shotTimer;
    Random rand;
    Texture asteroid_image;
    Sprite ship;
    Texture bullet_image;
    Bitmap bg_image2x;
    Rect bg_rect;
    Point bg_scroll;
    int numAsteroids = 0;

    final int ID_SHIP = 100;
    final int ID_ASTEROID = 200;
    final int ID_BULLET = 300;


    public Game() {
        canvas = null;
        paint = new Paint();
        timer = new Timer();
        shotTimer = new Timer();
        rand = new Random();
        asteroid_image = null;
        ship = null;
        bg_image2x = null;
        bg_rect = null;
        bg_scroll = null;
```

```
}

public void init() {
    setScreenOrientation(Engine.ScreenModes.LANDSCAPE);
    setFrameRate(60);
}

public void load() {
    createAsteroid();
    createShip();
    createBullet();
    createBackground();
}

public void draw() {
    canvas = getCanvas();
    Rect dest = new Rect(0,0,getScreenWidth(),getScreenHeight());
    canvas.drawBitmap(bg_image2x, bg_rect, dest, paint);
    drawText("Scrolling Shooter Demo", 10, 20);
    drawText("Scroll: " + toString(bg_scroll), 10, 50);
    drawText("Rect: " + toString(bg_rect), 10, 80);
    drawText("Sprite group size: " + getGroupSize() , 10, 110);
}

public void update() {
    scrollBackground();
    getUserInput();
    ship.animate();

    if (numAsteroids < 10)
        addRandomAsteroid();
}

/**
 * Abstract collision() method called by engine!
 */
public void collision(Sprite sprite) {
    Sprite other = sprite.getOffender();

    switch(sprite.getIdentifier()) {
    case ID_ASTEROID:
        if (other.getIdentifier() == ID_ASTEROID) {
            //try to keep asteroids off each other
            other.position.y += 1;
        }
        break;
```

```
    case ID_SHIP:
        if (other.getIdentifier() == ID_ASTEROID) {
            /*
             * uncomment this if you want asteroids to hit the ship
             */
            //other.setAlive(false);
        }
        break;

    case ID_BULLET:
        if (other.getIdentifier() == ID_ASTEROID) {
            numAsteroids--;
            sprite.setAlive(false);
            other.setAlive(false);
        }
        break;
    }
}

/**
 * Add collidable warping sprites
 */
public void createAsteroid() {
    asteroid_image = new Texture(this);
    if (!asteroid_image.loadFromAsset("asteroid_sheet.png")) {
        fatalError("Error loading asteroid_sheet");
    }
}

public void addRandomAsteroid() {
    int w = getScreenWidth();
    int h = getScreenHeight();
    RectF boundary = new RectF(-180,0,w,h-60);

    Sprite ast = new Sprite(this, 60, 60, 8);
    ast.setTexture(asteroid_image);

    ast.position = new Float2(100+w+rand.nextInt(w),
            rand.nextInt(h-60));

    ast.addAnimation(new FrameAnimation(0, 63, 1));
    Float2 vel = new Float2((0.5f+rand.nextFloat())*-10.0f, 0);
    ast.addAnimation(new WarpBehavior(boundary, 60, 60, vel));
    ast.setFrame(rand.nextInt(63));
    ast.setScale(1.5f + rand.nextFloat());
    ast.setCollidable(true);
    ast.setName("asteroid");
    ast.setIdentifier(ID_ASTEROID);
```

```
        addToGroup(ast);
        numAsteroids++;

}

/**
 * Create ship
 */
public void createShip() {
    int h = getScreenHeight();

    ship = new Sprite(this);
    if (!ship.getTexture().loadFromAsset("ship3.png")) {
        fatalError("Error loading ship3");
    }
    //note changes over previous hour
    ship.position = new Float2(20, h/2);
    ship.addAnimation(new ThrobAnimation(0.8f, 1.2f, 0.001f, true));
    ship.addAnimation(new FenceBehavior(new RectF(0,0,200,h-64)));
    ship.setName("ship");
    ship.setIdentifier(ID_SHIP);
    ship.setCollidable(true);
    addToGroup(ship);
}

/**
 * Load bullet image
 */
public void createBullet() {
    bullet_image = new Texture(this);
    if (!bullet_image.loadFromAsset("flare.png")) {
        fatalError("Error loading flare");
    }
}

/**
 * Create background
 */
public void createBackground() {
    Texture tex = new Texture(this);
    if (!tex.loadFromAsset("space.png")) {
        fatalError("Error loading space");
    }

    //make a bitmap 2x screen width
    int w = getScreenWidth();
    int h = getScreenHeight();
    int w2 = w*2;
```

```
    bg_image2x = Bitmap.createBitmap(w2, getScreenHeight(),
            Config.ARGB_8888);
    Canvas can = new Canvas(bg_image2x);

    //stretch bitmap over background
    Rect dst = new Rect(0, 0, w-1, h);
    can.drawBitmap(tex.getBitmap(), null, dst, null);
    dst = new Rect(w, 0, w2, h);
    can.drawBitmap(tex.getBitmap(), null, dst, null);

    //draw red line between two halves of background
    paint.setStyle(Style.STROKE);
    paint.setColor(Color.RED);
    can.drawLine(w, 0, w, h, paint);

    //set initial scroll values
    bg_rect = new Rect(0,0,getScreenWidth(),getScreenHeight());
    bg_scroll = new Point(0,0);
}

/**
 * Get user touch input
 */
public void getUserInput() {
    Point leftTouch=null, rightTouch=null;
    int inputs = getTouchInputs();

    if (inputs > 1) {
        leftTouch = getTouchPoint(0);
        rightTouch = getTouchPoint(1);
    }
    else if (inputs == 1) {
        leftTouch = rightTouch = getTouchPoint(0);
    }

    //left side of screen moves ship up/down
    if (leftTouch != null) {
        if (leftTouch.x < 200) {
            if (leftTouch.y < ship.position.y) {
                ship.position.y -= 5.0f;
            }
            else {
                ship.position.y += 5.0f;
            }
        }
    }
```

```java
        //right side of screen fires bullets
        if (rightTouch != null) {
            if (rightTouch.x > 200) {
                fireBullet();
            }
        }
    }

    /**
     * Fire a single bullet from the ship's position
     */
    public void fireBullet() {
        if (!shotTimer.stopwatch(200)) return;

        Sprite bullet = new Sprite(this);
        bullet.setIdentifier(ID_BULLET);
        bullet.setTexture(bullet_image);
        bullet.position.x = ship.position.x + 128;
        bullet.position.y = ship.position.y + 24;
        bullet.setCollidable(true);
        double angle = 0.0;
        float speed = 20.0f;
        int lifetime = 2500; //milliseconds
        bullet.addAnimation(new VelocityBehavior(angle, speed,
                lifetime));
        addToGroup(bullet);
    }

    /**
     * Scroll the background
     */
    public void scrollBackground() {
        bg_scroll.x += 10.0f;
        bg_rect.left = bg_scroll.x;
        bg_rect.right = bg_rect.left + getScreenWidth()-1;
        if (bg_scroll.x + bg_rect.width() > bg_image2x.getWidth()) {
            int diff = bg_scroll.x - bg_rect.width();
            bg_scroll.x = diff;
        }

    }
}
```

Summary

That wraps up two fairly awesome hours on building a scrolling shoot-'em-up game. In the previous hour, you learned about velocity and put that knowledge to use this hour in a game with a scrolling background. Together with the code developed earlier, the rudimentary Android engine is really taking shape. Now there isn't much more to cover for 2D game programming, but in the final hour coming up you will be building one more game example to demonstrate the final revision of the engine code.

Q&A

Q. There is quite a bit of gameplay code to be discussed when it comes to the collision system demonstrated here and in Hour 21. The way in which collision testing occurs can have a big impact on the speed of the game and apparent logic. For instance, if a bullet goes through an asteroid without hitting, the player will assume the game is broken, when it's really a matter of working with the sprite identifiers properly. What are your experiences with this issue while working on the game?

A. Answers will vary.

Q. There is another type of side-scrolling genre we might have dabbled in—a *platformer* game, similar to Nintendo's Mario Brothers franchise. A game with platforms and jumping tends to be data driven (from level data). How much of a difference do you think it would be to code a platformer after having studied the code for a shoot-'em-up?

A. Answers will vary.

Workshop

Quiz

1. Which `Engine` method performs a collision test between two `Sprite` objects?

2. Which key `Sprite` method makes it possible to perform a collision test with the scale factor included?

3. Which `Bitmap` method creates an image in memory?

Answers

1. `collisionCheck()`

2. `Sprite.getBoundsScaled()`

3. `createBitmap()`

Activities

The shoot-'em-up game demo is a good starting point for a more interesting game, but it needs a designer. See what you can do with it! For starters, make it so the player has to avoid the asteroids, and getting hit takes away "health" from the ship. You might show the player's "health" with a green bar on the screen. Next, keep track of the score by giving players points whenever they shoot an asteroid. Finally—and this is a *really cool idea*, if I do say so myself—make it so that hitting an asteroid makes it break up into several smaller asteroids, rather than just removing it from play. That is sure to have a big impact on the challenge, but it will make the game so much more interesting.

HOUR 24
Ball and Paddle Game

What You'll Learn in This Hour:

▶ Creating the ball and paddle game
▶ Automated ball movement
▶ Automated paddle restriction

The purpose of this hour is to demonstrate how you can quickly and easily make a complete game using the simple Android engine developed over the past few hours of this book. It will also provide a nice break from the space shoot-'em-up style game from the last two hours. This is a single game, developed in one hour, and kept to a minimum on gameplay to show how useful the engine is for other game genres. Because we have barely touched portrait-oriented games in this book, the ball and paddle game will run in portrait mode.

Creating the Ball and Paddle Game

The ball and paddle game is shown in Figure 24.1. This is an example of a game that runs in portrait mode. Because we have spent most of the hours focusing on games in the landscape orientation, this is an interesting contrast.

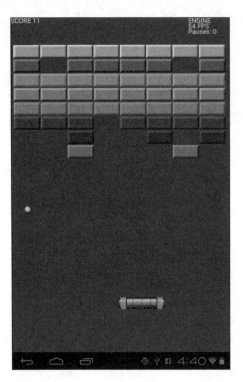

FIGURE 24.1
A simple example of the classic ball and paddle game.

Automated Ball Movement

The gameplay is known to most programmers because it dates back to some very old arcade games, notably Atari's *Breakout* and Taito's *Arkanoid*. One of the key behaviors of this type of game is a ball that follows a rather simple path on the screen, bouncing or rebounding off the edges. To increase the fun factor, the ball will often change its speed or angle after hitting a block or the player's paddle, which throws some randomness into the game and makes it more interesting. Figure 24.2 shows the basic bouncing ball logic.

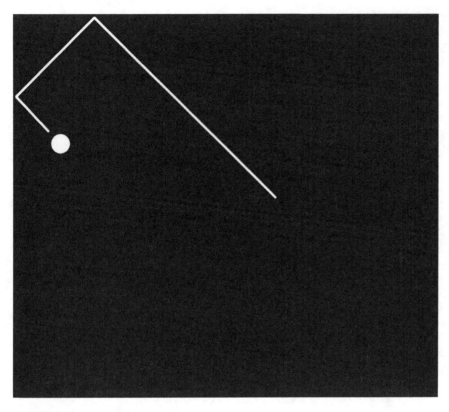

FIGURE 24.2
Keeping a sprite within a specified boundary by "bouncing" off the "walls."

Based on our `Animation` class, we can code a behavior that simulates this type of ball movement logic so that it can be automated. The new class is called `ReboundBehavior`.

```
/**
 * ReboundBehavior class - derived from Animation
 * Requires game.engine.Engine to build.
 */
package android.program;
import android.graphics.*;
import android.renderscript.Float2;
import game.engine.*;
```

```
public class ReboundBehavior extends Animation {
    private RectF p_bounds;
    private Float2 p_velocity;
    private Point p_size;

    public ReboundBehavior(RectF bounds, Point size, Float2 velocity) {
        animating = true;
        p_bounds = bounds;
        p_velocity = velocity;
        p_size = size;
    }

    @Override
    public Float2 adjustPosition(Float2 original) {
        Float2 modified = original;
        modified.x += p_velocity.x;
        modified.y += p_velocity.y;

        if (modified.x < p_bounds.left)
            p_velocity.x *= -1;
        else if (modified.x > p_bounds.right-p_size.x)
            p_velocity.x *= -1;

        if (modified.y < p_bounds.top)
            p_velocity.y *= -1;
        else if (modified.y > p_bounds.bottom-p_size.y)
            p_velocity.y *= -1;

        return modified;
    }
}
```

The *worker* method in ReboundBehavior is adjustPosition(). The logic of this method involves checking the position of the sprite against a boundary (passed as a RectF parameter to the class constructor). When the sprite reaches the edge of the boundary, its direction is changed so that it moves in the opposite direction. The two axes, X and Y, are each handled separately.

Automated Paddle Restriction

Another behavior of this sort of game involves bounding the player's paddle near the bottom of the screen and preventing it from going off either the left or right edge. In some games of this type, the paddle can move only left or right, not up or down. In this example, the paddle can move in both axes but is limited to a small portion of the bottom of the screen. Figure 24.3 illustrates the situation, with the paddle sprite limited to the region shown (where the jointed line represents the paddle's movement). This behavior was coded a while back, so we can reuse the FenceBehavior class again, which is shown here.

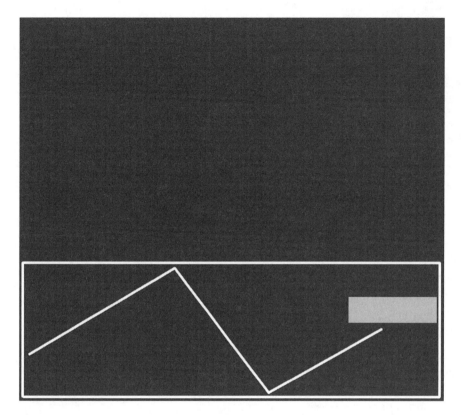

FIGURE 24.3
"Fencing" a sprite within a certain boundary.

```
/**
 * FenceBehavior Class
 */
package game.engine;
import android.graphics.RectF;
import android.renderscript.Float2;

public class FenceBehavior extends Animation {
    private RectF p_fence;

    public FenceBehavior(RectF fence) {
        p_fence = fence;
        animating = true;
    }
```

```
@Override
public Float2 adjustPosition(Float2 original) {
    Float2 modified = original;

    if (modified.x < p_fence.left)
        modified.x = p_fence.left;
    else if (modified.x > p_fence.right)
        modified.x = p_fence.right;
    if (modified.y < p_fence.top)
        modified.y = p_fence.top;
    else if (modified.y > p_fence.bottom)
        modified.y = p_fence.bottom;

    return modified;
    }
}
```

Although `FenceBehavior` is similar to `ReboundBehavior`, velocity is not involved, so it stops the sprite's movement when it touches one of the four sides of the boundary.

The Ball and Paddle Source Code

Now we'll go over the source code for the sample game for this hour. First are the imports, global variables, and game startup and initialization. As you can see from the code listing, the layout of the blocks for the "game level" is defined in an integer array called int [] level. Next, we have the game's constructor and the init() event.

WATCH OUT
_____

The game should run at about 50 fps with smooth movement of the ball and responsive touch tracking. If the game runs poorly, check running apps for example projects from previous hours (or other Android games) that may still be taking up processor cycles in the background (if they do not respond properly to the pause/resume events).

Also, be sure to launch the game with the device already in portrait orientation so the game doesn't have to flip. The engine can set the orientation at startup but cannot handle dynamic flipping. If it flips after startup, the frame rate will drop and the game will stutter.

_____

```
/**
 * H24 Ball and Paddle Game
 * Requires game.engine.Engine to build.
 */

package android.program;
import java.util.Random;
import android.graphics.*;
```

```
import android.renderscript.*;
import game.engine.*;

public class Game extends game.engine.Engine {
    Canvas canvas=null;
    Paint paint=null;
    Random rand=null;
    Point touch=null;
    int score=0;

    final int PADDLE_ID = 100;
    final float PADDLE_SPEED = 5.0f;
    Sprite paddle=null;

    final int BALL_ID = 200;
    Sprite ball=null;

    final int BLOCK_ID = 300;
    final int BLOCK_WIDTH = 96;
    final int BLOCK_HEIGHT = 48;
    Texture block_image=null;

    final int LEVEL_WIDTH = 8;
    final int LEVEL_HEIGHT = 8;
    final int[] level = {
            1,1,1,1,1,1,1,1,
            2,0,2,2,2,2,0,2,
            3,3,3,3,3,3,3,3,
            4,4,4,4,4,4,4,4,
            5,5,5,5,5,5,5,5,
            6,6,6,6,6,6,6,6,
            7,0,7,7,7,7,0,7,
            8,8,8,8,8,8,8,8 };

    public Game() {
        paint = new Paint();
        paint.setColor(Color.rgb(100,80,40));
        rand = new Random();
    }

    public void init() {
        setScreenOrientation(Engine.ScreenModes.PORTRAIT);
        setFrameRate(60);
    }
```

The next section of code includes the load() event, which is called by the engine to allow loading of game assets. Of particular interest in this method is how each of the sprites are created and then added to the engine's entity manager with a call to `addToGroup()`. You may recall from Hour 20, "Entity Grouping," that the engine has a `LinkedList` of `Sprites`. After a sprite has been added to the list, it is automatically animated, drawn, and updated according to any attached animations or behaviors. Take note of the calls to `addToGroup()` here to understand more clearly how the game works with so few lines of code.

```
public void load() {
    int w = getScreenWidth();
    int h = getScreenHeight();

    //load block image
    block_image = new Texture(this);
    if (!block_image.loadFromAsset("blocks.png")) {
        fatalError("Error loading blocks");
    }

    //position blocks for game level
    for (int y = 0; y < LEVEL_HEIGHT; y++) {
        for (int x = 0; x < LEVEL_WIDTH; x++) {
            Sprite block = new Sprite(this, BLOCK_WIDTH,
                BLOCK_HEIGHT, 4);
            block.setTexture(block_image);
            int index = level[y * LEVEL_WIDTH + x]-1;
            block.setFrame(index);
            block.position.x = 10 + x * (BLOCK_WIDTH+1);
            block.position.y = 100 + y * (BLOCK_HEIGHT+4);
            block.setCollidable(true);
            block.setIdentifier(BLOCK_ID);
            addToGroup(block);
        }
    }

    //load paddle image
    paddle = new Sprite(this);
    if (!paddle.getTexture().loadFromAsset("paddle.png")) {
        fatalError("Error loading paddle");
    }

    //init paddle sprite
    paddle.position = new Float2(w/2,h-200);
    RectF rect = new RectF(0,h-250,w-180,h-52);
    //keep paddle near bottom of screen
    paddle.addAnimation(new FenceBehavior(rect));
    paddle.setCollidable(true);
    paddle.setIdentifier(PADDLE_ID);
    addToGroup(paddle);
```

```
    //load ball image
    ball = new Sprite(this);
    if (!ball.getTexture().loadFromAsset("ball.png")) {
        fatalError("Error loading ball");
    }

    //init ball sprite
    ball.position = new Float2(200,h-300);
    ball.setVelocity(new Float2(4.0f,-6.0f));
    //keep ball inside screen boundary
    Point size = ball.getSize();
    ball.addAnimation(new ReboundBehavior(
            new RectF(0, 0, w-size.x, h-size.y),
            size, ball.getVelocity()) );
    ball.setCollidable(true);
    ball.setIdentifier(BALL_ID);
    addToGroup(ball);
}
```

Next up is the draw() event, the update() event, and finally the collision() event, all called from the engine's threaded loop. Because the blocks, paddle, and ball were added to the internal entity manager, we do not need to manually move or draw any of these objects in the game. So there's actually more setup code than gameplay code in a simple game like this. In fact, we're not too far removed from a fully scripted game at this point (using a script language such as Lua, for instance). Collisions in this game are also fairly simple; the same ball-rebounding logic is used when the ball hits either a block or the paddle. The main difference between the two events is that hitting a block adds to the player's score.

```
public void draw() {
    canvas = getCanvas();
    //clear the screen
    canvas.drawPaint(paint);

    //display the score
    drawText("SCORE " + toString(score),0,20);
}

public void update() {
    int inputs = getTouchInputs();
    if (inputs > 0) {
        touch = getTouchPoint(0);
        if (touch.y > getScreenHeight()-250) {
            paddle.position.x = touch.x - paddle.getWidth()/2;
            paddle.position.y = touch.y - 50;
        }
    }
}
```

```java
public void collision(Sprite sprite) {
    switch (sprite.getIdentifier()) {
    case BALL_ID:
        Float2 vel = sprite.getVelocity();

        Sprite other = sprite.getOffender();
        switch (other.getIdentifier()) {
        case BLOCK_ID:
            score++;
            other.setAlive(false);
            vel.y *= -1;
            sprite.setVelocity(vel);
            sprite.position.y += vel.y*2;
            break;

        case PADDLE_ID:
            //make sure ball bounces up
            vel.y = -1 * Math.abs(vel.y);
            sprite.setVelocity(vel);
            sprite.position.y += vel.y;
            break;
        }
        break;
    }
}
```

That is the end of the source code. Remarkably short, isn't it? Granted, there is only one level to the game and no way to lose—you just keep playing until clearing the level or exiting. But it's a start, as it was meant to be. The purpose of this project was twofold: first, to show how easy it is to make a game using the code in this book; second, to give you a framework for making your own ball and paddle game. With all the functionality now working, all that is missing is some creative design to give it some flair and improve the fun factor. There also must be a way to lose—by missing the ball, that is. The rest is up to you! Modify this game, enhance it, and begin improving the engine to suit your own Android game development needs in the future.

Summary

That about sums up the entire book! This hour explored the source code for a simple game to show how the Android game engine presented in this book might be used for a variety of games. Although we did not get into OpenGL ES and do any 3D rendering—which would take several hundred more pages just to explain lighting, cameras, shaders, and the like—I believe you now have all the tools and know-how you need to build your own high-performance Android games!

When you have finished your first game and put it up on the Google Play marketplace for Android apps, drop me a line! Here is the QR barcode for my website.

Q&A

Q. What are some core improvements you would make to the engine to increase its usefulness for your favorite game genre?

A. Answers will vary.

Q. Do you think the animation and behavior system used in this game is an improvement over coding game logic manually with helper methods in the main code listing or in a class for a game object, such as a `Paddle` class, for instance?

A. Answers will vary.

Workshop

Quiz

1. What is the name of the behavior class used to move the ball in the ball and paddle game?

2. What is the name of the `Engine` method used to add a sprite to the entity manager?

3. What is the name of the behavior class used to keep the player's paddle sprite in a region near the bottom of the screen?

Answers

1. `ReboundBehavior`

2. `addToGroup()`

3. `FenceBehavior`

Activities

You will probably want to see what interesting new gameplay you can add to the ball and paddle game demonstrated this hour. See what you can do with it as a learning exercise. At minimum, you should give the player some "lives," take away a life when the ball hits the bottom of the screen, and then reset the ball again. You could also give the player an extra life after reaching a certain number of points or by hitting a special block. You might also cause certain blocks to drop power-up items or launch multiple balls or any number of other interesting gameplay improvements.

Index

initializing, 214

playing, 217

R (resource identifiers), 215

audio files, with SoundPool

asset file extensions, 218

Audio Demo Program, 220-221

initializing, 218

loading resources, 218-219

playing, 219

multiple sounds, 218

R (resource identifiers), 219

AudioManager.STREAM_MUSIC parameter, 218

autorotation on screens, 159-160

AVD (Android Virtual Device) emulator

versus Android devices, 63-64

AVD Manager, 31, 33-34

creating, 32-33

limitations, 64

multi-touch input

receiving basic data, 149

receiving/storing values, 150-155

options

CPU/ABI field, 32

RAM size, 64

SD card field, 33

Skin, 106

Target field, 32, 56

WVGA800 display, 33, 64

running, 33-35, 54-59

single-touch input, 144

axis directions

accelerometer sensor, 161, 164

linear acceleration sensor, 169

B

back buffers, 111, 113-115

background scrolling, seamless texture, 371-374

BaseSensor class, 208-209

Basic Graphics Demo, 95-98, 129

beginDrawing() method, Engine class, 262, 365

Bitmap class, 111

alpha channels for transparencies, 121-124

android.graphics.Bitmap namespace, 112

assets

adding, 115-118

AssetManager class, 117-118

copying, 121, 271

error handling, 119

InputStream object, 118

istream.close() method, 119

linking, 121

back buffer, 111, 113-115

background scrolling, 372-374

Bitmap Loading Demo, 120, 125-126, 129-130

Config.ARGB_8888 parameter, 112, 119

file formats, 115

front buffer, 111

methods

BitmapFactory.decodeStream(), 118-119

createBitmap(), 112, 373-374

drawBitmap(), 120

Texture class, 246

BitmapFactory.decodeStream() method, 118-119

Bitmap knight [ ], 135

Bitmap Loading Demo, 120, 125-126, 129-130

bitmaps and animation, 269

Runnable Animation Demo, 134-140

walking character, 134-140

Bitmap knight [ ], 135

drawBitmap() method, 135

frames, 135

InputStream object, 135

for loops, 135

BMP file format, 115

bounding circles (radial) collision detection, 335-336

bounding rectangles (box) collision detection, 333-336

Box2D physics library, 233

box (bounding rectangles) collision detection, 333-336

boxes, 93-94

Breakout, 386

Buffered Graphics Demo, 113-115

buffers, front and back, 111, 113-115

C

C++ and Android NDK

libraries, 8

supplementing Android SDK, 8

support

for Open GL ES 2.0, 8

for Open SL ES 2.0, 8

Canvas class, 89-90

Basic Graphics Demo, 95-98, 129

game engines
components, 227
design goals, 226-227
engine core component, 227
Engine class, 235-243
TextPrinter class, 244-246
Texture class, 246-247
Timer class, 243-244
Engine Test Demo Project
creating, 247-248
logging demo, 252-253
source code, 249-251
Game Engine Library project,
229-233, 288
android.engine.VectorMath
class, 229
.APK file (Android
Package), 233
creating, 230-232
DotProduct() method, 229
VectorMath class, 229
main thread component, 228
rendering component, 228
startup component, 227-228
Unity, 226
game examples
Ball and Paddle, 385
automated ball movement,
386-388
automated paddle
restriction, 388-390
source code, 390-394
Shoot-'Em-Up
output, 375-394
source code, 374-395
getBitmap() method, Texture
class, 246
getBounds() method, Sprite class,
342-343, 368

getBoundsScaled() method, Sprite
class, 342-343
getCanvas() method, Sprite
class, 262
getCollidable() method, Sprite
class, 342-343
getCollided() method, Sprite class,
342-343
getGroup() method, Engine
class, 368
getHolder() method, Canvas class,
132, 228
getIdentifier() method, Sprite
class, 342-343
getName() method, Sprite class,
342-343
getOffender() method, Sprite
class, 342-343
getSensorList() method,
SensorManager class, 163
GIF file format,   115
GIMP graphic editor
alpha channels for
transparencies, 121-124
converting assets from one
format to another, 115-116
Gingerbread code name, 10
Google Drive app, 10
GPS location service versus
sensors, 158
Graphics Demo project code,
86-87
Canvas class, 89-90
drawColor() method, 89
graphics shapes, 90
onDraw() method, 88-89
DrawView class, 88-89
MainActivity class, 88-89
package and import
statements, 88
Paint class, 89
View class, 90

gravity sensors, 194
algorithm, 181
constants/values, 182
converting 3D to 2D
coordinate, 183
Float2 or Float3 classes,
182-183
initializing, 181
onSensorChanged() method,
182
reading, 182
testing, 183-188
GSM 6.10 WAV (mobile) audio
format, 217
gyroscope sensors, 194-195, 210

H

H15 Game Engine Library, 248
H16 Game Engine Library, 263
H16 Sprite Demo, 262
H17 Game Engine Library, 270
H19 Game Engine Library, 322
H23 Game Engine Library,
367, 375
H23 Velocity Scrolling Demo, 375
hand-held video game systems, 7
Helios Service Release, Eclipse
IDE, 16, 25
Honeycomb code name, 10, 69

I

IBM PCs, 7
Ice Cream Sandwich code name,
3-4, 10, 69
Amazon Kindle Fire, 69
identity matrix, 300

IDEs (integrated development environments), 16

init() method, 252

InputStream object, 118, 135

int change constructor, 287

int maxAlpha constructor, 287

int() method, 390

int minAlpha constructor, 287

invalidate() method, 130

iOS/Apple, Android as derivative of, 9

iOS/Apple versus Android and Windows Phone

  hardware control, 3

  licensing, 4-6

  market share, 4, 9, 12

iPad

  adult toy, 7

  versus Android, 9

  development of, 9

iPhone

  adult toy, 7

  versus Android 4, 4

  development from iPod, 9

  and Palm Pilot, 9

  Plants vs. Zombies, 7

  and Pocket PC, 9

  release in 2007, 9

  Unity game engine support, 226

iPod

  versus Android, 9

  iPhone development, 9

istream.close() method, 119

iTunes, development of, 9

J

JAR (Java Archive) utility, 269

Java

  compiler requirements, 140

  importance of experience, 8

  JAR (Java Archive) utility, 269

  modulus operator, 273

  new classes, 288-289

  programming games, 7

  similar to C# language, 78

Java Development Kit. See JDK

Javadoc for self-documented code, 103-104

.java extension, 8

Java Runtime Environment. See JRE

JDK (Java Development Kit), 8

  Enterprise Edition, 16

  installing, with Eclipse, 16

  Java Standard Edition 7, 16

  NetBeans

    downloading, 17

    installing, 16-20

    installing, default locations, 19-20

    license agreement, 18-20

    plug-in for, 16

    versions available, 17

Jelly Bean code name, 3, 10, 69

JPEG file format, 115

JRE (Java Runtime Environment), 8, 16

K

Katz, Phil, 233

Kindle Fire, Amazon

  Android 2.2 Eclair, 69

Android 4.0 Ice Cream Sandwich, 69

sensors reported, 164

L

landscape orientation, 99, 159-160

licensing

  Android OS/devices, 4, 6, 10

  iOS/Apple, 4-6

lifetimes for programs (activities), 79

  foreground, 79

  visible, 79

light detector sensor, 195

Linear Acceleration Demo, 171-177

linear acceleration sensors, 193, 210

  versus accelerometer, 169

  initializing sensor, 170-171

  methods

    onPause(), 171

    onResume(), 171

    registerListener(), 171

    unregisterListener(), 171

  reading sensor, 171

  velocity, 170

  X and Y values, 169

lines, 93

LinkedList object, 321, 392

  adding properties, 322

  initializing, 322

Linux

  and Android development, 8, 66

  basis for Android 4, 3

  versus iOS and Windows Phone OS, licensing, 4

T

Taito's Arkanoid, 386

Target Platform table, NetBeans IDE, 51

Teach Yourself Windows Phone 7 Game Programming in 24 Hours, 6

TextPrinter class, 244-246

texture atlas. *See sprite sheets*

Texture class

Bitmap object, 246

core engine classes, 246-247

drawSheetFrame() method, 273

getBitmap() method, 246

Sprite class, 261

TextView widget, **63, 83**

threaded game loops

Context parameter, 131

methods

invalidate(), 130

onDraw(), 131-132

Runnable class, 130

run() method, 130-132

SurfaceView class, 131

Thread object, 131

pause() method, 131

resume() method, 131

Thread object, 131

pause() method, 131

resume() method, 131

Thread.sleep() method, Timer class, 243

ThrobAnimation class, 291-292, 324-325

Timer class methods, **243-244**

stopwatch(), 243

System.currentTimeMillis(), 243

Thread.sleep(), 243

toDegrees() method, Math class, **305, 350**

toRadians() method, Math class, **305, 350**

Toshiba Thrive 7" tablet, 69

sensors reported, 163

toString() method, Engine class, **368**

touch input

multi-touch input

MotionEvent parameter, 151

MotionEvent parameter, getX() and getY() methods, 149

Multi-touch Demo, 151-155

onTouch() method, 151

Point() points, 151

receiving basic data, 149

receiving/storing values, 150-155

single-touch input

MotionEvent parameter, 144-147

get.PointerCount() method, 149

MOVE event, 144

OnTouchListener, 143-148

onTouch() method, 144-147

Single Touch Input Demo, 144-148

testing on emulator, 144

UP event, 144

View class, 143-148

transparencies, alpha channels, **121-124**

triangles, **95**

Tricorder Demo (sensors)

classes

Accelerometer, 209

BaseSensor, 208-209

CompassSensor, 211

GyroscopeSensor, 210

LinearAcceleration, 210

PressureSensor, 210

ProximitySensor, 210

SensorPanel, 202-203

Sensors, 205

events, trapping, 205-206

events, unused accuracy, 207

helper methods, 201-202

panels, 199-200

panels, drawing, 201

pausing and resuming, 207-208

printing text lines, 203-204

updating sensors, 200-201

TYPE sensors

ACCELEROMETER, 157

AMBIENT_TEMPERATURE, 157

GRAVITY, 157, 181, 182

GYROSCOPE, 157

LIGHT, 157

LINEAR_ACCELERATION, 157, 171

MAGNETIC_FIELD, 157

PRESSURE, 157

PROXIMITY, 158, 177

RELATIVE_HUMIDITY, 158

ROTATION_VECTOR, 158

Essential Resources for Android Developers

informit.com/android

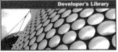

Sams **Teach Yourself**

When you only have time
for the answers™

Whatever your need and whatever your time frame, there's a Sams **Teach Yourself** book for you. With a Sams **Teach Yourself** book as your guide, you can quickly get up to speed on just about any new product or technology—in the absolute shortest period of time possible. Guaranteed.

Learning how to do new things with your computer shouldn't be tedious or time-consuming. Sams **Teach Yourself** makes learning anything quick, easy, and even a little bit fun.

Sams Teach Yourself Google TV App Development in 24 Hours

Carmen Delessio
ISBN-13: 9780672336034

HTML, CSS and JavaScript All in One
Julie C. Meloni
ISBN-13: 9780672333323

Sams Teach Yourself JavaScript in 24 Hours
Phil Ballard / Michael Moncur
ISBN-13: 9780672336089

Sams Teach Yourself Node.js in 24 Hours
George Ornbo
ISBN-13: 9780672335952

Sams Teach Yourself jQuery Mobile in 24 Hours
Phillip Dutson
ISBN-13: 9780672335945

FREE
Online Edition

Safari
Books Online

Your purchase of **Sams Teach Yourself Android Game Programming in 24 Hours** includes access to a free online edition for 45 days through the Safari Books Online subscription service. Nearly every Sams book is available online through Safari Books Online, along with thousands of books and videos from publishers such as Addison-Wesley Professional, Cisco Press, Exam Cram, IBM Press, O'Reilly Media, Prentice Hall, Que, and VMware Press.

Safari Books Online is a digital library providing searchable, on-demand access to thousands of technology, digital media, and professional development books and videos from leading publishers. With one monthly or yearly subscription price, you get unlimited access to learning tools and information on topics including mobile app and software development, tips and tricks on using your favorite gadgets, networking, project management, graphic design, and much more.

Activate your FREE Online Edition at
informit.com/safarifree

STEP 1: Enter the coupon code: GRBMMXA.

STEP 2: New Safari users, complete the brief registration form.
Safari subscribers, just log in.

If you have difficulty registering on Safari or accessing the online edition,
please e-mail customer-service@safaribooksonline.com